COMING
HOME
AGAIN

COMING HOME AGAIN

A Family-of-Origin Consultation

JAMES L. FRAMO, PhD
TIMOTHY T. WEBER, PhD
FELISE B. LEVINE, PhD

Brunner-Routledge

New York and Hove

Published in 2003 by
Brunner-Routledge
29 West 35th Street
New York, NY 10001
www.brunner-routledge.com

Published in Great Britain by
Brunner-Routledge
27 Church Road
Hove, East Sussex
BN3 2FA
www.brunner-routledge.co.uk

10 9 8 7 6 5 4 3 2 1

Library of Congress Cataloging-in-Publication Data
Framo, James L.
    Coming home again : a family-of-origin consultation / James L. Framo,
    Timothy T. Weber, Felise B. Levine.
        p. cm.
    Includes bibliographical references and index.
    ISBN 1-58391-373-4 (hbk.)
        1. Family psychotherapy—Case studies.   2. Weber, Timothy T.   3. Weber family.
    4. Framo, James L.   5. Levine, Felise B.   I. Weber, Timothy T.   II. Levine, Felise B.
    III. Title.

RC488.5 .F698 2003
616.89'156—dc21

                                                                                2002152050

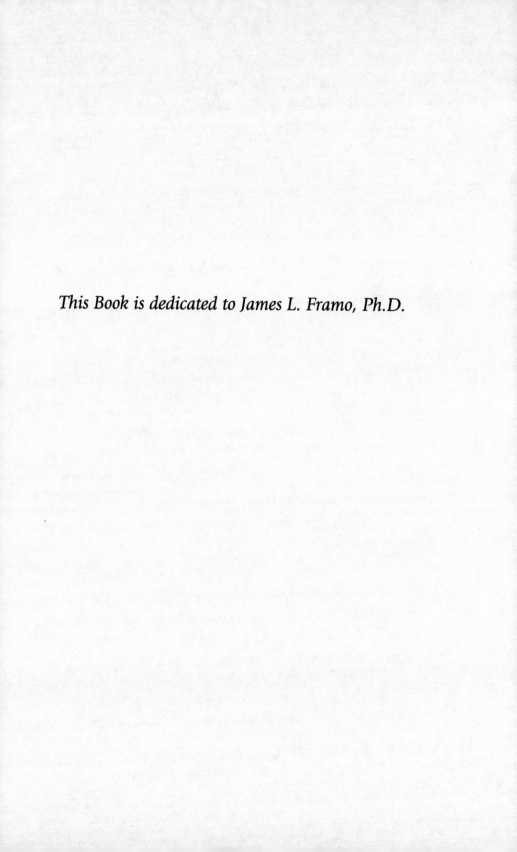

This Book is dedicated to James L. Framo, Ph.D.

CONTENTS

ACKNOWLEDGMENTS

This volume is the fruition of a long and rich journey, a blending to-gether of two hearts—the heart of James L. Framo and the heart of the Weber family who generously offered their story as the substance of this book. The Webers' openness throughout these conversations, never in-tended for publication during the consultation itself, has been made public in this volume for one reason—to encourage all families to deepen their intimacy through conversations of caring and honesty. If the readers of this volume find their hearts opening more and more to the possibilities within families, this story will have helped evolve its purpose.

Pulsating through this volume is the heart of James L. Framo whose decades of professional work and passion sparked the ideas and meth-ods in working with families of origin. While editing the final pages of this work, Jim died suddenly at his home in San Diego on August 22, 2001. He was 78 years old. Jim's spirit breathes through these pages. His intellect, compassion, bravado, wit, imagination, commitment, vulner-ability, and profound respect for families permeates these pages. We miss him dearly as husband, friend, and colleague. Words cannot express who he was to us and what gifts he left with us. This volume is dedicated to Jim.

We also want to thank colleagues who have been formative in shap-ing our thinking and professional evolution through the years—Lyman Wynne, Susan McDaniel, and Donald Williamson. We owe theoretical debts to Murray Bowen, Ivan Boszormenyi-Nagy, and Carl Whitaker.

We give particular gratitude to the faculty and staff at The Leadership Institute of Seattle (LIOS) at Bastyr University in Kenmore, Washington. Good colleagues both hold us and challenge us to find and creatively use our best gifts. LIOS has been that kind of place. Debi Vogel has been the "administrative center" for this project, contributing her "eagle eye" over the text and bringing her tenacity and affection for many years.

Finally, we continue to "love and work" in this world largely because we are embedded within our respective families. Timothy's wife, Misty, has been a steady companion through the inception of the family-of-origin consultation and the generation of this book. Often joining us around the table in San Diego, she has injected questions and observations that have enriched our reflections on the depth of family life. Within these relationships of love and continuing opportunities for learning and transformation in our families, we ourselves continue to evolve.

This volume is a product of our mutual friendship and growth together.

Timothy Weber
Felise Levine
October, 2002

PART I

PROLOGUE

Chapter 1

PREFACE

JAMES L. FRAMO, PhD

This book is the outcome of a unique venture in the field of psycho-therapy. The case-study format of a full-length family-of-origin consulta-tion with interspersed commentary by the therapists is new to the family therapy literature. The door to the treatment room is open therein, re-vealing not only the inner life and workings of a family, but also the interventions and private thoughts of the therapist conducting the con-sultation sessions. In the human encounter that takes place in the subjec-tive space between the world of the family and the world of the therapist, the wonder of therapeutic change can take place.

Book-length case studies ($n = 1$) are rare in the psychotherapy field, even in the family therapy literature (Chasin, Grunebaum, & Herzog, 1990; Keeney & Silverstein, 1981; Napier & Whitaker, 1978; Paul & Paul, 1975; Satir & Baldwin, 1983; Whitaker & Bumberry, 1988). Clinical anecdotes, brief case examples, and snapshots of therapist–family transactions give a pallid description of how psychotherapy is actually done. A longitudi-nal approach revealing the internal reflections of the family members as they evolve over time gives a truer picture of the natural flow of family transactions, and of the effectiveness of the therapist's interventions. Within the limitations of the printed word, one has the opportunity in this book to examine the natural *process* of psychotherapy, particularly as applied to conjoint family sessions including parents and adult siblings.

What are family-of-origin consultations, and what are they trying to accomplish? From my theoretical perspective, I see present-day inner con-flicts, marital relationship problems, and parenting difficulties as largely stemming from reparative efforts to cancel out, replicate, defend against, master, or heal earlier conflicts and relationship patterns from the family of origin. Early in my psychotherapy experience with troubled individu-als, couples, and families it became apparent to me that the kinds of

3

conflicts people have with themselves, their partners, and their children have much to do with what they are still working out from their families of origin. Most people who enter psychotherapy spend a lot of time talking *about* their original families. Some years ago I took the unusual step of having clients actually bring in their parents and brothers and sisters for family-of-origin consultations, taking the problems back to where they began, thus providing a direct route to etiological factors. Adult clients in individual, marital, divorce, or family therapy are prepared to deal directly with parents and siblings about the important issues and relationship problems that have existed among them in the past and the present (such problems as open or silent warfare between parents, clashing of needs, family cutoffs, feelings of rejection, distant fathers and intrusive mothers, sibling competition, unfulfilled longings, parentification of children, etc.). The context of the family-of-origin sessions gives permission for the family members to discuss with each other the painful, difficult issues that had always been avoided; the safe setting allows honest exchange about previously forbidden topics to occur. Family-of-origin sessions, which I consider to be the major surgery of psychotherapy, usually bring about beneficial changes on the individual level, in the marital system, and in the family of origin itself.

This book had an uncommon genesis, and its conceptualization and development have followed an arduous, lengthy course. It all began when I was scheduled to give a seminar on my work with family-of-origin consultations. Prior to the workshop, I received a letter from Dr. Timothy Weber offering his family of origin to be interviewed at the workshop. I had been using Dr. Weber's article (Weber, McKeever, & McDaniel, 1985) in one of my classes, but did not realize until later that this was the same Dr. Weber. When I did make the connection, I wondered why this family therapist, who had a theoretical orientation different from mine (structural-strategic), would be interested in intergenerational work—much less be willing to put his family of origin in my hands. His letter gave a short description of his family:

> My father, Paul (age 67), lives with his second wife. He has a doctorate in theology, was campus pastor at a university, but spent most of his professional career as president of a college (1958–1983). He retired in 1983. He had a serious brain tumor in 1967, but has had only two incidents of speech loss since that time. My mother, Elizabeth, died in 1978, at the age of 53, from sudden heart failure. She was a preschool teacher (as are my wife, and sister, Katie). My father married Linda (age 50) in 1982. Stepfamily issues abound, even though most of us were out of the home when my father remarried. I am the oldest sibling (age 36). My brother Thomas (age 34) is mentally retarded from birth, and lives in a Lutheran home. He probably is the most "aware" of all the siblings, and took my mother's place as the family "switch-

board" after she died. He's the one who calls all of us and passes information through the family. My sister Katie (age 33) lives in another state with Steve, her husband, and her daughter, Mary (age 3). Katie is a teacher in a public school. Ann (age 23) is married to Mark, works as a food manager at a college, and lives in a nearby state. She became diabetic at age 13. She is now heavily involved in a charismatic congregation with Mark, somewhat to the dismay of my Lutheran father. Lynn (age 19) has now completed her freshman year at the same university my father graduated from. She probably is the most "freed up" one of the bunch.

Our family is both common and unique. We have had our share of somatic crises over the years, partly because—like good Lutherans—we tried to be "proper and well-behaved," leaving much buried and unfinished. My mother's death is an example. Although we have talked, we have not talked. We are getting better, however—more daring. I see this seminar as an opportunity for our family to be with each other in a way that will generate more growth amongst us, with each one of us, and with our respective nuclear families. All these perceptions, of course, are my own.

There were a number of aspects of this offer that appealed to me. First, I was glad to have a family to interview at the seminar instead of having to show a videotape of a family-of-origin consultation. Live interviews are risky and unpredictable, and harder work for the therapist, but they do impart a sense of immediacy and realness about human struggles. Although demonstration interviews in front of an audience are not exactly the same as those conducted in private, nonetheless they are a truer approximation of what actually happens in psychotherapy than are videotaped excerpts. They show how clients communicate their experiences, the way the therapist assesses and intervenes in the system, the mistakes therapists make, the empty periods of psychotherapy, the human encounter between clients and therapists, and those rare moments of constructive change. Videotaped treatment sessions are carefully selected, and are usually edited to delete ineffective interventions, the periods where nothing seems to be happening, and they are packaged to highlight the dramatic changes brought about by brilliant therapeutic moves. Audiences of therapists usually then feel inadequate, thinking, "I could never do therapy like that."

There were other reasons I wanted to respond positively to Dr. Weber's letter. The family was being offered by an individual who was not only strongly motivated to work on family issues but a family therapist-psychologist who had some acquaintance with my work. Further, I was intrigued and challenged by the unique features and dynamics of the family. As I read the brief family history I began to shape a map of the family in my head, and to form some ideas of areas and themes I would want to pursue. I could also foresee some of the potential difficulties that lay ahead in working with this family. The loss of the mother seemed to me to be the key event in the family history, and I anticipated dealing with the mourning and aftershocks of that tragedy. I wondered whether I could connect with this father, a former college president, and whether I would be dealing with religious matters that were beyond my experience. I considered the effects of having a retarded child in the family, the impact of chronic illnesses in the family, and I was alert to the complex dynamics of the sibling relationships. Since I find the presence of siblings to be critical to the outcome of the family-of-origin sessions, I was pleased that there were five siblings in this family, and I knew I would want all of them in the family meetings. The significance of sibling relationships has been underrecognized by the mental health professions (Bank & Kahn, 1982; Bank & Lewis, 1988).

Because one major goal of family-of-origin consultations is to have the family members work out and resolve, face to face, whatever hard issues exist among them, it was fortunate, indeed, that the person organizing the family for this demonstration interview appeared to have fairly clear ideas about what he wanted to accomplish. I looked forward to finding out what the rest of the family wanted out of the experience.

I saw Dr. Weber alone in a preparation interview in order to get a detailed family history, and to assist him in preparing his agenda of issues to be dealt with in the sessions. Then I saw the whole family for 2 hours the next day, and an additional 2 hours the following day. (This family-of-origin procedure is fully described in Framo, 1992; a summary of my intergenerational approach is in Chapter 2 of this volume.) All interviews were held on stage in front of an audience of approximately 150 workshop participants, all mental health professionals. The interviews had a twofold purpose: The first was to provide the audience with a training experience in my family-of-origin method; the second was to provide the participating family with a therapeutic experience that could be useful to their relationships. The family was aware of the live audience and that all sessions were videotaped.

About six months after the initial family-of-origin consultations, Tim Weber called and asked whether I would be willing to do a follow-up consultation with his family. I was open to the suggestion because I believed in follow-ups and was also interested in whether and what kind of changes had taken place in the family. I proposed that my wife, Dr. Felise Levine, a psychologist-family therapist, join me in conducting the sessions. Felise and I, as a cotherapy team, had conducted numerous family-of-origin sessions, as well as individual, marital, and couples group therapies. A male–female team, working in consonance, adds an important gender expansion to the process. Tim agreed enthusiastically with the cotherapy format. The follow-up sessions were held a year after the first consultations, and included some spouses of the siblings for part of the consultations. That consultation was videotaped as well.

Over the course of several years we ran into Tim at professional conferences and had, over time, developed a collegial relationship with him. He brought us up to date on developments in his family, and told us he had been so impressed with the power of the family-of-origin approach that he had begun utilizing the method with his own clients.

Several years after the follow-up consultations with Tim's family, he wrote to me and Felise stating that he believed family-of-origin work was underrepresented in family therapy literature. He asked whether we would be interested in collaborating with him on an article or book on this intergenerational approach, particularly with reference to the consultation with his own family. Tim had also mentioned to his family his interest in writing a book about their experience. Although they have expressed concerns about their family life being disclosed to the public, they eventually agreed to the publication of the book. Felise and I were intrigued by the idea of writing a book about our work with Tim's family, so we accepted his invitation.

Then began a series of three-way discussions over a period of years on how such a book could be fashioned. The guiding concept of the book was to give a faithful account of the entire series of consultations by using the actual words spoken by family members and therapists during the sessions. We agreed that Tim would write about his own private thoughts, fears, and plans before, between, and following each of the sessions. Furthermore, the therapists decided to relate, in as honest a way as possible, their own personal associations and strategies that accompanied their interventions. This aspect of the psychotherapy process is rarely reported in the psychotherapy literature. What goes on in the mind of the consultant or therapist when he or she treats people whose emotions, utterances, and stories traverse the range of human experience? What feelings are aroused in therapists during treatment sessions?

An interesting parallel process accompanied our review of the videotaped sessions. While observing the family interactions and affective events, Felise, Tim, and I intermittently associated to events in our own families, and we three got more personal with each other in our disclosures. Conversations took place back and forth as we revealed information about our families and ourselves, and this sharing created an intimate space. Occasionally we moved from personal material to the higher levels of abstraction of theory construction as we speculated about aspects of family systems theory as applied to family-of-origin work. The self-disclosures, however, led to a kind of easy familiarity and comradeship that came to provide a safe envelope for the creating of this book project.

One barrier with this particular book was the confidentiality issue: our struggle over whether Tim should be himself in the book. For some time we explored having Tim be one of his clients whom he had referred for a family-of-origin session. However, we believed that Tim's recording of his experiences between sessions added a level of authenticity that could not be contrived as coming from one of his clients. Although the family had consented to the live interviews, allowing the book to be published with Tim using his real identity was another decision. Clearly this compromised the anonymity of the family. We are appreciative of the conflict family members went through in allowing Tim to appear as himself. We recognize their decision to allow him to be identified is a gift to Tim and to the field, for it allows this text to remain an honest account of the family-of-origin sessions. We also want to acknowledge Tim's father for his help in transcribing the videotaped consultations.

The nature of this enterprise required that Tim wear several hats. First, he was a member of the family being studied. Second, he had to step back and take the metaposition as a family clinician. Bowen (1978) stated that this stance could be looked upon as one of the first steps toward differentiation. A third hat for Tim was as a colleague with me and Felise as authors of a book. Felise and I also came to approach the clinical material from two vantage points. When we reviewed the videotapes of the sessions in Tim's presence, we responded with the requisite clinical detachment, but every now and then we would realize that we were not just discussing a mother, father, sister, or brother in a family, but we were discussing *Tim's* family! Despite our gender and age differences, and our ethnic and religious diversity (a WASP minister, a nonpracticing Catholic with an Italian background, and a secular Jew), our three-way collaboration developed into a friendship that persists to this day. Out of all this creative confusion has resulted a document that is novel in the mental health field.

Finally, because this family did not seem to have much fun of a frivolous, nonserious nature, we set aside a portion of the royalties to go into a play fund for the family to enjoy together. Again, we are indebted to this family for making this book possible.

Chapter 2

INTRODUCTION

JAMES L. FRAMO, PhD

In 1992, a book on the most important aspect of my work was published: *Family-of-Origin Therapy: An Intergenerational Approach* (Framo, 1992). The theoretical foundation for that approach was contained in my paper "Symptoms from a Family Transactional Viewpoint," originally published in 1970, and reprinted in my book of collected papers (Framo, 1982). This model addresses the hidden transgenerational forces that exercise critical influences on present-day intimate relationships. That is, current internal conflicts, as they play out in one's marital relationship, one's relationship with one's children, parents, or siblings, are viewed as metabolized residues of relationship paradigms that existed earlier in the family of origin. Employing object relations theory (Fairbairn, 1954), I have postulated that in their choice of intimate relationships, particularly a spouse, people attempt to make an interpersonal resolution of intrapsychic conflicts derived from their family of origin. Transference distortions from the past are lived through one's intimates, anachronistically. The introjects that were established by early identification with parental figures and other aspects of their family life became templates for later intimate relationships, sometimes leading to unrealistic and bizarre expectations of one's spouse, children, and other intimates. It is postulated that this process is fundamental to the distress and misery that we see clinically in individuals, couples, and families.

Rather than having adult clients work out their problems via the relationship with the therapist or depending on the therapist's techniques, I got the idea that many people could get their lives together by going

---

*In order to respect the privacy of family members, the first names of family members, except Timothy Weber, the second author of this book, are pseudonyms in the transcript and narrative.

back to where the problems began. Instead of the clients making a father, mother, sister, or brother out of the therapist, I would have them deal with the original transference figures by bringing them in for sessions. I thought that if I could help the original family to revisit old struggles and deal with the past and current hard issues, an opportunity existed for reconstructive change to occur on multiple system levels.

In the early days of doing this work, I was unprepared for the intensity of fear people have about bringing in their family of origin, but over the years I have developed methods for handling these natural apprehensions and for conducting family-of-origin sessions. The great resistance of clients toward bringing in their family of origin testifies to the great power of this approach. I believe this pivotal, intense, brief intervention can bring about more basic therapeutic changes than several years of psychotherapy for the individual family members. In this sense, I view family-of-origin therapy as the ultimate brief therapy—an important point considering the trend in the mental health professions toward short-term treatment.

Although most therapists recognize the importance of the family of origin in shaping people's lives, very few have utilized the family of origin as a therapeutic resource (Framo, 1976). Indeed, many therapists who do individual therapy regard the family of origin of their adult clients as the enemy, as noxious, and as undermining the treatment. Trying to help their clients become more independent and free of their families, they see as part of their task keeping the family at bay, or emphasizing the negative features of the parents (e.g., Forward, 1989).

In the family-of-origin sessions as I conduct them (usually with my wife, Dr. Felise Levine, as cotherapist), the family members are helped to articulate, sort out, and work through their honest and mixed feelings about other family members and family events. In this context of safety, an atmosphere is created where one can tell the people one loves what is in one's heart without the sky falling in. The family members usually engage each other with long-buried truths and secrets, and reveal the range of passions that exist in most families: ambivalence, jealousy, yearnings, unrequited love, disappointments, devotion, compassionate sacrifice, rivalrous feelings, nostalgic memories, unreserved love and admiration, anger and hurt, and so on. Family-of-origin consultations not only reveal how a family works, but also facilitate the family members' understanding of each others' motives and intentions, particularly regarding perceived past injustices. Old painful memories are usually reappraised and redefined; family cutoffs are usually repaired. This process enables longstanding misunderstandings, disputes, grievances, false beliefs, miscalculations, and wounds to be healed, eventually leading to discovery of positive qualities in each other and, ultimately, forgiveness. Eugene

O'Neill, in a letter to his wife about his autobiographical play, *A Long Day's Journey Into Night*, wrote, "I give you the original script of this play of old sorrow, written in tears and blood . . . truth in love enabled me to face my dead at last and write this play—write it with deep pity and understanding and forgiveness for all four haunted members of my family" (O'Neill, 1955). Had O'Neill come to terms with his family in family-of-origin sessions while they were still alive, some of the agony in his family might have been alleviated. But, then, the world would have been diminished by the loss of a great play.

In describing the procedures I have developed in preparing clients for family-of-origin sessions and for conducting them, I need to point out that there are two general kinds of clients who have these sessions. One category consists of those clients who are in ongoing marital or individual therapy with me and/or Felise. The other category is composed of adults who are not in treatment with either of us, but who request a family-of-origin consultation (as is the case in this book). These requests come from all over the country, typically from therapists, and are usually motivated by the desire to come to terms with parents before they die.

A detailed description of the methods I use is contained in Framo (1992). What follows is a brief summary of the 5-hour procedure.

- Clients in ongoing treatment are prepared for sessions over the course of the therapy, whereas those who are not regular clients are seen either alone or with their partner for a prior preparation session.
- The purpose of the preparation session for those who request these family meetings is to collect a detailed family history, and to assist the client in coming up with an agenda of issues the client wants to take up with his/her family. The partner can also help with this preparation phase. The client is also coached on how to involve reluctant family members, and is told to inform their family members that they are free to bring up whatever issues they wish when they come in.
- Clients in both categories need considerable support in managing their anxieties at the prospect of telling the truth to their family members, and being self-disclosing.
- The spouse of the client is not ordinarily included in family-of-origin sessions, primarily because the client's priority at this time is to deal with issues with parents and siblings, not his or her issues with the spouse.
- Two 2-hour sessions are held with the client and his or her parents, brothers, and sisters, with a break between the two segments. The breaks vary in length from several hours to overnight. During this break the family members struggle to integrate the varied perspectives expressed in the prior 2 hours. Various family members often discuss the ses-

sions on their own during the break. Subtle shifts and changes in attitude often emerge, even on the part of those who keep their thoughts to themselves.

- The safe context of the sessions, where disloyalty to the family is legitimized, allows grievances and love to be expressed in open fashion. Adult sons and daughters hear their parents' stories and get to know more about what the parents had to struggle with in their lives. The parents become more real and human to their sons and daughters instead of being mythic figures who are either denigrated or idealized. Sibling issues are dealt with, and alienated family members usually become more accepting of each other.

- Some of my regular clients have follow-up family-of-origin sessions, or continue their individual or marital therapy. A follow-up debriefing session is usually held with the clients who request family-of-origin sessions in order to process the experience and explore the relevance of the sessions to their present lives. Some of these clients return to their own therapists and use the family-of-origin experience to accelerate and further their treatment.

It needs to be emphasized that family-of-origin consultations are not a general method of psychotherapy. This procedure is a highly specialized intervention that can be utilized by therapists who recognize that their clients cannot progress until they work out some important matters with parents and siblings. In that sense, the family-of-origin consultation should not be looked upon as an emergency procedure or crisis intervention.

Throughout this volume, the terms family-of-origin *consultation* and family-of-origin *therapy* have been used interchangeably. Although in a strict sense the family-of-origin model is not therapy per se, because the incoming family members are not patients or clients who are explicitly agreeing to an ongoing therapy contract, nonetheless the method has many of the characteristics of therapy. Certainly, therapeutic changes take place in most cases as a result of the procedure. The therapists (or consultants) are using therapy skills in facilitating the family members to work on their issues with each other, although we consider our primary role in these sessions to be that of facilitators rather than therapists. On the other hand, the consultation model (Wynne, McDaniel, & Weber, 1986) consists of a consultant entering a system (such as a family) temporarily, guiding interactions, offering observations, and exiting without any long-term commitment. The distinctions between the two models are, therefore, blurred. Both models are brief interventions, both shake up the system sufficiently to bring about change, both foster the inherent resources of the family, and both do not usually contract for continuing work together.

Those therapists who are interested in applying this method to their clients, or are interested in having family-of-origin sessions themselves, will find in this book how this particular intergenerational method was used with an actual family. (Parenthetically, I do believe that therapists who plan to do this work should first have family-of-origin sessions themselves.) Using actual verbatim transcripts and descriptions of the family's interactions, the therapist's interventions, the therapist's personal associations, the personal associations of family members, and the family members' responses to the interventions, the reader can follow, step-by-step, the stages of a family-of-origin consultation. Although intergenerational family therapy has become one of the major theories in family therapy (Boszormenyi-Nagy & Krasner, 1986; Bowen, 1978; Freeman, 1992; Hargrave, 1997; Headley, 1977; Hovestadt & Fine, 1987; Roberto, 1992; Satir & Baldwin, 1983; Searight, 1997; Whitaker, 1989; Williamson, 1991), there is a paucity of information about its clinical application, and how this approach is used with real families.

OUTLINE OF CHAPTERS

In Chapter 3, Tim Weber, one of the authors of this book, who was also a member of the family being presented, gives a detailed account of his personal struggle in organizing the consultation. In a remarkable document, he describes his fears, expectations, fantasies, hoped-for results, anticipated reactions of family members, his qualms about what could go wrong, and other considerations that enter into preparing for a family-of-origin meeting. This chapter gives an inside view of some of the apprehensions that precede the prospect of bringing one's family together for the purpose of telling and hearing the truth, changing roles, breaking family rules, setting the record straight, reconnecting with emotionally distant or belligerent family members, and trying to make sure no one, especially parents, gets hurt in the process. Although the entire book gives some idea of what can be accomplished in family-of-origin consultations, this section of the book will be useful for people planning to have sessions with their original family, especially concerning strategies for involving and gathering together the family, deciding what one wants to do with one's family, and managing one's anxieties.

Chapter 4 contains excerpts from the preparation interview of Tim alone; in this session he gave a family history, and was helped to develop his agenda and prepare emotionally for the family sessions. Chapter 6 presents the proceedings of the first 2 hours of the consultation with the whole family, where they all primarily dealt with the major event in their lives—the loss of mother and wife—and the many intense and ambivalent feelings they carried in response to her living and dying. In Chapter

8, the second 2 hours of the consultation, which occurred on the following day, the major themes were centered on relationships of the adult children with the father, as well as the sibling relationships. Tim, in Chapters 5, 7, 9, and 12, narrates his reflections and reactions to each of these sessions. He discusses in a frank, open way the thoughts and feelings that got stirred up in him by the consultations. He also reports on his perceptions of the reactions of other family members. Chapters 10 and 11 consist of the 4 hours of the follow-up consultation with the family, which occurred 1 year after the first consultation, and included both Felise and myself as cotherapists. Two spouses of the young adults were present in the second half of the follow-up consultation. In Chapter 12 Tim reports on his reactions to the follow-up consultation.

Because we didn't wish to rely just on Tim's report of his family members' responses, in later months Felise interviewed by phone all family members who had participated in the family-of-origin consultation. They were asked about their thoughts and feelings relative to the sessions. The findings of these phone interviews are incorporated in Chapter 13, "Authors' Trialogue."

Chapter 13 consists of excerpts from a tape-recorded, free-wheeling trialogue among the three authors. Tim stepped out of his role as family member to comment as a family therapist professional about the dynamics of his family and his role in it—taking distance and viewing his own family with some objectivity. We three discussed this intergenerational method itself and its applicability, not only to this family but also to various clinical problems.

MULTIPLE VOICES

This family's story is told in multiple voices. The central voice—the bulk of the book—is that of the family itself, as revealed in the selected verbatim transcripts of the actual words spoken by the family members during the family-of-origin consultations. The remaining family transactions, not directly quoted, are presented in the form of descriptive summaries. If we had printed every word of the 9 hours of consultation this book would consist of many volumes.

A distinctive feature of this book is that the therapists' statements, questions, and therapeutic interventions are also reported as they actually occurred (myself in the first consultation and the cotherapy team in the follow-up consultation). Unlike other published case histories, we emphasize that we have taken no literary license to modify the words spoken by the family members or therapists. That is to say, the transcript is a faithful, verbatim account of what was said, a "true" nonfictionalized record of what happened in real time. To be sure, we deleted some material (to include all of it would have required many volumes) but we did not change what was left in. My assessment of the family's dynamics, and comments about the rationale for my techniques and strategies, are distributed throughout the transcript. Sometimes I compare events and experiences in the consultation with this family with those observed in other family-of-origin sessions. I go further: I report on the private, inner associations and feelings I had while conducting the sessions, only some of which were communicated to the family. Indeed, sometimes the ghosts of my own family of origin made their presence felt in the therapy room (Framo, 1968).

Another uncommon feature of this book is that Felise makes meta-comments throughout the text on my interventions, style, and intergenerational method. Felise and I are a husband–wife cotherapy team who have conducted numerous family-of-origin consultations together. We know each other well, and know each other's thinking and therapy styles. Felise also gives her own views of the family's dynamics, as well as her ideas about treatment.

The person of the therapist and the use of self of the therapist in psychotherapy has been a recurrent area of exploration (e.g., Aponte, 1992; Ferber, Mendelsohn, & Napier, 1972; Levine, 1997; Weber & Levine, 1995). It may surprise or chagrin people to discover that therapists are human, sometimes uncertain, fallible, have their own blind spots and areas of vulnerability, their own set of values, and are not all-knowing like the Wizard of Oz was supposed to be. Our candidness in discussing the basis of our therapeutic moves and subjective personal associations reveals some of the nuances and intricacies of this innovative method, and shows how the theory is translated into clinical practice.

In many ways, Tim had the most difficult task of all. As a family member he could speak from the inside, like a double agent, and tell the story behind the story. At the same time, like all of us, Tim was subject to the powerful influence of his own family forces. When you are with your family you are not the same person that you are with other people; in general, your immature personality features emerge, along with your vulnerabilities. How to keep your head straight while immersed in the crosscurrents of your family is one of life's most challenging questions—a puzzle that Murray Bowen spent a lifetime trying to solve (Bowen, 1978). Because Tim is also a psychologist-family therapist, he contributes his own voice as a participant-observer. That he achieved the appropriate balance between these two roles was quite a feat.

The weaving together of all these voices and stories has been the challenge of this book, the result of a generative, collaborative effort on the part of the three authors.

There are certain naturalistic universals of family life. Families can provide the deepest satisfactions of living—love, devotion, attachment,

joy and fun, belonging, loyalty, familiar sounds and smells, the taste of
family food, family games, rituals, and vacations, and the kind of unconditional acceptance for which no price is too high to pay. At the same
time, every family, like every individual, has its demons and dark side. All
families have to deal with the backstage or underground currents of family life, such as family secrets, conflicts over who gets more, jealousy, guilt,
anger, competition, scapegoating, family discrimination, losses, neglect,
unfairness, emotional unavailability, conditional acceptance, crossing of
boundaries, deleterious alliances, abuse in its various forms, exploita-
tion, and generational heritages.

It should come as no surprise that, like all families, the family in this
book had its issues. But what the transcripts of the consultations more
compellingly reveal is how this normal family—having a foundation of
commitment, of trustworthiness, and deep caring for each other—con-
tended with their crises, losses, and relationship struggles. Their courage
in letting the world know how they dealt with their difficulties should
make therapy seem less frightening and intimidating, and perhaps encourage other families to seek help when help is necessary. The resilience
of this family in the face of tragedy is testimony to their coping abilities
and resources (Wolin & Wolin, 1993). The family therapy literature is
replete with accounts of so-called "dysfunctional families," whereas reports of how normal families survive life's exigencies are few in number
(Lewis, Beavers, Gossett, & Phillips, 1976; Walsh, 1993).

When the adult children "come home again" in these family-of-origin consultations they reevaluate and attempt to complete old, unfinished business with the original transference figures—the people who
always mattered most to them. The reader can follow in this book the
entire course of one of these consultations where family members are
given the opportunity, in a safe context, to work out, face-to-face, the
impasses that have existed among them. One can witness the movement
of this family from the pain of mourning its losses and expressing its
longings to a place of rediscovery and connecting of themselves and each
other, enabling them to move on with greater freedom of choice.

Now let the story begin.

PART II

THE INITIAL
FAMILY
CONSULTATION

Chapter 3

RECRUITING THE FAMILY

Fears, Perils, and Hopes

TIMOTHY T. WEBER, PhD

SEIZING THE OPPORTUNITY

What precipitated my interest in doing some work with my own family was receiving a letter from the American Board of Professional Psychology announcing an institute on "Intergenerational Marital and Family Therapy" with Jim Framo. The announcement described the institute as follows:

> In this workshop, Dr. Framo will present his method of working with families of origin. This powerful intervention is based on the premise that coming to terms with parents and siblings before they die will have beneficial effects on one's current intimate relationships. That is to say, marital and divorce problems can be alleviated by preparing clients to face the issues from the past directly with their families of origin.

I was drawn to the letter. For a number of years I had been eager to spend some time with Jim Framo, after having read about his intergenerational approach in graduate school and postgraduate training. I was beginning to have an increasing interest in incorporating family of origin work in my own professional practice as a clinical psychologist and family therapist. I had been requesting patients to work with their families, and did not want to continue to ask them to do things that I had not done myself. I had to experience this work myself to genuinely request it of my patients, and to better understand the emotional journey behind these ventures into the family.

But there was a more personal drive. In reading the announcement, I was struck by the words "coming to terms with parents and siblings before they die." I had not done so with my mother before her death 8 years prior. The night my mother died of coronary failure, at the age of 53, the spark for this family of origin work was ignited. Her death was so unexpected, so shocking, so stunning. I was unprepared. Before her death, I naively believed that there was time, surely enough time to work out the murky drama of family relationships. Whatever was not worked out, unfinished, could be resolved as life settled down.

My mother's sudden death, however, left me without any direct, face-to-face chance for conversation and closure. I felt unfinished, sad, and angry at myself. From that experience I learned how important it is to be aware of the quickness of life, and to not let relationships drift. I did not want to make the same mistake again.

I not only had things to say to my father and siblings before any of us died, but I wanted to hear what they had to say to me. I believed that if I could live more consciously, more aware with this original group, then I would be able to live more intentionally and intimately with others in my life. I also knew I would have a clearer direction for my own life's journey if I could engage my family members more intentionally.

I knew that part of what I needed to do was to define myself more clearly in relationship with my family members while staying engaged with them in a receptive mode. Instead of fleeing or fighting them, I wanted to encounter them with my own beliefs, perceptions, values without being dogmatic. I wanted to be open to their viewpoints with reflectiveness instead of reactivity. I wanted to be more open to differences between us, moving away from this penchant of trying to convince them of my "truth." I wanted to respect instead of trying to reform. I was becoming clearer about this process of "defining myself" (Kerr & Bowen, 1988) and knew that this journey was arduous, especially for an offspring from the German Lutheran tradition where the rigidity of truth is like skin—it sticks tight.

CRAZY IDEAS

I began to imagine more than merely attending this Framo workshop. Why not volunteer my family as a "demonstration family" for the workshop. For years I had gently toyed with the idea of bringing my family together for a consultation with Jim. Now, especially if we didn't have to pay for this consultation (getting things cheap, on sale, or free are prized family values) how could we pass up this opportunity!

I also believed my family would be more receptive to Jim's style that I perceived as gentle, but still provocative—an embodiment of the "velvet hammer." I remember being very protective of my family (and also myself) at this point, wanting to choose the best "surgeon" for the operation. Although I was mindful of what Jim's impact would be on the entire family, I was most concerned about my father. Would my father "click" with Jim? Would they fight? Would my father allow Jim to enter our family? I felt like I was setting up a blind date. I didn't want my father coming back to me later saying, "I can't believe what you got me into!"

Before doing anything else, I decided to consult my wife, Annie, about this risky plan. I knew I would need her support if I were to proceed with gathering together my family. I also wanted to get a "reality check" from her, being uncertain about bringing my family together as a demonstration family before a group of strange mental health professionals. Would I be making things worse? Would I be stirring up trouble that could not be resolved? I had heard my patients asking these questions and regarded them as resistive. Now I heard those same questions in mine and regarded them with respect.

Annie was stunned when I told her I wanted to gather my family for this institute. Her reaction was not based so much on the crazy idea (she knew I was highly prone to such unorthodox thinking). Rather, she was incredulous that my family would accept such a proposal: "Your family will never do this. They are private people. They won't talk to you about their growing up."

As we talked, she became more enthusiastic and supportive, recognizing an opportunity for our marriage and family life. Annie had always been bothered by my skill in putting her in the place of my mother, and was bothered by my emotional distancing. She believed she was more connected than I was to members of my family, especially my sisters, and she wanted me to develop a closer relationship with my siblings. She thought I needed to work on sensitivity, compassion, consideration, vulnerability, and warmth. She said, "I'd like to see you give to your family what they need. I like your family, and I don't like them to be critical of you." Her endorsement and continuing consultation through the process were grounding and guiding. Annie also thought that this consultation would improve my parenting, and would increase intimacy between us, possibly shifting my pattern of overworking, distancing, and "living on the edge"—patterns that had developed in my family of origin.

We thought about reasons not to proceed with this idea. Would we open up wounds that could not be closed? Would I say things that could not be heard and would remain unforgiven? Worse yet, would I be heard and still be unforgiven? Would I not forgive or listen? Would I find out about secrets that I didn't want to know? Would all of this be boring so that family members would complain that I wasted their time? Just a hair away from the worry of boredom was this worry: would one or more of us die in the process? Was this the right time and place...maybe another time and place?

There is never a right time and right place. If this work weren't risky it wouldn't be useful. I believed that the potential side effects were worth it. We were hopeful enough that going back to my family and facing my family members eyeball to eyeball would somehow help me be more free of the legacies, ghosts, and patterns that were boggling us.

I NEED YOUR HELP TO HELP ME

Before contacting Jim about the possibility of our family being the demonstration family, I wanted to test out this idea with my father and siblings. The most important task was to assess whether there was any interest for this kind of venture. If I sensed at least some interest, I resolved to put all my energy toward enlisting family members for the consultation.

I was anxious as I anticipated calling family members. My anxiety was less about how they would respond and more about myself. Did I really want to go through with this? Was the cost too great? What might I hear about myself that I did not want to hear? What was I afraid to say to whom? Worries about how my family would respond to this inquiry masked more potent worries within my own heart. As much as I wanted healing in our family, I wanted healing for myself. This self-focus needed to be the primary driver. I could not change them; working on that never works anyway. The primary target of this project had to be me, my change, or else this work would fail.

I invited them to join me in this consultation because "I need your help to help me." This position was different from their perception of the invincible son and brother who did not need help. I described to them my stuckness, my isolation, the strain in my marriage and parenting, and my emotional constriction. I also identified some of the painful, unresolved issues in the family that I wanted to work through, such as the agony around my mother's life and death and my own regrets; the distance between myself and my father; and isolation from my siblings.

In contacting family members I wanted to state clearly: (a) that I wanted this consultation for myself; (b) that I needed the help of other family members; (c) that I had specific issues I wanted to work on in the consultation; and (d) that they would also have the opportunity to work on matters they deemed important. Naming some of the concerns I wanted to address helped give focus to my request and accented the note of urgency within me.

Throughout my life, I had been perceived as the "hero" in the family, the special privileged one, the only child to be seen and baptized by my maternal grandfather, destined to proudly carry on the family tradition. I was the firstborn, a male, and a success in virtually everything I did. (Although, looking back, I believe I carefully arranged most everything in my life so that the outcome would be successful, avoiding most opportunities that had a significant degree of risk. I was expert in leading a highly restricted but successful life.) My parents and siblings looked to me as an example of achievement. But at this point I wanted to come to my family in a completely different way. My call for their help grew out of this authentic need to be more than who I had been.

PROBING THE SYSTEM—FATHER

I decided to contact my father first. This would be a test of my own personal authority (Williamson, 1991). Would I be able to state clearly to him my opinion, my pain, my request? I had dealt with intimidation, historically, by distancing from my father and others. Approaching him in this manner—as peer with a need—was a shift away from distancing and toward engaging. By taking this risk, I also was intending to build more trust in our relationship. Just contacting him with this request was already a first step in changing our relationship.

I believed that if my father would agree to this consultation the rest of the family would follow. I wanted to respect the family hierarchy. If he accepted, other family members would be given tacit "permission" to also accept. Loyalty to my father was solid enough that it would be difficult for other family members to decide against my father.

I had some feelings of disloyalty as I thought about approaching my father. The development of personal authority is often laced with feelings of disloyalty. I had strong doubts about my father's receptivity to the idea of a family of origin meeting. When I went to graduate school in clinical psychology my father was concerned that I would be too focused on my feelings, doing this "navel gazing" as he called it. Although he supported my graduate education in psychology, he always seemed to be a distant critic of the profession and its limitations. He came from the "old school" and thought psychology placed too much emphasis on feelings.

Then there were also feelings of father loyalty in this invitation. I believed my father had painful regrets, most unspoken, about not having been in the emotional life of the family over the years as much as he could have been. This consultation with the family could be one potent means of dealing with those regrets. I could help him by inviting him to help me and others in the family in a forum that would have a big emotional price tag for him and yet ultimately be rewarding.

I wondered whether he would perceive this family consultation as too emotionally costly and painful. Worrisome to me was my perception of my father's personality—preacher, intellectual, emotionally closed to others, closed to himself, but very pleasant in a social role. I also believed he would be frightened about any family gathering that would review our history, especially events surrounding my mother's death and an examination of her life. Would he be afraid of being criticized as father and husband, partly responsible for my mother's struggles and the frailties in his children? (Having children of my own heightened my awareness around parental mistakes and the raw feelings about being told about those mistakes.) I also wondered whether he feared that this consultation would push family members away from each other rather than bringing them closer together. He had been expressing concerns about the family's increasing geographical distance from each other as we matured and moved away from home.

Throughout my life I had experienced him, similar to how many children experience their fathers, as emotionally distant and more wedded to his work. I could not recall many meaningful and personal conversations with my father in all our years together. Our relationship was marked by respect, politeness, caution, handshakes. I had sought out his opinion occasionally over the years on such matters as my girlfriends, education, theological issues. We had talked about his life changes such as his remarriage and retirement. I think he had been seeing me more as an adult; he was interested in my opinions.

I called my father one evening, outlining the conditions in my own life that sparked such a request for the family to gather to help me. He was flabbergasted. Why in the world would his heroic son need this kind of assistance? Was he going off the deep end? I also added that the family meeting (I said "meeting" because he knew "meetings," but not "therapy") might benefit the entire family. We could use the gathering to deal with important matters such as our history as a family, and our relationships, my mother's life and death, my brother Thomas's mental retardation, how we might work to strengthen our relationships with each other. I told him that I was becoming more aware of how strange it was that, for all we had experienced together as a family, we had never really talked—not at all—together in one family group for any length of time about what happened to us and what really matters. How could families live together for decades and not come together in this way? I then briefly described what I knew about Jim: his expertise in the field and his integration of both compassion and incisiveness. I concluded by describing some of the logistics—professional institute, demonstration family, working in front of an audience of other therapists. In conclusion, as a clincher, I threw in, "It won't cost you anything, Dad!"

My father's response stunned me: "I think it would be okay. Why not?" His unequivocal openness to the invitation was unlike the father I knew. But, then, did I know him? He then added, possibly to establish some logic to the idea, "I'll do anything to help science." I had been poised for some fight, as least a challenge. Now I was taken off guard, prepared for a battle that was not happening. My perceptions were changing even at this gathering point. I was delighted, but confused. I had to reconsider certain assumptions about my father's rigidity.

There was another part of me that was respecting the new part of my father emerging in the moment. To be sure, I had respected his professional stature and achievements. But I had rarely seen the personal side of him and his more adventuresome spirit. He was willing to enter a completely unpredictable event, not as an expert but as a novice. He was willing to risk discomfort. I decided to tell him how much I appreciated his openness to the idea. Trying to temper my enthusiasm, he added, "Often things like this are played up, but they really don't result in much." I had heard this before from him. One of my father's themes in life was to dampen enthusiasm and pride so that he and others might not be disappointed if the anticipated outcomes did not materialize. He had told me, as if this was one way he cared, that if disappointment does follow, the downfall would not be as severe.

My father needed to frame this consultation in a way that would help him move forward. I needed to respect his language, his view of the world, without trying to convert him to my view. I had to continue with what I could get, not rebuking him for what I did not have. Focusing on what he was giving me, I was pleased that he simply was willing to enter a completely unpredictable and challenging situation that was important to me, his son.

PROBING THE SYSTEM—SIBLINGS

After calling my father I turned to Katie, the oldest of my three younger sisters. She was the one sibling who would challenge me the most. I valued her position as a "senior sibling" in her somewhat maternal role in the family. She would have a good deal of influence with my other two sisters, Ann and Lynn.

But it was this contentious spirit between Katie and me that bothered me the most. I had teased her when we were children. I remember one lengthy summer vacation in my preteen years when my verbal jabs to her were regularly returned with her deep nail scratches to my skin. These contests between us were more than sibling rivalry. She believed that I, as older brother, had not supported her as younger sister, and that she had been left with tension-filled domestic and maternal responsibilities at home while I escaped these duties as the heroic "boy knight" outside the home. It was like we were acting out the parental drama, not uncommon for siblings. I remembered only a trace of compassion and tender affection between us. It seems we reflected the mood of strain within our home, living metaphors of our household tension. I was uncomfortable with the prevailing mood between us, yet I was even more uneasy in talking about it with her.

I doubted that Katie would be open to this proposal of a family consultation, perhaps seeing this as another one of my heroic acts to which again she would have to succumb. Annie also anticipated that Katie would not want to come. She had heard Katie's criticisms of me over the years, and believed that Katie would be reluctant to join with me in this venture.

Katie seemed to be taken aback by my call as I put forward the kind of invitation she had never heard from me. She asked, as if I were on drugs, "Why do you want to do this?" Again, I repeated my major theme—that this coming together was for me, and I needed the help of other family members. She may have been hearing a different side of me that was new and puzzling to her, possibly attractive. Then again, I was also placing myself in the center of the family and asking others to follow me. Was she perceiving me, again, as the hero at work? I explained to her that I had seen Jim work; I liked him because he was "gentle" (maybe if I saw gentleness she would have hope of gentleness in me) and I really wanted the help of other family members so that I could work on some issues that had been bothering me: dimensions of myself that were not right. I also added that there were issues in the family that I wanted to talk about, such as our mother's life and death, and our own sibling relationship that had been strained.

If she even agreed to join the venture, she was making it clear that she was doing this for me, that it was a gift. I don't think I have appreciated and acknowledged Katie's depth of sacrifice for me and for the family. Here again, it appeared that I was getting and she was giving. It was my hope that the strained threads of all our relationships could be repaired and strengthened. In my mind, this was for our family, not only myself. But from her perspective, this was another costly sacrifice for another member in the family—me. I was not acknowledging to her that she was giving me this gift. And I also wanted to say to her, "Katie, don't you see that I am trying to help the family, not just myself!" We were two family members blinded to the gifts we were trying to offer each other. As we concluded our conversation Katie said, "I'll think about it."

As I had anticipated, my other two sisters, Lynn and Ann, were receptive to the idea and supportive of me sending a letter to Jim. I'm sure they were influenced by our father's endorsement and Katie's partial openness. My father and Katie seemed complementary to each other. My father took care of the head ("This is a good idea to help science") and Katie took care of the heart ("Why would you want to put the family through this?"). In a crazy way, I felt like a child asking my "parents" (my father and Katie, who replaced my mother) for their support. When I presented the possibility to Lynn, she rebounded with delight, "Oh, wow!" She said that because she had already had general psychology in college, "I'll know some of the terms."

I did not contact my brother Thomas in this preliminary stage. He had been living in a residential home for the retarded since he was about 15 years old. Looking back, I should have acknowledged him by informing him of my intentions and efforts, asking for his response. It has always been difficult for me to talk with him. His level of understanding usually is minimal, and our conversations typically are strained with his stuttering, seemingly endless repetition of simple questions, and minimal interaction. It is sad for me to say that it feels like I never have had a brother. In many ways I have felt like an only child—I with myself and three younger sisters that seem to form their own family. I also have felt driven, like I am trying to live two lives: my life and the life of my brother, making up for what he has been unable to do.

CONTINUING THE PREPARATION

Having received the tentative approval of family members to go ahead with the consultation, I wrote to Jim Framo, who accepted our offer as a demonstration family for his workshop. Jim explained the procedure of what would happen at the workshop. He said he would spend 1 hour interviewing me, getting a brief family history, assessing what I wanted, my goals, and preparing an agenda of issues to be dealt with. He told me he wanted to meet with the family for 2 hours on each of the following 2 days. He stated that it was necessary for all the family members to attend the sessions. We also reviewed the procedures of signing consent forms, agreeing to be videotaped, and the structure of the workshop as a training session.

When he began to describe his procedure by saying, "I'll start by asking people to say something positive about the family," I was pleased. I knew it would be easier for my family to engage in the consultation with this kind of support. I was focused on protecting my family. The idea of starting with something positive was comforting. Jim told me to ask family members to think about what issues they wanted to raise during the family sessions. I knew that I had to keep the focus on myself as the one who was seeking help from my family while, at the same time, broadening the goals of the consultation to include the agendas of other family members. The balance seemed delicate. Jim concluded by asking me to get back to him once I had obtained the consent of all family members.

That same night I called all the other family members. My father and youngest sister, Lynn, were receptive. I informed them of the plan Jim had discussed with me. Before calling Katie I committed myself to support her in any way I could so that she could attend the family consultation. I said that I would pay her airfare, and I offered to bring my son, Ty, so that her daughter would have a playmate. I wanted to smooth out as many of the logistical humps as I could so that all family members could focus on the emotional processes between us. In this age of jet travel and mobility, it is not as difficult as it may seem to convene family members for these consultations. The major resistance is not logistics or technology, but fear.

My call to my middle sister, Ann, was probably the most personal and extensive of all the conversations I had with family members at this stage. I had not spoken with her for any length of time for about 6 months. We talked about our relationship and its history, how she and I had distanced from one another, how she hardly knew me and Katie, her older siblings. She was heartened that Lynn and she had been getting closer during the past year. She added, sadly, that Dad had seen her once in the last 6 months although they lived only 90 minutes from each other.

Conversations with my sisters usually took the shape of a triangle, with both of us talking about my father and our concerns about his various predicaments in life. Gossiping about him could bring me and my sisters closer together without ever having to really talk about ourselves. I was also dimly aware that when we talked about my father we also seemed to be talking about me indirectly. His intellectualization, his distancing, his quirks were all mine, too.

I began to realize that our family had used this triangulating through our history as a way of managing stress, fearful of dealing openly and directly with each other. My father and I had often gossiped about my mother. I had talked with one sister about another sister and my brother. All of us would talk about my brother without talking directly to him, because he would take offense or not understand. I had suspicions that my sisters were talking about me without coming to me directly. I believe, in our family, we carried around secrets about each other because we did not want to raise conflict, hurt others, or increase the tension within the home. We lived in a home where personal privacy was a dominant value at the cost of intimacy.

About a week later, Katie called back to share some concerns she had about this consultation. She described herself as a "private person" and said that she really did not want to talk about some things. I reassured her that she would have "veto power," and would not have to talk if she didn't want to. It seemed that she was fearful of being put on the spot and being coerced to say things she really didn't want to say. She pressed on, pushing for more specifics on what Jim would do. Perhaps this information would settle her, giving her structure and predictability. Katie said to me with both envy and irritation, "You are secure, you don't have to worry. Also, it's your profession." Again, she was following my lead, doing what I wanted to do, feeling one down to older brother.

I tried to convey to her what I knew. I told her that I could not exactly predict what Jim would do. If she wanted to know more specifics, I suggested that she call him, and I gave her his phone numbers. I was concerned that I was being cast into the role of "expert," an insider in the world of mental health, rather than as another family member. I had to move out of this role, wanting all questions about the institute and the arrangements to be referred to Jim. I also did not want to comment on matters I really could not speak about. I reiterated that Jim was "gentle," and found myself amplifying this trait to calm family members in their worry about being "under the knife of a shrink." Katie seemed to be only mildly calmed.

Shifting the balance from my role as family hero and helper to needy struggler was essential. I know I had to send a letter to the family, elevating this goal and deferring questions about the consultation to Jim and his previous work. I sent the following letter to each family member, along with a copy of Jim's article on the method of these family-of-origin meetings (Framo, 1976):

> Dear Family,
>
> I appreciate that each of you is willing to participate in the upcoming sessions with Jim Framo, especially since our meetings will be in front of a seminar of family therapists. I hope that these two meetings will help me at my "stuck points" such as overwork, hesitancy toward intimacy, and withdrawal. I also hope to strengthen my bonds with each of you.
>
> Dr. Framo has informed me to pass on to you that he will meet with us from 10 a.m. to 12 noon on both Tuesday and Wednesday (four hours total). He will interview me for one hour on Monday to get some family history, and to help me clarify what I want out of these consultations.
>
> I would like to videotape the meetings. However, my video equipment was stolen from my office last week, and so now I am forced to explore means of getting the equipment. My immediate interest in taping is to have the tape available for our own review, and our spouses' review if we wish. Dr. Framo has requested a copy of the tape if we tape.
>
> I have enclosed an article that Dr. Framo wrote a number of years ago on these family-of-origin meetings.
>
> If you have any questions please give me a call.
>
> Love, Tim

In preparation for the actual family consultation, the relationship dynamics within the family were actually shifting. These changes in the preconsultation phase can be as impactful as changes brought about as a result of the consultation. The old family drama wasn't working as it once did. New lines were being added; old lines were being questioned. Characters began to act out of character.

I felt especially supported by my wife during this preparation phase. I wondered how difficult it could have been had Annie resisted my intention to meet with my family. I found myself sharing with her often, using her as a consultant, seeking her encouragement, which she gave in abundance. I didn't want to exclude her too much from this process. Had I blocked her off and moved ahead without her, perhaps she would have come to resent my getting closer to my family and moving away from her. Williamson (1991) noted the importance of having a supportive spouse in doing this work. As he wrote, "It is difficult to fight a war (or transform relationships) simultaneously on two fronts" (p. 68).

Unlike Annie, my family members expressed mounting concerns. Thomas told me that Katie was "scared of the meeting," as he had found out in talking with her. Here he was playing one of his familial roles: the emotional switchboard, conveying information back and forth between family members. Lynn was worried that the family meeting would destroy the progress that she believed we had been making in the family over the last several years. My sisters were anxious that these family meetings would spark a catastrophe of some sort, upsetting the delicate emotional ecology of our family.

Without being prompted by me, Lynn talked about how mother's death was more of a concern to her now than when mother had died. Specifically, she was reacting to a comment that my father had made to her, "You're just like Mom." Apparently, my father saw Lynn's abrupt mood changes as being similar to the mood variations in my mother. This deepening conversation between us was something different. Simply anticipating a family consultation can begin to create change, evoking from family members memories, images, beliefs, feelings that are latent but now acknowledged.

Linda, my father's wife, informed me that during the family consultation she would be going away for a few days when we were meeting. She said, "I don't want to interfere." She was respecting the boundaries of our family of origin, allowing us to have a space to retreat to between the meetings. Had she been present our conversations between the meetings might have been diluted by her benign interference. As it turned out, conversations among us between the meetings were as important as our conversations during the meetings.

When I saw old, familiar behaviors from my family of origin—distancing, cutoff, isolation, blame—being duplicated across contexts in marriage, work, friendships, it became increasingly difficult for me to blame these behaviors on context—where I was instead of who I was. I had to take more responsibility for these behaviors. I could only move so many times, be in so many relationships. As I was getting older, I saw the same problems repeating themselves regardless of who I was with, where I was living, what I was doing.

We had been a religious family—Lutheran Christian. The long roots of both my father's and mother's generations extended firmly into the soil of American Lutheranism. My father was a Lutheran pastor. My mother was a Lutheran teacher. There were dozens of Lutheran pastors and teachers that dotted the landscape of our family tree. No wonder I went to a Lutheran seminary! Functioning in some Lutheran vocation, minimally being active in the Lutheran church, was the "union card" of family loyalty.

Our family faithfully followed this historical drama, incorporating Lutheran symbols and traditions within our family culture. Two of my sisters, Katie and Lynn, and I attended Lutheran schools from kindergarten through college. I continued my loyalty by going on to a Lutheran seminary. This was the same Lutheran seminary my father had attended in his preparation for the ministry. (If I first paid this debt, then I was entitled to go on to graduate school in clinical psychology. I had merited this privilege.)

My other sister, Ann, was more adventuresome than any of us, and attended a state university. She also "jumped ship" and joined a nondenominational church, continuing in this different tradition with her husband. I remember when they were married, the wedding seemed so different (more low key, informal, no clergy vestments, hymns not in the Lutheran hymnbook) that I felt odd being in this different religious culture, and somewhat of an accomplice in this act of disloyalty to our ancestors. The moment you are most aware of family norms is not when you are keeping them, but when you are breaking them!

Despite the tendency toward restrictiveness and insulation from cultural diversity within our German–Lutheran–Christian religious heritage, there were many values in this tradition that I came to appreciate: a deep faith that seemed to both ground us and give us a vision of abiding hope; a commitment to service in the wider community beyond a narcissistic service to ourselves; a tenacity in human relationships buttressed by the core value of forgiveness; using our resources as gifts for others rather than as fuel for consumptive materialism; a sense of participating in a very important story stretching back eons into Judeo-Christian roots and a confidence that this story will stretch well into the future. I was well aware of all the criticisms of the church, many of them justified, some not. What I knew was that this tradition in my family was foundational and strong, bequeathing to me identity, community, confidence, and mission.

Yet in spite of all these benefits, something was missing. I was missing a vitality, a vibrancy that springs forth when people begin to strip the varnish of pretense and secrecy. I was missing warmth. I wanted us to be more welcoming of our full selves, not just the partial self of success. I had been working overtime in life, too compulsively, pushing away my foibles and trying to polish the ones I could not push away. I think I had been trying the same project with my family, cutting myself off from whatever I saw as negative, embarrassing, shameful. I saw others in my family locked into this same position.

Although I indeed wanted to upgrade my relationship with other family members, I did not want risk-taking and truth-telling to be sacrificed for "better relationships." Too many families are propped up like a house of thin cards that easily topple when truth is spoken. Especially in my family's history with its professionalism, religiosity, and public life, it seemed like we were often posing publicly for others, and then carried that "smile for the camera" pose into our private lives, hiding what we easily declared as "dirty." Yes, we were competent and had the awards to prove it. But we were much more than this. There was much more power and life in each of us, in our family, that was untapped, hidden deep. This was our family soul, and we needed to find it.

MOTHER AND FATHER—ELIZABETH AND PAUL

One of the most compelling reasons behind this quest was to come to terms with my family about my mother's life and death. Her sudden death at the age of 53 left me shaken and regretful. I had not treated her with respect and understanding. But as much as my relationship with her was between her and me, there was also a communal–familial dimension to this history that I needed to know and grasp. All of us experienced her in similar and different ways. We each held a different part of my mother, and to know her I had to seek out those parts of my mother planted in the memories and lives of my family members. We had to meet and talk. (After these family of origin meetings I did interview my mother's siblings and some of her friends in an effort to know her more completely.)

My fantasy was that I would die at age 53, suddenly, as my mother and her father before her. He also died unexpectedly in the night on January 2, 1950, from a heart attack, only two months after baptizing me, his first grandchild. My mother died at the same age as her father, about the same time of year, of a similar cause in the heart region of the body. This historical linkage across the generations was uncanny and frightening. I was intimidated by this story and the fantasies of what it meant for me.

It seemed to me that my family wanted to honor her by keeping her life and times locked up in their private memories. For me, this secrecy would dishonor her, and also would make it more likely that the aggravating parts of her personality would haunt us with power. Also, "pasteurizing" my mother by deleting her unattractive traits and only focusing on her assets would also dishonor her. She was all of her. And all of her was vital, energetic, brimming with electrical charges—some of which shocked and hurt, others of which cared, and others of which ignited abundant creativity and imagination.

A way to give back to my mother would be, in a public setting with family witnesses, to admit and correct the wrongs I had done to her. I had not been fair to my mother in her living years. I had split my parents into the "good parent" and "bad parent." I had idealized my father, minimizing his faults, and had denigrated my mother. One of my worst fantasies growing up was that my mother's anger would kill my father, and he would die young. My mother surprised me and died first. Repeatedly in our home I was taking sides in this triangle, defending my father and trying to protect him against my mother.

This fixed triangle, and my illusion that reinforced it, kept me from knowing my parents as people and dealing with them more justly. I had not seen clearly the burdens my mother carried, her struggles, the heavy load encumbering her. I also had not seen my father's frailties. She had a glorious reputation for gathering people for celebrations, children in her classrooms and adults at parties. Her gatherings were always beyond what was expected. And she gathered us as family. By gathering the family together in this family of origin consultation, I was continuing her tradition, but with my own spin: loyal and differentiated. I wondered how she would have liked the "party" we were soon to begin.

SHIFTING FAULT LINES

There were other events that contributed to the force behind this family-of-origin project. The landscape of my life and my family of origin had been shifting significantly. When these contexts shift, "fault lines" appear on the relational landscape that create opportunity for change.

One factor furthering my interest in conveying my family of origin were the births of my children. As I was thrust more into my father role, I began to think of myself as less of a child of a parent and more of a parent of a child. This shift created within me enlarged empathy for both of my parents. Now I knew some of what they must have been up against. I wanted to ask my mother: "What was it like being a parent?" "How did you handle this and that?" "Did you struggle with balancing your own life with life as a parent?" "How did you deal with us when we wouldn't listen to you?" "What did you do to stay alive as a parent?" "How was your marriage affected by having children?" I did ask these questions of my father, but I would have loved to ask them of my mother.

Having children also began to compel me to think of how I wanted my family to be. There were high stakes here. The power of influencing their lives seemed enormous. I wanted to bring the best of me into this project of parenting, and to do that, I needed to be different—more aware, present, open, feeling, welcoming, work through conflict, warm.

But to do this with my family of procreation, I felt I had to do this with my family of origin. Call it a loyalty issue. I needed to change my relationships with family-of-origin members first, which would, I thought, free me up to do the same with my wife and children. I had to honor my family of origin first. I felt I would be disloyal if I were to devote my energy of change to my wife and children without at least genuinely trying to be different with my first family. I didn't want to get into the trap of some people who are absolutely unwilling—because of undying loyalty to their parents—to have better marriages than their parents did. If a sincere effort is made with the first family, a greater "permission" within the self is granted, releasing energy and commitment for others.

Another shifting fault line in the relational landscape was my father's retirement from being a college president in 1983. He had held this position for a quarter of a century. Now that he was retiring from this position of authority, perhaps I was feeling more peerlike with him. I was ascending my career, and he was descending. Our professional trajectories were intersecting, opening up the possibility that we would relate more as friends. Maybe I was feeling more gutsy while perceiving him as less imposing.

My father's remarriage and the creation of a new blended family was another fault line. I had a longing to preserve the "old family" in the midst of this change where the boundary around family was widening to include my father's new wife and her children. What had happened to our family in all this change? I feared its dissolution before I hardly knew this family of ours. I had to grasp, know, encounter this group before I could let it safely blend with others. I wanted to regroup, reconsolidate, and mark out that this was family. My father was being pulled into another family, and Lynn, the last child, was leaving home. Before we all left, we had to come together.

Another shift in the relational landscape was the death of my maternal grandmother, Nana. She was the family historian. For decades she had been compiling notes on her extended family history. Eventually she used these notes to write a dramatic novel, entitled *The Miners*, that chronicled her family history from its European roots to the coal fields of central Pennsylvania in the late 1800s and early 1900s. I read that book in its entirety shortly after her death. I was struck by the power of this story in linking me to my own heritage, and emerged from this reading with a sense of wonder and gratefulness for the story, and for Nana who kept the story alive. With her death, there was a vacuum in the family. I wanted to honor her and fill this gap in our family by being a collector of stories and the transmitter of family tales. This family-of-origin work linked me with this tradition.

GETTING TO KNOW MY FAMILY

It was only about one week before we would be leaving for the family-of-origin consultation with Jim. As I began to focus more on each of my family members, I took notes on my feelings and impressions, what I wanted to ask each of them, and what I wanted to tell. What I knew was that I hardly knew them. Even at the level of being aware of basic information about each of them, there were noticeable gaps in my awareness. I remember one encounter I recently had with Katie, who had challenged me on how much I knew of her life. She put me to the test on the spot: "Tim," she said with determination and challenge, "I bet you don't even know what grade I teach. Do you? Do you?" This challenge felt like a technical form of a duel even though it was Katie's plea to me simply to be seen and heard. I gulped hard at that moment, knowing that I didn't know for sure, but not wanting to admit it. Katie was right, even though I could guess and possibly get the correct answer. We then talked about our disconnectedness from each other's lives. She also had to acknowledge that she didn't know much about me outside of the general longitude–latitude information about my life.

Moments like these with Katie highlighted my family style: distance, focused on self, cut off, low in inquiry. I entertained several hypotheses as to why I was this way, including my favorite: For much of my life I protected myself from the family tension by leaving the house, numbing myself from family pain by not knowing, immersing myself into my own life. I was not only low on information about family members, the most basic component of "knowing," I also knew little of the life inside each of them—passions, dreams, fears, goals, hurts, commitments, values—those interior dramas that drive the self.

As I wrote about my family members, I tried to "de-glob" them from "family" to individuals. I already have noted impressions of each of my family members, and my sense of the nature of the relationship I had with each of them.

About my father: I loved him for the support he had given me as I grew up. I realized he was proud of me, and his pride in me had helped me push myself farther. I wished that he had taken more leadership in the family when my mother was alive, instead of letting his leadership drain outside of the family. I wanted him to have seen the difficulties in the family and to have addressed them with action and leadership. (Perhaps this was one reason I became a clinical psychologist specializing in work with marriage and family life.) In our family, he would often repeat the phrase, "Think positively." This seemed to be his major intervention, after which he would often sink in resignation as if the words carried no weight. I also wanted to know more about what had been going on with him in his struggle with my mother. There was much I didn't know about his personal struggles.

I also wanted to move out of the role of a parent–child relationship with him into more of a friend-friend relationship. I did not want to give him up as father, but I did want to relate to him in a more open and intimate way. Although Williamson (1991) has taken the position that self-differentiation is partly a function of "declaring independence" from the parent and regarding him or her as "former parent," I believed I could see my father as "father" but relate to him with both intimacy and reverence, not intimidation where I would allow his presence and will to organize my responses.

I also had experienced my father as having a "critical lens" at life, where he would look at problems not so much for what was going right, but primarily for what was going wrong. He seemed to deflate optimism and enthusiasm, looking more mournfully than hopefully on life. I saw this criticalness and cloudy spirit within myself. True laughter and fun were hard for me to connect with, as if they were some alien being. As I lived too much on the serious edge, I saw my father within me.

I also often experienced my father as distant, as if he were having some petit mal seizure, dissociating, off somewhere else. I wanted to experience the "more" within my father, believing that he had more within himself, that he was less mechanical and more human. Seeing more in him would give me more hope for myself. Sometimes I fantasized that my parents' destinies were to be my destiny. What happened to them, by and large, would happen to me. I didn't like this feeling of historical determinism and did believe, quite to the contrary from time to time, that I could shape a life for myself quite different from my parents. This belief about the resources of the self was growing. But I still wanted to believe and see more capacity in my father as a way of upgrading my fate.

I also noted that I had not told my father that I loved him. Sometimes when I tried to blurt out those words I would say, "We love you, Dad." I had trouble personalizing my love for him. Sweetness, warmth, and play were not things between us. He seemed so serious, and so did I. I wanted to make my love for him more authentic, love coming from the heart and not coming out of duty.

About Thomas: I saw him as a very sensitive person, tuned in to other family members in ways that the rest of us were not. It seemed that all of us except Thomas had been caught up with our lives and careers. Thomas, on the other hand, because of his retardation, did not have any of these diversionary experiences. He was the one who held information about each of us and would often share that information in his role of the switchboard operator. He kept the light burning around my mother's life and death, not wanting to let her go, at least not yet, until we all recounted her story.

Thomas was difficult for me to be with—stuttering, repetition of questions, only mechanical inquiries about my own life, moody with a short fuse. In checking with family members about this consultation, I gained Thomas's compliance by speaking with my father. In the family meeting, I did want to address Thomas's retardation with Thomas present. We had talked about him apart from him, protecting him from our thoughts and feelings about him. We may have been saying, "He won't understand. He'll blow up. We'll hurt him." I believed this process kept Thomas diminished. Furthermore, we family members had not really come together to talk about his retardation and his impact on our lives.

Next to my mother, Thomas had been the most central figure in our family, shaping how we would organize ourselves and setting the family's mood. As Thomas grew older, it seemed like he was a "minefield" in public places; at any moment, without provocation, he could blow up and seemingly was beyond control. I wanted to bring this "secret" about his retardation out in the open. I also believed that talking about his retardation would be a gift to Thomas. He must have been continually frustrated throughout his life, having this disability, but not having us as a family talk with him about his disability in a straight and direct manner.

About Katie: She, Thomas, and I were the siblings that formed the first sibling subsystem, while Ann and Lynn formed the second sibling subsystem. Katie, in fact, bridged both subsystems, functioning as a "mother surrogate" for Ann and Lynn as she lived at home until her junior year in college. Thomas was between us in age. We had much in common in our struggles, experienced much of the same history together, and could have been resources for one another. But we were not. We both seemed to have trouble having fun, were serious with life and our missions, and were cautious. Maybe part of our conflict with each other was masked mourning for what we both did not have with Thomas: our lost brother between us.

About Ann: I also experienced distance with her. One of the factors that reinforced this distance was her moving outside the Lutheran tradition into another denominational experience. I saw Ann as having been deeply embedded within the family's emotionality with little power as the middle child. I believe her diabetes was partly a consequence of being so emotionally entwined within the family that she either had to act out or get sick; she "chose" the latter. Similar to Thomas's retardation, her diabetes had not really been discussed within the family setting. This was another "taboo" topic. I wanted to hear how other members of the family reacted to her diabetes. I wanted to hear how she was handling her own diabetes, if she wanted any help from me, and what she could tell me about the disease and its impact on her life. I was proud of her for moving in an independent direction, attending a public university and linking with another Christian religious community.

About Lynn: I had few notes for her. I realized I still saw her as a little girl, and knew her much less than anyone else. I was 17 years old when she was born, and spent most of my life away from her. I did enjoy her best gift to me: her fun-loving freedom, her gutsy attempts to "speak the truth," her laughter. She seemed to do all of this much better than any of us.

THE WEEKEND BEFORE

I was grateful that we all would be in the same place during these meetings, without interference from our work or other family members. This kind of protected space and time would allow us space for retreat as well as opportunities to continue our learning between the meetings. Perhaps I perceived this upcoming experience as more weighty and critical than anyone else. My father talked about the upcoming "interrogations" (his words to describe the family conversation) and, once again, reiterated that he was going along with this "for research." My father's means of getting safe distance? I knew I had to welcome a diversity of individual styles as family members approached these meetings.

My own anxieties came out in my dreams. For weeks before the family meetings, I dreamt often of my own dying. I wondered whether this dream reflected my fear that in the consultation there would be a good deal of hurt and pain so that somebody else or I would die. Even in my waking state, I had fantasies of some catastrophe happening after these meetings, particularly that my father or I would die. I think that I was anticipating having to talk with my father about my difficulties with him and that I, because of this criticism, would kill my father as I had feared my mother was killing my father when she was alive.

In these days before the meeting, I also began to experience numerous physiological reactions. I felt very tight with "kinks" throughout my body and both aches and pains attacking my body, as if they were saying, "Why are you making such a mistake like doing this?" I wanted to be free of this somaticizing tendency, but had to admit that my body feels what my mind does not allow. At the same time, I also feared that all of this would be a nonevent, and that everyone—family members and Jim— would be bored. Nothing would happen, and I would come away from these meetings feeling that the others and I were invincibly stuck forever.

I saw this pattern in the other family members. On the one hand, I did not hear of any major anticipation from anyone else. No bright hopes or possibilities were entertained publicly. What I did hear was the fear that these meetings would do harm to the family and that, at best, we would come out of this major surgery with no deep scars. As I talked with my father and sisters, I did not get the sense from anyone that this "major surgery of psychotherapy" (Framo, 1992) would even produce a "better patient" than the patient who entered surgery. The only hope was that the patient simply would survive the operation.

On the other hand, I did see continuing change in other family members, as I had been seeing in incremental ways over the previous weeks. My father's wife, Linda, observed during the weekend before the consultation that changes were already happening in the family, especially in the way we had been talking with each other more frequently and more personally. Each family member had been reading Jim's 1976 article, which I had distributed earlier (like they were cramming for the final exam). As we were getting ready to go to bed on the night before the meeting, we were standing around the stairs, talking about the article and its impact on our lives—family history, traumas, themes. Katie was even taking notes, and I was stepping back.

Right before the session, my clear agenda and goals for the meeting seemed to be eroding. It seemed that weeks before these meetings I had my agenda and themes neatly organized into 1-2-3-4. However, as time grew closer for the consultation, my thoughts (now following my body) were becoming more disorganized. Now I felt more like a mosaic.

I was preparing myself for the hour interview with Jim. He already knew something about our family history from the letter I had sent him months ago. I wanted to be clear about my agenda, but in some ways my clarity was rapidly eroding. I thought about the positives within our family life and, clearly, there were some: like our family vacations, and the help on homework that both my parents gave me. But I also did not want to diminish at all the desperation I felt that something had to be different within me certainly, and hopefully within the family. I felt a struggle to claim gifts in our family while not gossiping over the pain in our history. I wanted to make a case to Jim that "I/we need help here!" Too many times in our family history, our distress signals from sea had not been seen, and we had continued floundering in the waters.

I was determined not to let this happen again as I went to bed the night before my interview with Jim.

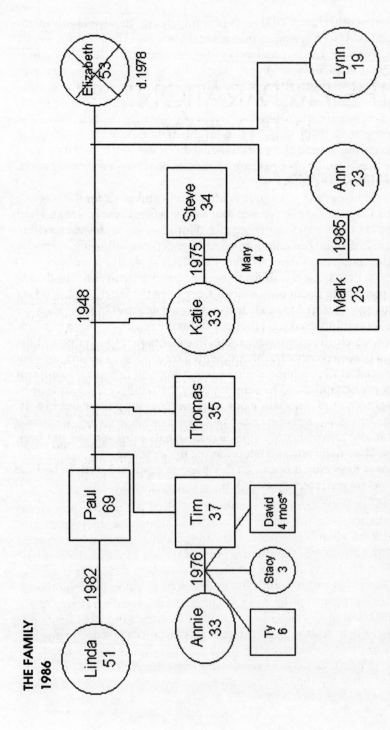

THE FAMILY
1986

GENOGRAM at the time of the first family consultation. David was born between the first and second consultations. He was four months old at the 1987 consultation and was present with the family during the second two hours of the second consultation.

Chapter 4

THE PREPARATION INTERVIEW

JAMES L. FRAMO, PhD

The following interview with Tim Weber was conducted in front of participants of a workshop I presented on my work with family of origin. Prior to the family meetings I see the initiating person alone, or occasionally with a spouse or sibling, in order to prepare that individual for the meeting with his or her family of origin. A primary goal of the preparation sessions is to collaborate with the client in developing an agenda of issues to be dealt with during the consultation. In order to do this, it is necessary to gather a detailed family history, including such information as who is in the family; the client's characterization of each family member; key events in the family; a sense of the family's ways, style, and emotional atmosphere; the positive strengths in the family; and so on. The recounting of the family history reveals the issues in the family, some of which are loaded. I negotiate with the client as to which issues he or she feels safe to bring up. If the spouse or a sibling is present, their views about the issues in the family are elicited. Throughout the preparation interview the client's inevitable fears and anxieties need to be reduced. Guidelines are offered the client, as well as reassurance that the consultant will not allow matters to get out of hand. As the family's story unfolds, as viewed through the client's perspective, I develop hypotheses about the family dynamics and form tentative intervention strategies.

The ensuing interview is an example of how I prepare clients for family-of-origin sessions—although in this instance I was dealing with a motivated professional who had done a lot of advance preparation.

My personal associations to the interview material, in italics, are interspersed through the transcript. My commentaries include my assessment of the individual and family dynamics, the thinking behind my interventions, explication of my intergenerational methods, and how these proceedings compare to those of other family-of-origin sessions, as well as disclosure of my own private reflections, conjectures, and the subjective associations and feelings aroused in me by the transactions.

FRAMO: From the material sent me beforehand, I gather that you've given quite a bit of thought to what you want to do here. What were your motives in wanting to have a session with your family?

TIM: My motives were clearer several months ago than they are now . . . We've had a very difficult family history. I think we've managed to come out of that history fairly reasonably, but we've had a very difficult family history. I think at times we've gone on automatic pilot through the years that I've been alive, and I don't think we've talked about what we've been through. I heard about your work and wanted to take advantage of this opportunity.

Tim reported that his father had been a campus pastor for 10 years, and then became a president of a college for 25 years. Father is now retired. During the period when father was campus pastor, the children (PKs—Preacher's Kids) were on stage a lot. They had to look good and present themselves as a "together" family. Tim said that father was often away, especially when working on his doctorate in theology. Mom taught preschool during those years, and her own children were in her classes.

FRAMO: I understand your mom died.

(Framo: This sounds abrupt, but I wanted to get to the heart of the matter early on.)

TIM: She died in 1978.

FRAMO: Of what?

TIM: Heart failure. She collapsed on the morning of the twenty-first of December, and she was taken to the hospital and she sort of went in and out of comas throughout the day. They thought she was going to be okay in the morning, but by night she went into a deeper coma and then she died about one o'clock that night.

FRAMO: Tell me about your mom.

TIM: My mother was a very powerful and emotional force in our family. Our family sort of revolved around the moods of my mother, and when she died it was . . . I had been out of the house for some time—since the late sixties—but my sisters had lived in the house long after I had left, and it has been very, very difficult on them, and so when she died there was, in a sense, I think, some relief, but . . .

FRAMO: Relief?

TIM: Relief that she had died.

FRAMO: In what sense? What do you mean?

TIM: The tension in the house was gone.

FRAMO: About what?

TIM: Her moods were very intense, and she would often get mad at us kids. Less so me. I think my sisters were the ones that really absorbed a lot of her emotional energy. My sisters tell me stories about how she was to them. But I didn't receive, myself, that kind of emotional negative energy from her. So when she died there was a sort of a relief that she wasn't around, but there has been a lot of sadness in her absence, too.

(Framo: I had not expected this response. I assumed Tim meant that his mother's death brought relief from her suffering. I knew that his family would need help in dealing with the mourning, guilt, and aftershocks of that tragedy.)

FRAMO: Has the whole family really dealt with her death, *as* a family?

TIM: Well, the night before we had her funeral—the day before Christmas Eve (and this is one of my problems in roles in the family, and one I think I want to do something about)—I gathered the family around and I took out a tape recorder and I said, "I think it's important we talk about Mom. Talk about what we liked and what we didn't like about her, what some of our memories are." A number of people in the family didn't want to do that, especially my oldest sister. But we did it anyway. And then, periodically Dad wants to take us out to the cemetery, to go out there and talk about Mom, and we sometimes do that and sometimes don't, finding reasons not to do it. We've made attempts, but I think there's a lot of unfinished business.

FRAMO: Do you want to deal with this tomorrow?

TIM: Yeah.

FRAMO: Is that sort of high on your list?

TIM: That's one of the issues. As I'm thinking about this meeting, it's like a mosaic. It's not well organized. As I said, less well organized than it was two months ago. It's more of a mosaic of feelings and impressions, and my mother's death is one of the issues I want to deal with.

(Framo: Tim's lack of clarity and confusion is typical of clients preparing for family-of-origin sessions. Their attempts to sort out the myriad of memories, thoughts, and feelings about themselves and their family are experienced as overwhelming at times. It's as if they are saying, "There is so much. Where do I even begin?" This dilemma takes care of itself as the guided interview progresses.)

Tim went on to describe the rest of the family. He is the oldest, and the next oldest is his brother, Thomas, age 34, who is mentally retarded. Thomas lives in a group home; he has lived away from home since he was 14 or 15. Thomas has been considered the family switchboard because he is the one who calls family members the most and passes on information. Tim described his brother as being marginally retarded, and when asked why Thomas was not living at home Tim said Thomas has severe emotional outbursts on occasion at home, and he does better living with other retarded people.

The next oldest is Katie, age 33, a schoolteacher who is married with one child. Tim described her as the big sister who assisted mom around the house and took care of her two little sisters. Tim did not have to do work around the house; he got off the hook by staying out of the house. Tim said Katie was resentful of him because he had lots of advantages and privileges she never got, including parental and grandparental attention. He thought these circumstances were the basis of the strong competition that has existed between them. Interestingly, Tim thought the sexism that existed in the family was because the females ganged up on the males, although he conceded that maybe the males did the same thing to the females.

Tim's sister Ann is age 23, married, and the first child who went to a non-Lutheran college, and who married a non-Lutheran who is very religious in a charismatic sense. These movements away from the Lutheran church were difficult for dad to deal with. Ann has insulin-dependent diabetes, having been diagnosed at age 13. She is now a food service manager. Tim said Ann was lots of fun as a child, but in her teenage years she became serious, quiet, and closed in.

The youngest child in the family is Lynn, age 19, unmarried and in college. Tim described her as the most free in the family. He said, "She kids around with people and trusts others."

When asked how the family members felt about the forthcoming family session, Tim said Lynn was looking forward to it because she's studying psychology. Ann says she has dealt with the family already, and because of her religious beliefs she has nothing to fear. Katie, who said the family should wear black to the meeting, was the most reluctant to come to the family meeting.

FRAMO: How was your parents' marriage?

(Framo: This question, which I routinely ask, touches on one of the most sensitive issues in a family. Since the family is not present during the preparation session, statements made by the initiating client are usually more unguarded and uncensored. At the time, Tim had no idea that his family, especially his dad, would ever hear his frank views. Indeed, family members who do listen to recorded prep sessions are often shocked at what they hear. I did wonder whether the father would permit discussion of his marital relationship.)

TIM: [long pause] Rough.

FRAMO: You said you stayed out of the house a lot. What were you staying away from?

TIM: The tension in the house.

FRAMO: Between who and who?

TIM: Between my mom and dad, my mom and me, my mom and the rest of the kids.

FRAMO: What went on between Mom and Dad?

TIM: Arguing and long-distancing. The dinner table was a good example of what went on. The dinner table was a very unpleasant experience. We would often get into a lot of fights, and my dad would say, "Let's just think positively. Let's just think positively." It's an echo; I keep hearing it at the dinner table. But there was tension and fighting, and it was very hard for people to just stay in the house, so I was in sports all year long—baseball, basketball, football. So I was out of the house all the time.

FRAMO: Which parent did you feel closer to?

TIM: Well, I thought while I was growing up that I felt closer to my dad. But I think I felt closer to my mother. I think I took the place of my father in the family, and mom and I had a lot of stuff going on between us. My dad was gone, and I always thought my dad would die first, and I was angry at my mom for killing my dad, and I was concerned. I told her, "You're going to kill him. You're going to kill him and he's going to die of a heart attack."

(Framo: In order to get maximum information in the preparation interview, I try to ask factual questions rather than those designed to elicit emotions. I ignored the oedipal hint, but did silently take note of Tim's reference to "killing," and of his protective attitude toward his father.)

FRAMO: From what? The arguing?

TIM: From the arguments . . . the fights . . . the tension. I was afraid my father would die. Then, in 1967, my dad had a brain tumor in his left frontal lobe, benign, the size of a grapefruit.

FRAMO: Grapefruit?

TIM: Yeah, it was huge. They took it out and he has . . . It was a tough year. It was my senior year of high school. And that year Ann was born and my mom had been having multiple medical problems, Dad had a brain tumor, and everyone was going crazy. But he managed to survive.

(Framo: This unusual combination of calamitous illnesses, plus the strain of taking care of a retarded child, must have created considerable stress and dread in this family. Preoccupation with death and somatization of conflicts in the family were likely outcomes.)

Tim related that his father lost speech initially from the brain tumor, but regained it after surgery. He has had two re-occurrences of temporary speech loss since that time, the last one four years ago. Father recently went for a physical exam, and the doctor said he was doing fine.

FRAMO: How would you describe your relationship with your dad now?

TIM: (pause) Better.

FRAMO: Better than what?

TIM: Better than it used to be. I think there was so much tension in the house that I don't remember really relating to anybody in a way that I really felt was productive and intimate. I remember just having to deal with people and protect myself. He's remarried now . . . My stepmother keeps him alive, and he's much more open now. Whenever I go to him, though, he reaches out his hand to shake his hands with me, and I push his hand away and hug him. Intimacy, affection, and saying loving things to each other is very hard in my family. I think it's easier to get mad at each other than it is to love each other.

FRAMO: So one of the things you'd like to do is get into some positive stuff.

(Levine: It is typical for Jim to use simple, down-to-earth language with clients, even with therapists who are clients.)
(Framo: From time to time I remind clients in the preparation interview to tell their family the things they liked about their family. If family-of-origin sessions consisted only of complaints or what went wrong the family members would become discouraged about whether that they could ever have a better way of being with each other.)

TIM: Yeah, yeah. To say to him "I love you" is very hard. I have prac-ticed saying, "We love you, dad," uh [nervous laugh] in the car sometimes, sneaking in, "I really like what you did." But it's really hard to look at him and just say "I love you." I think I'm . . . There's some anger there at him, also, from when I was growing up. I felt real sympathetic toward him and angry toward my mother. But, having been in therapy, now I think I had a skewed vision of that history. I think my mom was angry that he was so distant, so hard to engage, and I think that she engaged us to be his substitute, and I feel more angry toward him than I did when I was growing up.

FRAMO: How was your father affected by your mom's death?

TIM: Well, he's told me that he is sad she died, but he has also told me that it was a relief. I start to think about murder and homicide, and have wishes that somebody would be gone. Well, it's like it's good that she died.

FRAMO: Where does murder come in?

TIM: It's not that he would have murdered her, but it's like for him to say that he's somewhat glad that she died . . . since there is less tension in the house. We're just burying this person, and we're glad she's gone and we're getting rid of her. You know. I even say it myself, and it's hard for me to say.

(*Framo: I was reminded here of Carl Whitaker's belief that whenever death occurs it is experienced as murder. Tim goes back and forth, painfully seeking the answer to the mystery of who is to blame for eliminating mom. I anticipated that guilt and blame would be major themes in this family.*)

FRAMO: So there's a lot of ambivalence about Mom, still?

TIM: Yeah, I think so.

FRAMO: Who was the most severely affected by her death?

TIM: [pause] I don't know. It's hard to say. My brother talked about it the most. My sister, Lynn, was eleven or twelve when she died. And I just recently talked to her, and she said she's thinking more about mom now than she did when mom died because my dad will go to Lynn and say, "You remind me of mother." And Lynn is starting to fear that she is falling into the steps of my mom, and so she's thinking more about mom than she ever did. I've thought about my mom a lot. I talk about my mom a lot in therapy. I don't know whether I still need to do some work on that. I think I do, and I don't know quite what it is. I don't know who was most affected. I think we were all affected in different ways.

(Framo: Because of his honesty, openness, and relative ease in disclosing his inner self, I had already guessed that Tim had been in individual therapy.)

FRAMO: Then perhaps this is one of the big topics we need to talk about in the family. What other issues do you want to deal with?

TIM: Oh, I have certain difficulties with some things that I don't know how to connect to my family, but again in this mosaic thing, I work too much and don't know how to play. Dad is a real hard worker, and my mom was a hard worker. Saturdays were spent working. We never played.

FRAMO: Your family didn't go on picnics or go to the fair?

TIM: We took summer vacations. We did that well. We traveled across the country to visit relatives and would stay in cheap motels and visit relatives, and we did that okay. But as far as just taking time off and having fun, we never did that. And there's something about this work stuff and no play.

FRAMO: I would like to suggest that you be self-disclosing to your family. Tell the family some things about yourself that maybe they don't know. Is there anything about you that you would like to tell them?

(Levine: Jim is coaching Tim to set up an atmosphere of openness by beginning the sessions with his family with self-disclosure.)

TIM: That I work too much and don't play enough?

FRAMO: That would be one thing.

TIM: That I have trouble being intimate? That I hid behind professional roles and accomplishments?

FRAMO: Do you hear that from your wife or . . .

TIM: Yeah. And she's right. I hide behind professional identity. When I'm with people I try to get them to see my role rather than my person. I don't know if I'm really comfortable with my person outside of my role.

FRAMO: Can you tell that to your father?

(Framo: I suspected that Tim and his father shared this apparent characteristic of emotional distance from intimates, and was suggesting that by exchanging this information they could help each other.)

TIM: I think I can.

FRAMO: Is he like that?

TIM: I think he might be. When he retired it was real hard for him.

FRAMO: I got the impression that your father sort of hid behind his professional role.

TIM: I think he's changing that a little bit.

FRAMO: Well, did you feel really close to your dad?

TIM: Not much. I can't remember really doing much with him. I don't have any real strong images of doing something with my father.

FRAMO: What issues would you like to take up with each of your siblings?

(Framo: Sibling relationships have been largely ignored by mental health professionals. I have found the presence of siblings to be critical to the outcome of family-of-origin sessions, and have gone so far as to cancel sessions when siblings were not to be included.)

TIM: With Katie, it's our competition. She puts me down . . . A lot.

FRAMO: Have you told her that?

TIM: Yeah. I gave her little digs. Not major digs. With Thomas it's the fact that sometimes I just forget him. I forget that he's around.

FRAMO: Is he the guy in the family you forget to introduce?

TIM: Yeah, and I might say I have a retarded brother. I don't say my brother's Thomas and he is retarded. It's like, "I have a retarded brother," and jump to the next sibling.

FRAMO: How do the girls in the family view him?

TIM: I don't know. And I don't think we've ever sat around as a family and talked about his retardation in front of him.

FRAMO: Do you want to bring that up?

TIM: Yeah, I think I'd like to do that, and I think we owe it to him to talk about his retardation. I was out of the house, really, when Ann and Lynn were growing up, so in some sense I don't know them.

FRAMO: Can you tell them that?

TIM: Yeah.

FRAMO: Would you like to get to know them better?

(Framo: One of my goals of family-of-origin sessions is to establish connections between emotionally distant family members. Being in the same room and dialoguing about usually avoided topics gives the family members the opportunity to get to know each other better. Getting to know one's intimates [parents,

siblings, spouses] as real people is a key element of family-of-origin sessions. This process is usually painful and surprising as one discovers that these others have perspectives and feelings different from one's own. The end result is more family authenticity and enrichment.)

TIM: Yeah. I was really happy that Lynn has decided to come to my house for Thanksgiving because these girls, Katie, Ann, and Lynn, will talk among themselves and will make phone calls. Lynn will call Katie, but I didn't get a call from Lynn throughout the year, and I didn't call her either.

FRAMO: What do you think is the touchiest issue in this family, Tim? The part about the relief about mom's being gone?

TIM: My mother's presence. The touchiest one was my mom's presence in the family, and what that did to all of us; more so than my brother's retardation. We went through a lot of terrible experiences with his retardation. We would go to public places and he would have a temper tantrum and just blow up. Sometimes he would run out of the house nude, into the streets, yelling and screaming at us. He might do that on a trip, so that was tough to deal with. My mom's more civilized temper tantrums were harder to deal with, so I guess that's the touchiest subject to deal with. Also, I think there is a lot of anger toward my father. My sisters have said to me, before this family meeting, "We are afraid. We don't want to make Dad angry or sad."

FRAMO: What are they angry at him about?

TIM: I think they might be angry at him because of the way he treated Mom.

FRAMO: They, too, had mixed feelings about Mom.

TIM: Oh yeah. I think that nobody really loved my mother when we were growing up, and I really regret that. I really regret not having sat down with her and told her, "I love you." Because there were many things that she gave us. Fortunately, in the year or two before she died, she and I were beginning to have some talks. When I'd come home we'd stay up a little bit and talk to each other. She came to my graduation and my dad did not. I graduated from the seminary and my dad didn't come, but my mom did.

(Framo: I was touched by Tim's recognition of the nurturing, positive side of Mom. It brought up for me my belated realization of the good stuff I got from my difficult mother. How to come to terms with ambivalence about one's parents is one of life's endless perplexities.)

Although he was a minister, Tim said it worked best for him to have an affiliation outside the church. He felt the church was a tough place to be as a sole occupation. Tim wondered whether he did with the ministry what he did with his home: that it was easier to be there without being there.

FRAMO: How much contact have you all had with each other in recent years? You live in one place; your dad lives in another state. Do you call him frequently or what?

TIM: We've had more contact since he got married to Linda.

FRAMO: How often do you talk to him on the phone?

TIM: Once every three weeks, maybe, on the average.

FRAMO: How much contact do you have with your brother?

TIM: Well, he'll call me once every two weeks.

FRAMO: And your sisters?

TIM: Well, I've had more contact with Katie over the last year, but I did not call Ann in this last year until I called her about this conference. And I had not talked…

FRAMO: You hadn't talked to Ann for a whole year?

TIM: Since maybe last Thanksgiving.

FRAMO: Hmmm, why so infrequent?

TIM: I was asking myself that same question. I don't know.

FRAMO: She hasn't called you either?

TIM: No.

FRAMO: Can you deal with her on that?

TIM: Yeah… It's like Ann and Lynn are a separate family. Me and Thomas and Katie are another family. We talk in our family about two separate families. Those two younger sisters are the other family.

FRAMO: Still, you hadn't talked to your sister Ann for six months. It's kind of long, don't you think?

(Framo: When dealing with disengaged families I encourage more contact among the members, which invariably occurs following the family meetings.)

(Levine: Jim speaks with his brother and sisters, who live in Philadelphia, every weekend. These long-distance calls are very important to them. It is hard for him to understand how siblings could be out of touch for as long as a year!)

TIM: Yeah it is. And when I did call we stayed on the phone and talked about some things, so it was real useful. Then when I came here three weeks ago I visited them and had dinner with them.

FRAMO: How do they feel about coming in? How does your dad feel about it?

TIM: Well, he said, "I'll do anything for research."

FRAMO: Should we indicate that we are doing this for research purposes? [laughs]

TIM: He said, "I'll do anything to help the scientific community."

FRAMO: Aha! That sounds kind of impersonal. Doesn't he think we're going to be dealing with some of this loaded stuff?

(Framo: I had already suggested to Tim that he inform his family that each family member has the freedom to raise issues or concerns in the family sessions. Moreover, the family should be told that we would be dealing with family issues, not just those of the initiating client. If this caveat is not given, some family members who had the expectation that they were just coming in to help the initiating client [their son, daughter, brother, sister] may feel betrayed when broader questions are raised.)

TIM: Oh, I told them that I really needed their help and that's why I was asking them to come. And later on, after they agreed to come in, I said that we will really need to think about issues that we need to bring up as a family.

FRAMO: Do you think your dad has any issues he wants to deal with?

TIM: I don't know. I think he does, but I don't know if he's going to do anything about it.

FRAMO: And your brother is looking forward to the session.

TIM: And Katie's going to wear black.

FRAMO: Sounds kind of significant.

TIM: She was speaking to Ann and told her to wear black too.

FRAMO: Do you think that's connected to your mom's death?

TIM: It may be.

FRAMO: How would you interpret it?

TIM: That she's trying to put a damper on the party. I was surprised that she agreed to do this.

FRAMO: I detect a note of bitterness between you two.

TIM: Katie and I are very competitive.

FRAMO: This is more than competition.

TIM: Bitterness, like I want to kill her? She and I got some stuff to work out.

(Framo: I was quite uncertain about the meaning of Tim's preoccupation with murder and killing, although many speculations tripped through my head. I decided to back off from this charged affect and come back to it later, perhaps when the family transactions made the meaning clearer . . . Tim was also giving plenty of advance notice that his relationship with his sister Katie was going to be a central issue. I suspected that Katie's comment about wearing black to the family sessions had to do with the depth of her distress about the family issues and about herself.)

(Levine: While family members often have catastrophic fantasies about what might happen in these family-of-origin session, we are only hearing Tim's interpretation of what Katie meant by her reference to black. In a follow-up discussion with Katie, she told me that there was a long-term understanding among the girls in the family that Mom's favorite color was black. She noted that the kitchen was black, there were black polka dots on doors, and that Mother often wore black. According to Katie, wearing black was a way of connecting to Mom. The contrast between Tim's interpretations, Jim's impression, and Katie's report is a reminder to us as therapists not to assume one member's point of view is representative of all members.)

FRAMO: Do you think that because you organized this, she's going to put a damper on it?

TIM: She could have said that.

FRAMO: Can you face her and say, "Hey, we've got some things to work out."

TIM: Yeah.

FRAMO: Does she have issues to discuss, do you know?

TIM: Well, last night . . . See, everybody has read your article [Framo, 1976] and they were all reading it last night in their little corners of the house, and I have tried to get out of interpreting the article. I said, "Well, if you have any questions . . . I really don't know what it's about, and you'll have to ask him [Framo] about it." So I've just been listening about how they are reading the article, and I went to bed and Katie and my dad were reading the article.

FRAMO: Are you going to have the family watch the videotape of the session?

TIM: I don't know how we're going the handle the videotape. They have consented to be videotaped, but who will watch it in the family . . . I don't know what's going to happen with that.

When questioned further about the family members' anticipations and fears about the forthcoming session, Tim related that Ann told him she was going to deal with the experience through her spirituality. Further details revealed how Ann had deviated from the Lutheran track by joining, with her husband, a fundamentalist religion where the emphasis was on prayer, healing, speaking in tongues, music, and joy. Her charismatic wedding was difficult for father; as a clergyman, he had participated in the wedding service.

Little information was gleaned about father's expectations and apprehensions about the family meeting.

FRAMO: And what do you think your dad will want to deal with? Do you think he'll bring up any issues at all?

TIM: I would be surprised, but he's also been told to think of issues he wants to bring up. I think that his general mood is, "Let's not break the family... Let's not go back fifteen years. We've come this far, so let's make sure we don't destroy the progress that we've made."

FRAMO: About Mom's death?

TIM: Yeah. We've come this far.

(Framo: Father's concern is understandable—namely, that the outcome of the family meetings is unknown and the procedure could possibly damage the equilibrium that the family, in his view, had achieved.)

(Levine: Also, we usually tell clients that we are very protective of parents. This statement helps alleviate some of their fears that we will allow the parents to be destroyed through uncontrolled parent bashing. In fact, Jim will not do a family-of-origin consultation with a client whose primary motivation is to get revenge or retaliate against a parent.)

FRAMO: What's going to happen, then, when you start touching on this?

TIM: Well, I've had two concerns about this family meeting. One is that it's going to be the most boring family-of-origin meeting that you've ever had because we don't want to rock the boat. The other is that it might explode and we'll never talk to each other again. And my hope is that it will get us moving in a way that really will help us all, but...

(Framo: The chance that a family-of-origin session would be boring was almost zero. The most common fear people have about family-of-origin sessions is that the family will be torn asunder. At this point, I should have offered anew my reassurance that I would contain strong emotions and not allow anyone to

get hurt. Further, I should have informed Tim that anger is a phase in all family-of-origin sessions, but that most families do get past that phase and get to the last phase of understanding and forgiveness of each other.)

FRAMO: Can you keep it from being boring?

TIM: Well, I'm trying to think of ways to do that . . . Right at the beginning.

FRAMO: Without explosion?

TIM: Right. I don't want to wait til day two to get something cooking. And I've wondered what I should do tonight about that because everybody will be there and Linda is out of the house.

(Levine: Usually during the first part of the family-of-origin session Jim will slow things down if the discussion gets too heated too fast to make sure the family is ready to address these issues.)

FRAMO: Do you want to start discussing some issues tonight?

TIM: Well, I don't really know whether to start things cooking. I think they already have cooked, in fact, just by reading the article that you wrote. People are talking about things. They were in the hallway last night until one-thirty talking. My dad and my sister. I was in bed. So it's already cooking, and I don't know really what to do at this point.

FRAMO: If it did explode, what would it explode around do you think?

TIM: [pause] Anger toward my father.

(Framo: In the prep session clients are encouraged to bring up in the family session family matters that they have thought about, been concerned about, fantasized about, but never verbalized. Perhaps the most difficult thing for people to do in family-of-origin sessions is to directly face the family member concerned and tell what is in one's heart. Like everybody else, Tim was most anxious about addressing his father face to face. I conjecture that this issue was where this family was stuck: how to confront Dad without hurting him. It is interesting that, in parallel fashion, I, too, wondered how I could understand, reach, or challenge the father in this family.)

FRAMO: For what? For the way he treated Mom?

TIM: Yeah. For the way he treated Mom.

FRAMO: For his emotional distance?

TIM: Yeah. For his uptightness with money. The money topic might come in. He's Motel Six.

FRAMO: Well, Motel Six is not so bad; you just pay extra for the television. [laughs]

(Framo: With this quip I begin to start changing the perception of Dad.)

TIM: [laughs] But we never paid extra for the television.

FRAMO: Why? Was he poor?

TIM: Well, not really poor, but he's not real rich and we've all maintained frugalness, I think in his footsteps. But I get a lot of this stuff, I think, that's aimed toward my father.

FRAMO: As the other male in the family? The oldest?

TIM: Yeah, the other nonretarded male and the oldest. I think that a lot of the stuff that comes to me in little digs is really meant for him.

FRAMO: Can you tell them this?

TIM: Yeah. I have so much stuff to tell that you're going to have to remind me.

FRAMO: You're going to have to think of them, but I'll be there to help facilitate this whole thing. I also am supportive toward the family coming in, because they're scared and they don't know what to expect. And I'm especially supportive of parents because it's really toughest on them.

(Framo: This statement is important, because no matter how angry clients are at parents, they will never forgive you, the therapist, if you join them in attacking the parents. Protectiveness toward parents is universal.)

TIM: Well that's what I told them. They thought, initially, that somebody would be here to analyze each one of them . . . Give them some kind of diagnostic report.

FRAMO: You let them know, though, that I'm there to help you all deal with each other?

(Framo: In family-of-origin sessions my role with the family is that of facilitator—i.e., to help the family members in working out things with each other. I attempt to create an atmosphere wherein honest dialogue can take place, eventuating in the family members listening to each other's experiences, clarifying misunderstandings, and using resources that they can find in themselves and in each other. I am not there to diagnose mental status or to "treat" them in the traditional sense. Along these lines, I suggest to clients that they invite their family to come in for a "family meeting" rather than family "therapy.")

TIM: Yeah. I said you were a consultant and you were here to help us talk to each other. I said you were a real positive guy. And I even showed them your picture in your book. And I said, "Look at this guy." Someone said, "Is he Jewish?"

FRAMO: [laughs] Someone said, "Is he Jewish?"

TIM: I said, "No. He's probably Italian or something like that."

(Levine: When family members ask personal questions I assume this reflects the high anxiety in the system. They are concerned about how different we are from them, and whether we can understand their culture. Although Jim does not ask about Tim's transference fantasies, I think these were important to explore.)

FRAMO: You know, also, I'd like you to start off with some positive stuff. Tell your family what were some good things that you thought happened in this family. They know there is going to be an audience, I presume. And I want to recommend, by the way, that the family certainly watch the videotape afterward . . . Tim, there's one issue you just alluded to. How much concern is there about Dad's getting old and approaching death?

TIM: We have not talked about that, but I'm concerned about it because after him I'm next in line. I've worried about his brain tumor, but there haven't been any serious repercussions from that to make me worry about his death. I want to deal with him before he dies. That's why this is such an opportunity. My fantasy is that after this meeting one of us is going to die in the next month. It's very scary to think that. I thought either it would happen before this meeting or after, and I hope I'm not talking about myself.

(Framo: Tim's obsessive thoughts and feelings about death, and his curious fantasy that either he or Dad might die after the family meeting, had all sorts of implications, but I could not sort them out at this time.)

FRAMO: What gives rise to that thought?

TIM: I don't know.

FRAMO: I thought you were going to say something else. That "I have this fantasy that my dad and I would really get close and would hug and the whole family would be closer." *That* would be the outcome rather than death.

(Framo: This is an example of a reframe about the purpose of the family meetings.)

TIM: I've thought about that. I hoped for what you said. I think about that, but the fantasy was, you know, somebody's going to get killed on an airplane coming up here, or somebody's going to die in a month after this meeting.

FRAMO: The question, maybe, has to do with whether or not you are the recipient of anger that should go to Dad. Or whether or not you are afraid that part of that anger is going to go to father. Is that it?

(Framo: I was not tracking well here, and made a premature interpretation. Like all premature or inexact interpretations it fell flat, especially since I don't know why I said it. My confusion may have been related to my own issues with death and anger. I did wonder whether the death theme was Tim's intrapsychic struggle alone or whether it had systemic meaning.)

(Levine: I think Jim was on target here, and Tim confirms this in his response, as he wonders about his own anger.)

TIM: Part of my anger?

FRAMO: The anger in the family. You've been protecting your father?

(Levine: Because Jim felt he was off base, he missed Tim's response and the possibility that Tim's murderous fantasies were a projection of Tim's own anger, as well as a reflection of anger in the family system.)

TIM: Maybe I'm concerned about that. I think I take too much responsibility in a lot of situations.

FRAMO: That's why you are a therapist.

TIM: Yeah . . . One thing I want to happen through this is that I just want to be a human being. Be a person. I've played a role too much in my life.

FRAMO: What do you think your major role was in your family? The responsible one, the oldest?

TIM: I think I've done everything just right. I've been a perfect son. I haven't done anything wrong.

FRAMO: If you had done anything wrong in your life would you be free to tell your family so that you won't look so perfect?

(Framo: I assumed that Tim's siblings saw him as they saw Dad, as above reproach.)

TIM: I crapped on the pool table when I was about three. This was in my father's church. I went down to the pool table and sat in the middle of the pool table, crapped, and a student discovered it. My dad remembers it, but doesn't quite know why I did it, and that's about the only thing I've done bad that they know about.

FRAMO: That they know about. I wonder if you want to let them know a few more things.

TIM: Well, some of the things, they're probably small, but I want to get out of the role of just being this "looking good" person. There's a lot of me that's really not good.

FRAMO: Tell them that.

TIM: Yeah.

FRAMO: Before we stop, Tim, would you like to talk a little about your present family, your own family?

(Framo: I always attempt to discover how themes from the family-of-origin carry over into the family of procreation.)

TIM: I am married to Annie, and then I have two kids, Ty and Stacy, who I brought with me on this trip. Annie is very close to my family, probably closer to my family than she is to her family. She is very close to Katie and Ann and Lynn. Her family is Lutheran. Her dad came from a Lutheran campus just like my dad. Many of the issues that I have with Annie, I think, come from my family, and that's part of the reason I want to work this out. My working too hard, not playing enough, trouble with intimacy, getting close, distancing from kids.

FRAMO: How does your wife feel about this session?

TIM: She really wanted me to do this. She had been encouraging me to do this for a long time. I have had the idea that I wanted to do this for several years. I was just looking for the right person and the right time.

FRAMO: Okay, Tim. I think we're going to stop now. We're going to do two hours tomorrow, and then two hours the next morning. I think one of the things you are going to see is the difference between the first two hours and the second two hours. Now that's the usual case, although I've seen some families get into the heavy stuff in the first two hours. But that's more unusual. So we'll see how it goes. I'm sorry now that I don't have Dr. Felise Levine, my wife and cotherapist, with me, but we'll do the best we can. It took a lot of courage, I think, on your part to begin this kind of work.

(Levine: In longing for a cotherapist, Jim was feeling the pressure of seeing the family alone.)

(Framo: Because of Tim's candor, insight, and motivation, I felt fairly confident about the forthcoming family sessions. Still, there are always apprehensions on the part of both clients and therapists before a first encounter. For example, some family members turn out to be very different from the way they were described by the client in the prep session. I was a bit concerned about interviewing a father who had some prominence, and I was a little uncomfortable at the prospect of seeing a family that was centered around a religious culture about which I knew little. Nonetheless, I was looking forward to meeting this interesting family and learning how they coped with the string of tragedies that had befallen them.

Chapter 5

THE NIGHT BEFORE
Anxiety and Anticipation

TIMOTHY T. WEBER, PhD

AFTER THE INTERVIEW

My one-hour interview with Jim had ended. I was bewildered and confused, side by side with a driving sense of urgency and mission. I felt an urgent responsibility to "make a case" for my family—that we were worthy of needing Jim's assistance, but that we also were not a "needy" family. It seems that I had been walking this "balance beam" much of my life— needing others without looking needy, being emotionally hungry while looking well fed. I have always feared being known too intimately, believing that if I were really known I would be a sure disappointment to the other, losing whatever respect and relationship I had. Jim was now that "other."

Driven by this urgency that we needed Jim's help, I neglected to identify positives about my family. I skewed the story of my family toward our pain, away from our strengths. Weeks later, after my father had watched the tape of my interview with Jim, he said with some irritation that he had not heard me talk about the good things in the family. The weighty atmosphere I had felt in the family over the years had made it difficult for me to be consciously mindful of our family health. I had been much more attentive to our struggles, the management of what seemed to be one crisis after another, the burying of my fears, and avoiding the surprises of disruption and explosion.

Yet we had much to celebrate over the years, even in the midst of some of our darkest moments. There were many gifts of intellect, creativity, resiliency, commitment, religion and faith, service and compassion to others, vacation jaunts, artistry, music, passion, drama, sacrifice for family. Why was I so inclined to forget our health? Remembering these strengths could be a resource for me in my own journey, and could also open up a more grateful heart in me toward members of my family.

I also thought about my father and his need to look back on our family's story with some integrity for what he had been able to generate. Did he perceive me only as critic and not celebrant of him and our family? How important was it for him to hear that he had "done good"? How could I affirm him genuinely, keeping my own integrity, without succumbing to the anxiety of not wanting to disappoint my father? How could I hold both at one and the same time—the hurts and the credits—and through both craft a deeper and more honest intimacy with him?

I also experienced during this interview a feeling of confusion, wondering whether my description of my family accurately reflected my own experience while also being somewhat fair to other family members. During the interview itself, I had forgotten that the interview was being taped and that other family members would have the opportunity to review the tape later. This temporary "amnesia" freed me up to speak more spontaneously. On the other hand, had I remembered that I was being taped, perhaps I would have been more cautious in what I said. As it was, I don't recall having any restraint in talking about my perceptions and the issues I believed were central to me and the family. If I had to do it over again I would do it the same: tape the initial interview and invite other family members to watch it. However, I would let other family members view the tape only after the family consultation, not before.

My sister Katie watched the interview and was stunned. She could not believe I saw the family the way I did. She couldn't believe I said this and that about the family. I began to defend my memory as "more true than yours," but soon stepped back from this assault on her memory. Our argument, I thought, was not about memory and truth but more about respect and authority, the emotional threads between us. Did I have enough respect for her to acknowledge her point of view and inquire even further as to what she remembered and valued?

Her stunned reaction helped me begin to appreciate the diversity of experiences within the same family. Each one of us is, in some sense, an "only child." None of us grows up in the same family. What we experience in the family is a partially shared reality, but is primarily shaped by our unique points of view and peculiar habits of remembering and forgetting. Any one family embodies the multiple realities of its members. I had been operating with a true and certain "map" of the family that shaped the way I thought, felt, and interacted with other family members. This diversity of stories within the family story threw into question the "truth" of my own way of remembering and forgetting. This was one of the beginning humbling moments for me, where the limits of my knowing were known more by me and my sister. How could our multiple realities come together to shape a family story with greater depth, texture, and honesty, uncovering more chambers of secrecy that would help us learn from one another?

My conversation with Jim had brought me closer to trusting him. He continued to cut sharply into my family life simply by his questions, while also applying the "anesthesia" of compassion and respect. He showed respect by inquiring rather than hypothesizing. He generally kept his hypotheses to himself. He did not spin forth any elegant theories of family functioning, but stayed simple and "naturalistic," inquiring about the family as a benevolent anthropologist. But there was less science to him, and more humanity. He had the spirit of an uncle who had been away from the family for a long time, and now was returning with some interested curiosity. I like therapists who enter as pretend uncles and aunts.

But I still wondered whether my father would like Jim. Deeper still, in spite of my initial openness toward Jim, I wondered whether I could really trust him to work with my life and the insides of our family. I had a feeling of going into major surgery and not knowing whether I could fully trust the surgeon. My fantasy was that we in the family had this "one chance." If this was a productive experience we could build on it. But if this were a disastrous experience, if Jim "blew it," I worried that we wouldn't recover, that I would be blamed, and that any possibility of doing this work as an entire family would be gone forever. If Jim was going to make some significant mistakes, I hoped that he would fail later rather than sooner, allowing the family to generate its capacity for forgiveness toward the beginning of our meetings.

STIRRINGS THE NIGHT BEFORE

My father picked me up outside of the auditorium after the interview. As we were driving home, I asked him to think about issues he might want to bring up during the family consultation. He quickly reported, "But *you* are the patient! We're coming to help you." Again, my father reiterated what he had said initially when I invited him to these consultations: He was here to help me, not himself. There was enough accuracy in his comment—that I needed help—and enough of his compassion for me to relinquish the potential debate around who really needed help. I was pleased he had agreed to attend. Pushing my own point of view would not promote healing, and would make it difficult for me to really see him.

As I accepted his proposal that he was there to help me, he then stated he had been feeling many regrets at not having been there for Mom as much as he should have. Was this his beginning confession to me? Did he want to acknowledge his own errors and regrets to lessen my anger toward him that could surface in the family meetings? When he acknowledged this regret, I felt more joined with him, although we did not talk much further about our mutual neglect of my mother, his wife. I wanted to push this conversation toward the family group. I believed the two of us were not alone in our sadness in having mistreated my mother.

Indeed, there was a momentum toward acknowledging the powerful presence of my mother in our lives. She had died eight years before, but clearly she had never been buried. She was much more than a ghost in our lives. I believed that our regrets kept us from seeing her more clearly as Elizabeth. Later that night, Ann told me, "I feel the most guilt for Mom's death than all of you." Guilt had this magnetic force in our family, as if the one who had the most guilt was the most connected to mother. How long would our penance last? The biggest challenge was to connect with her in a newer, fresher way.

Katie was crying the night before the family meeting, and explained her tears by saying, "I have PMS . . . Mom had it . . . and I have it too!" Her tears were an opening to even more disclosures. She said that she was angry at me for having been gone a lot, and putting more pressure on her to assume responsibility in the house. She added that she was hurt because I received all my parents' admiration, and that she had to follow in my footsteps to get some admiration. She felt sad that the love she received from our parents was conditional love. My first reaction to her disclosing all of this was admiration, and some jealousy. She seemed more fresh and raw in her encounter with me; I felt less free, more constrained.

I agreed with her that I have often assessed my sense of self based on my accomplishments and the continual approval and disapproval of others. I attempted to correct her assumption (or at least boldly represent my own point of view) that our parents had devoted much attention to my life and activities, and gave an example from my sports career where my parents were far more absent than present. I had always been irritated with Katie when she asserted this belief that I had this phenomenal attention and she did not. I was determined to let her know that I, too, had struggled with not being acknowledged, that I had to keep pressing on for success in some unlimited way, like success was "never enough." I was not the "hero" she wanted to make me, and she was not the one forgotten. We had to come together in our mutual hurt.

This evening conversation with Katie helped me also realize that I did not remember much about the family because I had attempted to leave the family physically and emotionally. The chaos and volatility of the family scared me, and I looked outside the family for my strength. These family consultations were a way I could "come home again."

I came to Thomas that evening, and told him I thought his mental retardation had been an important issue in the family and that we had not really ever talked about his retardation together as a family with him present. More regrets. Thomas responded, "That's okay, brother! Don't feel bad about it." Even Thomas was sensitive to how we all needed abundant absolution from each other. Confession and indirect pleadings for forgiveness formed the fabric of many of our conversations.

As the night went on, family members seemed to be more polite toward each other—more thank yous, more cracks of smiles, more sweetness in offering service. Were these acts of grace like shots of anesthesia, unconsciously designed to numb us partially from the stabs of disclosure tomorrow? Perhaps the message was "Please, go easy on me!"

The force of family anxiety, the necessary "propellant" for new conversations, was mounting. Katie took me aside and proclaimed, "They [other family members] don't know what we are getting into!" (In later years she told me that she was very concerned about the live audience, and the on-stage nature of the consultation, but at the time I thought her anxiety had only to do with the family-of-origin work.) I replied that I also didn't know what I was getting into. Katie was not impressed with my vulnerability. "You *do* this kind of stuff!" she pushed back. "We don't know how to talk about this!" For a while we debated this point with an unspoken awareness that we weren't discussing an issue as much as working through the anxiety prior to our family meetings. The more Katie expressed her anxiety, the more sedate I became, as if one of us were doing the anxiety work for both of us. If she worried more maybe I could worry less. How often had I depended on her to overfunction for me in this way?

Lee Headley (1977) once wrote, "No therapy approaches the emotional intensity of these intergenerational sessions." I was now struck by how that emotional intensity heightens long before the actual consultation sessions, sparking these kinds of disclosures and conversations between family members. Much tilling of the family's hardened emotional soil is done long before the family arrives for the first meeting.

The palliative for the increasing anxiety was Jim's leadership and conveying his deep belief and commitment that "healing of the hurts" is the central goal in these consultations. Jim also conveyed a hopeful challenge, predicting that "following this experience, the family can never again be the same." How would our family change? More importantly, how would I not be the same again in this family? Change in the family does not depend on the response of the other, but on the work of the self. Organizing myself to create some response in other family members was a futile and unhealthy goal. I had to make this challenge a personal one for me: "What will I do differently to make a difference in myself with others in this family?" This was the one most useful question that focused my anxiety for the work ahead. That night I had trouble sleeping. So did Katie. We were ready.

Chapter 6

THE FIRST
FAMILY MEETING
Remembering Mother

JAMES L. FRAMO, PhD

(Framo: Routinely, before the family sessions start, I state to the family the purpose of the family meetings: that they all have the opportunity to share their experiences of the family and to deal with issues that they may have had with each other in the past or in the present; that they have the opportunity, as a family, to discuss and exchange views about the critical events that have taken place in the family; and that, as they review the good and bad memories of the family, they are likely to get to know each other better. What I neglected to do with this family, which I regularly do in family-of-origin sessions, was to inform them in advance that as issues come up they may get upset, cry, get angry, but that these feelings are phases to be worked through. I indicate that the ultimate purpose of the meetings is to improve the family relationships, and that my function is that of a facilitator in assisting them to deal with each other to achieve that goal.

In the opening phase of the interview I attempt to get to know a little about all the family members—each one's name, age, occupation, marital status, whether they have children, etc. I ask permission to address them by their first name. I also tell them that they are free to ask me questions about myself. I have found this approach helps diminish the hierarchical nature of the situation, and creates an atmosphere of trust and openness.)

FRAMO: What was it like growing up in this family? Anyone can answer that.

(Framo: This question, which I commonly use to get the process started, gives the family wide latitude to respond. It gives each family member the op-

portunity to relate his or her own experiences of family events and of other family members. The question usually elicits important family themes.)

KATIE: We were busy a lot, we were taught to strive for excellence. We took a lot of trips.

FRAMO: Intellectual achievement was important?

KATIE: Yes, intellectual achievement was important.

FRAMO: Did that come from Dad or Mom?

KATIE: Dad.

FRAMO: Uh huh.

KATIE: Entertainment came from Mom. [laughter by all]

FRAMO: Entertainment came from Mom?

KATIE: You know, we had a lot of receptions at our house and we were always in the limelight which was kind of fun sometimes.

FRAMO: Was there a negative side to this?

LYNN: Yes.

KATIE: Yes.

FRAMO: Let's hear about that.

LYNN: Well . . . It was a lot of work preparing these receptions and things like that. And I can remember that Mom was so incredibly meticulous, too. Everything had to be so exactly right, and she wasn't the type of person who prepared everything a week in advance like any normal person would. We'd prepare everything two hours in advance. It was very stressful on the whole family.

FRAMO: You mean all the kids were enlisted to help out?

LYNN: Well, well, no. [laughter] We were talking about this. We were like two different families, too. Tim was in college when I was born.

FRAMO: Right.

LYNN: And so what I remember is Ann, and myself, and Katie a little bit, but Thomas wasn't at home and Tim wasn't either . . . I think the girls helped out the most. The three of us, I can remember.

FRAMO: Oh, there were real differences between the males and the females? In doing things around the house?

ANN: Yeah.

LYNN: Yes.

FRAMO: Uh huh. How did you feel about doing all that work? [Dr. Framo looks in the direction of Ann and Lynn.]

LYNN: Hated it.

FRAMO: Dad, did you know about this?

DAD: Oh, indeed.

FRAMO: What was your perception of that? Did you help out?

DAD: Oh, indeed I did.

FRAMO: So it wasn't only the women who did the work?

DAD: Well, no. I tried to contribute whatever I possibly could.

LYNN: I think Dad helped out, but I don't know if he knew exactly what we were all under, 'cause you [Dad] were away a lot and you were with the important people. You were always having conferences, and then you would come to the house when everything was prepared and beautiful, and I think . . .

FRAMO: That's the way I like to entertain. [laughter by Dad and others . . . pause] I know from talking with Tim that Mom died. When?

(Framo: Following the light discussion of the household tasks and the division of roles by gender, I tentatively introduce the core issue of this family: Mom's death. I am testing the family's readiness to deal with this charged topic, palpating the family's emotional system.)

(Levine: While it's clear that Jim is moving toward a core issue—Mom's life and death—he inadvertently makes light of the unfairness and sexism Lynn is talking about.)

TIM: December 1978.

DAD: The twenty-second. [quietly]

FRAMO: And how would you all feel about talking a little bit about Mom?

ANN: We already have.

FRAMO: [looking at Ann] You already have? As a family? Everyone?

TIM: [a long sigh]

DAD: [very softly] I'm sure we have. [sighs]

TIM: Well, the night before her funeral we tape recorded a meeting which we had where we looked at Mom's life and what we had appreciated about her, what we did not appreciate about her, and how we were feeling at that point. That was the night before the funeral . . . But I don't think we've done it as a family since that time.

FRAMO: Uh huh.

TIM: We've had these little conversations over the phone, and here and there about Mom . . . Just last night, as a matter of fact [Tim looks at Katie], a little bit.

FRAMO: Um, I wonder, Dad, how you would feel about talking about your deceased wife?

DAD: [choked up and mumbling]

FRAMO: You want to save that for another time?

DAD: [softly] Yeah.

FRAMO: Would you rather wait?

DAD: [nodding his head yes]

FRAMO: Okay. [pause]

(Levine: Jim is titrating the session, feeling where the tender spots are, while at the same time respecting the defenses of family members. I admire his "palpating" and timing.)

The discussion then shifted to the expectation of intellectual achievement in the family. Tim related that he was paid for getting A's, which prompted Ann to say, "We didn't know that." Katie felt great pressure to get good grades, saying that failing a course was unthinkable. Dad said it wasn't the grade that counted, that what mattered was making the best use of one's abilities. Father was comfortable in his role as educator here. Lynn felt she had to live up to the standards set by Tim and Katie. She said she got plenty of B's in her life, and when she disclosed that she just got her first C, Dr. Framo asked her if they were going to write her out of the family. Lynn seemed to be the one in the family who was most free to challenge the family rules.

ANN: We were always going 100 miles an hour that we never had time, to use an old cliché, "to smell the roses." We didn't have time to recognize the important things.

TIM: I remember just a blur at home. We would be working so much and so fast that it was very difficult to stop. We would go, we would take good vacations. I really appreciate this family for—and Dad and Mom—for taking us on vacations. We saw the whole United States, and we went to places that were really great. And then sometimes we would stay at Motel 6s. [everyone laughs, especially Dad and Dr. Framo]

FRAMO: Dad never took you to the Mariott? [laughing]

TIM: Well, no. We are starting to go to Holiday Inns. [laughter again, especially from Dad and Dr. Framo]

(Framo: Occasionally I put a humorous slant on my comments in order to ease the tensions that are inherent in this situation. I noted that Tim, here, was following my suggestion about bringing up positive experiences of the family.)

TIM: But mostly we would stay at friends' houses and relatives. We saw a lot of people, and that was really great . . . Seeing people. I think that was really helpful . . . But, like on Saturdays, I remember getting up in the morning and working, and we would work until we went to bed.

FRAMO: So, in addition to intellectual achievement, this was really a work-oriented family?

(Framo: It was apparent by now that the work ethic, religion, achievement, frugality, and competence were high values in this family. It seemed to me that, because of father's position in the community, the family felt it had to appear as the perfect family. I also had the thought, at this point, that the presence of a retarded child must have had deep significance in this achievement-oriented family. Did the other children have to compensate for Thomas's retardation? Thomas's handicap certainly must have been very painful for both parents, each in his or her own way.)

TIM: Yeah. A lot of . . . And one of the difficulties I have now—my wife really lets me know it—it's just real hard for me to keep from working. I'm always busy, even when I come home I'm doing something.

FRAMO: Uh huh.

TIM: And she just wants me to...

FRAMO: Before you can rest and relax do you feel you have to earn it? You have to do your work first, and then you can enjoy relaxing?

(Framo: This statement of mine had more to do with me than with Tim. It is an example of how therapists can intrude their own stuff into the proceedings. In my family one could not indulge in pleasure while tasks remained undone.)

TIM: That thought doesn't occur to me, but my behavior is that I just keep on going.

FRAMO: Uh huh.

TIM: I don't really feel I have to earn my pleasure, but I just know I keep on going.

FRAMO: Katie, did you feel that way? That there wasn't time to "smell the roses"?

KATIE: Oh, yeah. We were always going. I remember my friends used to have a list that they had on Saturdays on the refrigerator. When they were done with their jobs they could go play. They would come over to our house, and I could never play because if I was ever done with a job there was another one to be done. And I remember working so slowly, and my mother commenting, "You're just a slow worker" and "How come you don't work fast like Vicki does?" And it was because I knew that when that job was done there would be another one to do.

ANN: What I'm thinking through right now is, I think there were extremes. Either it was really, really good—like our vacations—or it was really, really bad and, for me growing up, it was real confusing to me. What the difference was, you know . . .'Cause it could change like that within minutes depending upon the attitude of whoever was at home.

FRAMO: [holding up some mints]) Would anyone like a Breath Saver? [laughter by the family] I'll pass them around. Help yourself.

(Framo: I'm not quite sure why, at this point, instead of attending to Ann's important statement I offered the family some mints. A likely explanation is that Ann was probably referring to Mom's emotional turmoil, and I may have felt that the family was not yet ready to deal with that.)

LYNN: We should have had that before we came here. [as the mints get passed around the circle] [laughter]

FRAMO: Come on, Thomas, take one!

THOMAS: No thank you.

DAD: There's nothing in here that somehow is going to purify whatever's being said? [Dad laughs, as well as others]

FRAMO: Well, you can never tell. [laughter by Dr. Framo and the family]

DAD: Not one device that the psychologists are using today, is it? [laughter continues]

FRAMO: That's not a technique. I just figured I needed one for dry mouth and it wasn't polite to just not offer. [laughter continues]

DAD: With all the drugs going on these days, one never knows what he's getting or drinking. [as Dad gets up and hands the mints back to Dr. Framo] [laughter continues]

FRAMO: That's true. Well, these are not drugs. I don't think . . . They're sugar-free. In any event, I get the impression that there was a minimum of fun in this family.

(Framo: Despite the humor, it became apparent to me during this inter-change that my offering of the mints became a metaphor for the relationship between father and me. He had never been in a psychotherapeutic situation before, and he was probably anxious. Also, perhaps he was dubious about my intentions, and wondered whether I had some hidden methods of getting him to reveal painful secrets. In the midst of these double-entendres, I speculated that, unconsciously, he was transmitting such messages as: "I don't know if I can digest what you have to offer," or "I loan my family to you for the present, but can I trust you with my family?" or "I hope you know what you're getting into and can handle it." Although father had told Tim he came to the sessions in the service of research, I sensed he really wanted something for himself [forgive-ness?]. In any event, I chose not to deal with these speculative themes at this time, and instead proceeded to deal with the topic under discussion: the relative absence of fun in the family.)

(Levine. Jim's earliest roots are in psychoanalytic/psychodyamic theory. He moves easily between the intrapsychic and interpersonal perspectives.)

Although Katie and Tim spoke of going swimming on Saturday nights, going to Tim's sports activities, and attending faculty picnics, the second family (Ann and Lynn) had difficulty remembering fun times. Katie said she and Tim were part of a more defined family when they were growing up. It seemed, however, that more than age differences separated the two families.

KATIE: I feel like I am the bridge between the two, because I was part of this family but I was also the mother of those two girls [pointing to Ann and Lynn]. I felt like I was involved with them like a mother. So I feel like I'm in both families.

FRAMO: You had to take care of these two? [pointing to Ann and Lynn]

KATIE: Yes.

FRAMO: Really?

KATIE: Yes, I did, and I loved it. I tell you that was probably the biggest joy.

FRAMO: You never resented it? Didn't you want to go out and be with your friends?

KATIE: [crying] Oh, sometimes.

FRAMO: Why does that make you cry?

KATIE: [continuing to cry] I cry at everything. [Katie laughs, followed by the laughs of others]

FRAMO: Sometimes I do, too.

(Framo: I self-disclose in order to give Katie the freedom to fully express her feelings. It is Katie's affect that is providing the opening for me to start dealing with the sibling issue.)

KATIE: You'll see. [crying and laughing at the same time]

FRAMO: So part of you really enjoyed taking care of your sisters, and another part of you apparently felt overly responsible. Did you know about this? [turning to Tim]

TIM: I don't think I knew about it. What I know is that she resented a lot of burdens that she had to carry in the family.

FRAMO: She was the oldest daughter.

TIM: Yeah, and I really got away with a lot, probably . . . I got outside the family.

FRAMO: Yeah. You said your sisters looked on you, and your brother looked on you, as the fair-haired boy of the family.

DAD: [laughs loudly]

FRAMO: Katie, do you have any thoughts about that?

KATIE: I've told Tim that, yeah.

FRAMO: He got away with a lot?

KATIE: Yes, he did. He did. But I respect him. We were talking last night about competition . . . I don't feel there was competition between us . . . I was always envious of Tim.

FRAMO: Uh huh. [looking at Ann and Lynn] Did you two feel that, too?

LYNN: Of Tim?

FRAMO: That he got away with a lot?

LYNN: I really don't know Tim that well. I mean, I probably know him more now than I ever have, and I'm nineteen. He was eighteen when I was born, so I . . . I always thought of him as kind of a visitor [laughing] when he came home . . . Oh wow! [Lynn laughs, Dr. Framo laughs, and others] Because he was never around when I was growing up.

When Dr. Framo inquired as to how often Tim had been in contact with his sisters, it turned out there had been sporadic but infrequent contact. They did not write to each other, and periods as long as a year would go by between phone calls. The family did usually get together at holidays, however. The younger sisters said they were joyous when Tim came through for them, but then he would disappear for long periods. Tim had already discussed, in the prep session, his personal problem of emotionally distancing himself, like his dad.

FRAMO: Tim, I'm hearing a message from your two younger sisters.

TIM: We need to get back into contact?

FRAMO: It's more than that. They're longing for something from you: closeness.

TIM: I'm really happy that Lynn's coming to our house for Thanksgiving . . . She's planning on it.

FRAMO: Uh huh. You're their hero. Don't you hear that?

TIM: I think they may not know that I need them, too.

FRAMO: Tell them!

(Framo: A prominent feature of family-of-origin sessions is that the family members find it very difficult to address each other directly. When statements are made to me about someone in the family I sometimes suggest that the individual tell the person or persons directly. Tim, here, steps out of his perceived lofty role by exposing his vulnerability. He took the first step in closing the distance between him and his sisters.)

TIM: [nervous laughter from the family] I need you, too. I think you think I don't need anybody.

LYNN: Well, that's not true, because I think that you're wonderful . . . I think that a lot. Like we never have family reunions or anything like that . . . And that really bothers me. It's really sad that we've never gotten together as a family and talked. In fact, holidays are an excuse, and it's such a big effort to get together, and it shouldn't be that way. Money should be no object when it comes to togetherness as a family because that's what's happening these days: everybody is breaking apart. I think it's wonderful when you visit. You always stress how the family is so important.

FRAMO: Are you pleased that he organized this meeting?

LYNN: At first, no I wasn't. [laughing] I don't think I really knew what was going on until I arrived here today, and I saw this place where we're supposed to sit, and I think it's very brave of us. [Dr. Framo and Ann are laughing] I guess the whole family coming out here . . . That's what pleased me, not this meeting so much.

FRAMO: I understand. And also because, perhaps, Tim was the one who organized this because he wanted something to change in the family.

(Framo: I wanted to make sure the family understood that Tim's motive in initiating the family session was for the benefit of the whole family, not just for himself.)

LYNN: Yes, I think that was very important. I'm really glad that he did that.

FRAMO: What do you think needs changing in this family?

LYNN: Communication.

FRAMO: Well, that word can mean most anything. What do you mean by communication?

LYNN: Feelings. Not so much, "Hi. How's it going?" And I'm guilty of that, too.

FRAMO: Do you mean not just superficial stuff?

LYNN: Yeah. Very deep conversation. Because your family should be your best friends also, and I think that there's a lack of communication between everybody.

FRAMO: Everybody?

LYNN: Well, no. There's more communication, I suppose, between Ann and me, Katie and me, than there is between Tim and me because we don't know each other.

FRAMO: How about Dad? [looking at Lynn]

LYNN: Dad and I are very close, you know.

FRAMO: Uh huh.

LYNN: That's because when I was growing up, I suppose, there was a lot of pressure when Mom was around, and to get out of it I went to Dad.

Lynn further elaborated the theme of closeness between her and Dad by saying that Dad was the fun parent who took her to basketball games, sang songs to her, and gave her affection. Apparently she had more of a personal relationship with Dad than the other children did.

FRAMO: Tim had told me, though, that Thomas was kind of like the switchboard in the family; that he's the one who sort of has the job of keeping everybody in touch with each other... Is that true, Thomas?

(Framo: I did not pursue further, at this time, the theme of Mom as the taskmaster and Dad as the nurturer. I decided, instead, to bring Thomas into the discussion because he did not seem like part of the family. I had noticed that Thomas hardly ever volunteered comments, so I knew I had to draw him out.)

THOMAS: Yes, that's true.

FRAMO: How do you do that?

THOMAS: I make phone calls, a lot of phone calls.

FRAMO: You do? Who do you call?

THOMAS: Tim and Katie. I never call Ann, and I never call Lynn... I just call Tim and Katie.

FRAMO: But you help people to keep in touch with each other?

THOMAS: Yeah.

FRAMO: I see. [looking at the rest of the family] Do you agree with this, that that's Thomas's role?

LYNN: Yes . . . Thomas is very affectionate . . .

FRAMO: Right.

LYNN: [looking at Thomas] You know how you always say, "Give me a love," or something like that?

THOMAS: Yeah.

LYNN: That's wonderful.

FRAMO: Uh huh.

LYNN: I think that's really wonderful, and I think he has the idea better than any one of us here.

FRAMO: Of what?

LYNN: Togetherness. I mean he's so happy. He'll say, "I'm homesick," or "I really miss home."

FRAMO: Uh huh.

LYNN: And we take it for granted so much.

FRAMO: Yeah.

(Framo: I took silent note of the denial here that Thomas has been one of the family's problems.)

LYNN: Especially me. I mean, I'm home for three months and I can't wait to get back to school. I mean, how awful.

FRAMO: So Thomas is the one person in the family who wants more togetherness?

LYNN: I don't think he's the only person who wants the togetherness, but he displays it the best. We all have faults, and I think I lived in a dream world when it came to Dad.

FRAMO: Why? Do you mean he was perfect?

LYNN: He was perfect. He was my image of . . .

FRAMO: [pointing to Tim] I thought Tim was the perfect one?

LYNN: I don't know Tim very well.

FRAMO: Oh.

LYNN: I think he's great.

FRAMO: Uh huh.

LYNN: I think he's done a lot, and I really admire him for that, and I wish I could be that drive-oriented and intelligent and all that, you know.

FRAMO: Yeah.

LYNN: But when it comes to Dad, I put him on a pedestal. I thought he was absolutely . . . He could do no wrong. And as I've grown up, I , . .

DAD: [chuckling]

LYNN: You're a wonderful person, Dad, but everybody has faults and I'm beginning to see those faults now . . . I still think he's a wonderful person.

FRAMO: Right.

LYNN: But the magic . . . Reality has set in.

FRAMO: You know, all kids go through this disillusionment. Do you think he would be willing to listen if you were to tell him some of his faults?

LYNN: [pausing] Honestly?

FRAMO: Yeah.

LYNN: [laughing nervously]

FRAMO: My kids tell me at times. Sure . . . They tell me I holler too much sometimes, and so forth.

LYNN: I'd rather not, because he could probably double that fault-finding with me. [laughing]

(Framo: I normalize Lynn's apprehension and present myself as a not perfect dad for my own children. I was attempting, here, to make Dad more real. Although Lynn was the most revealing person in the family, she could not bring herself to criticize Dad. The siblings were not yet ready to deal with Dad, and neither was I. The father and I had not yet established a relationship.)

The family had already demonstrated how difficult it was for them to express negative feelings. It turned out that overt expression of positive feelings (hugging, kissing) did not come easily to them either. Father attributed this to the generation gap, saying this generation was not very demonstrative. Lynn said Dad was affectionate with her, and she also saw Mom as affectionate. Tim remembered Mom as very caring, but could not recall her being affectionate with him. Katie said Mom would request affection from her, but she did not want to give it to her. Katie further added that Dad would tuck them in at night and sing songs to them.

FRAMO: Katie, how do you see your mom? How would you describe her as a person? What was she like?

(Framo: I finally return to what I intuited as the most painful and sensitive topic of all: the family's mixed and confused feelings about Mom. I sensed that by this point in the interview the family trusted me enough to talk about Mom in some depth. I also knew that if the father had confidence in me the rest of the family would follow.)

KATIE: I think my mother changed over the years . . . She was two different people. In fact, we were talking about that. I think maybe she was three different descriptions, because my fondest memories were before I was five, around five . . . Those were happy, happy times. I remember them as happy . . . Um, and then I think, later on, my mom turned almost into Dr. Jeckyl and Mr. Hyde. Like one of the girls said, Ann I think, said it was either really, really good or it was so terrible you just wanted to hide.

FRAMO: What was she like when she was Mr. Hyde?

KATIE: Um . . . Well, I think I would like to premise the whole thing by saying, as we were talking, we think that maybe she was suffering from PMS.

FRAMO: Uh huh.

KATIE: At times it seemed as if everything was fine and happy, and she would go buy things like you wouldn't believe. I mean, she would take us shopping . . . It might have been at Goodwill, but we went shopping. [Katie laughs, as do others] And we would buy ten pairs of shoes. We may not have liked them, but she just went on in binges. She was a bingeing person. And then the other side was there has to be work to be done . . . And she would get to the point where she would just scream at you, just literally scream and be . . . You didn't understand her . . . I remember being hit, not as a child, this was when I was older. But it was because she was so frustrated. I just think she was such a frustrated person. And there was so much to be done, and she would stay up all night long . . . There were party times where she would stay up all night.

FRAMO: Was it confusing to you these two pictures of Mom?

KATIE: Oh, you don't know . . . Yeah . . . And maybe there would be a point where she'd—after the parties were over—she would crash, and she'd sleep all day, and she wouldn't talk to you, or she would get into the mood where she wouldn't talk to you for a day or two.

FRAMO: Didn't she ever complain about having to do all this entertaining?

KATIE: Yes. In analyzing it, I think; after her death unfortunately. That's where her positive strokes were: People would come to the parties and say, "Elizabeth, you mean you did all this yourself? I can't believe it!"

FRAMO: Uh huh.

KATIE: And she would say, "Yes I did." Her food was excellent, and her parties were magnificent.

(Framo: Although Mom may have gotten social rewards and inherent satisfaction from organizing these parties, I wondered whether she felt it her duty to work hard to uphold and support her husband's position in the church and the community.)

FRAMO: Uh huh.

KATIE: And she was a wonderful hostess.

FRAMO: But, as a daughter, you found her behavior confusing.

KATIE: Unfortunately, in the last years, yes.

FRAMO: So when you have these negative thoughts about Mom, you think about the times when things were really good.

(Framo: I try to balance the negative with the positive views of Mom, and I am aware that I will have to do this with each of these adult children. The ambivalence about mother in this family goes beyond the kind of natural ambivalence that everyone has about parents. I noticed at this point, however, that I had to be careful here because the potential for my countertransference was high. My own mother had conspicuous mood swings, and it was only recently that I had reevaluated my mom, years after her death, by remembering the really good things I got from her.)
(Levine: The capacity to hold ambivalence is both an intrapsychic and family system task.)

FRAMO: Yeah. Tim, how did you see Mom?

TIM: She and I fought a lot. I can remember sometimes, Thomas, there would be Mom, and you and me, and there would be a big fight . . . Remember? [looking at Thomas]

THOMAS: Yeah. I remember.

FRAMO: What were you fighting about?

TIM: Oh, I don't know. It could have been over anything. I stayed out of the house a lot. It was a very tense place. Dinnertime, when I was growing up, was very tense, and it was just hard to sit down and eat. And I remember Dad saying, "Let's talk about the positive," "Let's think about the positive." And he would try to calm things down. My mom would get up and have a temper tantrum, and then she'd cry and I'd feel like we did it. She was also a very caring person, and very supportive of me. She's the one, I think, who gave me a lot of courage to do things. She always said I was a good writer. She would look at my papers and would correct them, and she'd really encourage me in the arts. And I think any creativity I have is really a gift from her. So, and, she was really creative herself. She was a great performer, an entertainer, an artist . . .

(*Framo: There is a suggestion here that father wanted only the positive focused on—that negative things should be denied [such as Mom's condition]. This attitude supports the family's view of father as the good guy, or even as saintly. Also apparent in this long statement of Tim's is his attempt to neutralize his disturbance about Mom's behavior by shifting to gratefulness for her good qualities. I saw this shift as an indication of the pervasive guilt in this family.*)

FRAMO: Well, did you see, as Katie did, these two different sides to Mom? A Jeckyl and Hyde? Did you see her apparent marked changes?

TIM: I don't think I was in the house that much to see it from moment to moment. Um, I just remember it being . . . She was a difficult person to be around.

FRAMO: She was so tense, you mean?

TIM: Yeah.

FRAMO: Was she argumentative?

TIM: Yeah. It was hard to sit down and talk to her. I did that a few times before she died. I would come home, and I can remember sitting around with her in the house where Dad lives right now and just having a good talk with her. That happened toward the end of her life, and that was really good.

FRAMO: Uh huh. Did you ever wonder whether or not your mom had any sort of medical condition?

TIM: I don't think I was smart enough to think about that at the time.

FRAMO: When you look back on it now, do you think she did?

TIM: I think so.

FRAMO: Did she have high blood pressure or something?

TIM: No. But there's a lot of, um, physical problems in the family history: kidneys, and thyroid, and heart, and a lot of other things.

Her behavior was just so out of control that I think that something else was going on. She really took care of Thomas a lot. I
think being concerned about Thomas really took up a lot of her
energy, too.

*(Framo: If, indeed, no one knew what was going on with Mom, I won-
dered why she was not thoroughly evaluated medically. What must Dad be
thinking as he's listening to his children describe how irrational their mother
behaved? I should have asked him at this point, particularly whether he knew
how much the children were demoralized by her behavior. I took note, also, of
how difficult it must have been for Mom having to take care of a retarded,
disturbed child.)*

*(Levine: In the role of back-seat driver, I imagined all sorts of diagnostic
possibilities that could apply to mother, from organic conditions to bipolar disorder to personality disorders. But I think it would be a mistake to diagnose mother
on the basis of a partial case history after the fact.)*

FRAMO: Uh huh. Thomas, do you remember Mom?

THOMAS: Yes.

FRAMO: How would you describe Mom?

THOMAS: She was a nice person, but she yelled a lot.

FRAMO: She yelled a lot?

THOMAS: Yes.

FRAMO: Did you ever yell back at her?

THOMAS: Once in a while.

FRAMO: Uh huh. How about you, Lynn. How did you see Mom? Can you
         confirm what they're saying—these two sides to Mom?

*(Framo: Throughout the interview, I used Lynn's relative openness to gain
entry to the emotional heart of the family.)*

*(Levine: Like Whitaker, Jim was seeking a cotherapist from within the
family.)*

LYNN: Yeah, definitely. Definitely. I think it was a little worse . . .

FRAMO: Worse than they're saying?

LYNN: Well, I think the last years of her life were when I was home. And
         Ann was home, too. And it was incredible what we had to go
         through . . . Absolutely incredible. I can remember, um, some-
         times, she would hit us, and things like that.

FRAMO: Hit you out of the blue, you mean?

LYNN: Well, almost. It was a total change of personality. One minute she would just be, "Oh, I love you; I love you," or "You're the greatest daughter," or "You're so cute," and the next minute she would be angry at you for not wearing a pair of pants that she wanted you to wear . . .

FRAMO: Uh huh.

LYNN: For no reason at all, you know. [nervous laughter] And I can remember . . . And you couldn't reason with her either. Like . . . Clothes are very important in our family, and I can remember not wanting to wear a pair of anklets. I wanted to wear knee socks like all the other girls did. And that just set her off. I mean, something so trivial like that just set her off. She would get really, really angry, and it was incredible.

(Framo: "Incredible" is the acceptable word for "horrible.")

FRAMO: How did you react to that?

LYNN: I was a brat.

FRAMO: You yelled back at her like Thomas did?

LYNN: Oh, yeah. Yeah. I screamed and I yelled, and I cried. I think that Ann and Katie would take it more, but I wouldn't take it. I wouldn't take it. I couldn't understand why she would do that, 'cause I was so young and I didn't understand.

FRAMO: Uh huh.

LYNN: But then she would take us to Burgerville and would buy us . . . Take me out to lunch every day . . . Or, like Katie said, she would take us shopping, or she would sit by the piano, or do wonderful things . . . But then the next moment it was a total change of personality.

FRAMO: Did you wonder if something was wrong?

LYNN: Medically?

FRAMO: With her, yes, medically.

LYNN: I was way too young to know. This was like when I was five and six years old. I remember that Mom had cancer. I remember Dad telling me that it was malignant. I asked if I could go play with my friend that day. [Lynn laughs quietly] I had no idea what it meant.

FRAMO: Yes. How about you, Ann. How do you remember Mom?

ANN: I was the one that said there were such extremes, but I don't know if this would be completely true. But I think that out of all the kids I can identify with her more than anybody . . . Because if anyone's like her I am.

FRAMO: You are?

ANN: Yeah. We had probably more deep talks, because I was home a lot. Besides Dad, I was probably her...her closest companion. Because when she stayed up late at night I stayed up late at night. But at the same time, because I was always there, when those moods changed I was the first person she talked to.

FRAMO: Well, when she had these bad moods, how did you react?

ANN: I've got some of my Dad's personality in that everything is internalized.

FRAMO: You didn't challenge her the way Lynn did?

ANN: No. Sometimes I wish I would have, because growing up I would get so sick to my stomach that my stomach would be in knots. And I mean every time I sometimes think about this, I start shaking. Already you know just how nervewracking it was. What I do now is, just like my Mom: I cater, I cook, I work in restaurants . . .

(Framo: Ann, it will be recalled, is diabetic, and appears to somatize her conflicts.)

FRAMO: Are there other ways you are like your mom?

ANN: Probably in her desires. She always wanted to be a professional caterer, and that's what I became.

FRAMO: I see.

ANN: And her creativity with music. That also goes with Katie, but that's me, too.

FRAMO: Do you think you would have been better off if you were more like Lynn and just fought it out with her toe-to-toe?

ANN: [shaking her head no] Sometimes I think it would have been better for my health, but I like who I am. I really did love Mom, and I wish I had had more time to understand her and to just have really told her how much I loved her because I think it would have made a lot of difference. [begins to cry]

(Framo: I was personally touched by Ann's tears since I, too, had experienced that universal regret over not having had the opportunity to tell my parents before they died that I loved them. Ann is still struggling between loyalty to self and loyalty to her mother. Her anger toward her mother was dissociated and turned against the self. She has some awareness that she sacrificed her physical and mental health for the sake of a close relationship with her mother.)

Her guilt for not having done more for her mother is palpable. I consider the probability that the debt was paid by becoming her mother, the formulation being, "If I can't have her I will be her." This is how she makes sense of her life.)

(Levine: Jim is using psychoanalytic theory to explain Ann's identification with the lost object.)

FRAMO: Yes, yes. [Dr. Framo touches Ann on the shoulder since she is sitting next to him] [turning to the family] What are your thoughts about what Ann has just said? [the family is quiet]

LYNN: I agree. What Ann said is very important. [Lynn wipes tears from her eyes] I think Mom's death affects me now twice as much as it did when it happened. When it happened it was kind of like a blur. I was twelve years old. I can remember losing my mom and people said, "Oh, you poor little girl." [as Lynn is telling the story, the rest of the family members are crying] Hey, and I had a great dad. You know, I love my dad; I thought he was terrific, and I got away with murder when Mom died. I could do anything I wanted to.

FRAMO: Oh, I see. It was almost like the policeman of the family had left.

LYNN: Exactly. Exactly. It was almost . . . In a way it's sad, but it was almost like the pressure was off. [the rest of the family members are more noticeably crying now] It was finally over…

FRAMO: So you felt some relief?

(Levine: Jim puts the forbidden word "relief" to her feelings, which will enable them to elaborate more about Mom.)

LYNN: Yeah . . . I mean, I feel terrible saying that. She's probably up there going, "Lynn!!!" [Lynn laughs slightly]

(Framo: At this point, I had another personal association to the material. My mom, too, was the disciplinarian of the family [although the responsible one] and my dad was the fun parent. I recall that when I was about ten years old my mother went to the hospital for a week, and I had the most terrifying thought: "I hope she never comes home because then we can have fun." I couldn't believe that I could have such an awful thought, and immediately tried to undo my crime by praying and saying, "I didn't mean it." I had to be careful here not to mix my life story with theirs, a parallel process sometimes called projective identification.)

FRAMO: [laughs]

LYNN: But . . . Yeah, in a way I felt relief. It was really sad because Mom was always the one who was really a mom. I mean, she cooked and cleaned, and she really loved us.

FRAMO: Uh huh. [the rest of the family continues to cry quietly]

LYNN: And it's really hard when you're twelve to lose your mom when all these girls are having their moms take them to Bluebird meetings and things like that, you know; but your dad's there taking you . . . [Lynn laughs]

FRAMO: Uh huh.

LYNN: But the relief was there, the stress was over . . . No more parties. I could go shopping with my dad and spend money. You know, we could go out to dinner all the time. It was great.

(Framo: When I originally heard from Tim in the preparation sessions that there was relief when Mom died, my first thought was that Mom's death was welcomed because she was dying in great pain. It was apparent now that the relief was based on the realization that Mom's unreasonable behavior and rage reactions no longer needed to be dealt with. Of course, there were many feelings besides relief: devastating feelings of loss, grief, desolation, shock, abandonment, and guilt.)

FRAMO: Did you feel a sense of loss at the time?

LYNN: I did, but Ann took Mom's place.

FRAMO: How do you mean?

LYNN: She was my mom. And she loved me, too, just like Mom did. She took Mom's place in that way, and she was a lot more quiet, understanding; and I took advantage of her a lot. I could do that and she wouldn't fight back like Mom did. [Ann laughs] So it was an ideal situation for a little girl.

FRAMO: I hear you.

LYNN: But now, as I become older, I look back on it and, like Ann said, I wish we could have talked to her. I especially felt this in college when people were getting care packages, letters, things like that. Or when people would send them things on Easter. I never . . . I mean, I got letters and phone calls and things like that, but not like I really wanted to and . . .

FRAMO: Yes.

LYNN: . . . and the loss was there.

FRAMO: Yes.

LYNN: And I think that I'm mature enough now that I could have tried to be her best friend, just like the relationship that I would want with my kids: to have a little girl and to have us be best friends.

FRAMO: Lynn, how did you hear about Mom dying?

(Framo: I have found that one of the best ways to help people ease the pain of mourning over a death is to revive the acute grief experience by going over in great detail the specific events surrounding the death and the funeral. Recalling the separate pieces of the experience almost always gives rise to intense anguish as experiences are relived, but this process can also be very healing, especially if it's shared with other loved ones. This technique is especially useful for people whose bereavement was muted, absent, or incomplete at the time of the death. Aborted mourning usually results in later years in seemingly unrelated symptoms such as depression, somatic disorders, sexual difficulties, violence, or suicide. The sharing of the grief among family members has therapeutic and reparative effects (Paul, 1967).

LYNN: Um, I was at my friend's house, and I've known this friend ever since I was born. Her mom is like a mother to me. I can remember the night so vividly. When Mom passed out, and she was in the ambulance, the nurse came over and told us that it was a mild heart attack and she'd be fine and there was nothing to worry about. Then I went to another friend's house, and Ann and I were there, and we got a phone call and the doctor said she had a 50–50 chance of living. And it's like from saying, "You have a mild cold" to "You're dying." And we just sat there and couldn't believe it. [family members are all weeping]

FRAMO: Yes.

LYNN: My mom's best friend, Mrs. Brown, took me to her home. It was like being with a family. I can remember that night, I didn't sleep all night. I think Mrs. Brown got a phone call in the middle of the night [Lynn looks at Dad] saying that Mom had died; but she didn't want to wake me up and tell me that because she wanted to wait until Dad told me. And I can remember everything: sitting there in the hallway and having the doorbell ring, and Dad walking through the door, looking at me and, you know, just crying . . . It was awful. [Lynn weeps] [there is a long silence with no conversation]

(Framo: For only the second time in my career as a therapist I lost my distance and cried in a therapy session. I don't know if anyone noticed. The memories of old pains and sorrows about my own past losses, particularly the losses of my sons, surged through me in waves. My own losses enabled me to

understand where they were. I handled my own emotions by asking factual questions.)

(Levine: On the videotape Jim looks moved but his tears were not evident. He is clearly talking about the powerful internal feelings he was experiencing.)

FRAMO: Did you talk to your brother and the rest of your family at that time?

LYNN: No. [wipes tears from her eyes]

FRAMO: What did you do?

LYNN: [continues to cry] I can remember going into my friend's room, and Dad was there, and Mrs. Brown was there, and she just held me. And she was saying, "I'm sorry." I can just hear her saying those words: "I'm so sorry."

FRAMO: Who is your best friend?

LYNN: Her mother was my mother's best friend. They had taught pre-school together, and it was like the four of us—the two women and my friend and I—had grown up together . . . And so she just held me and said, "Oh, I'm so sorry." [Lynn continues to cry] Then I can remember Dad telling me that all the kids were fine. And that's the last that I remember. I mean, everything after that is a blur. I don't remember what happened.

FRAMO: You don't remember the funeral?

LYNN: Oh, yes, I remember the funeral . . . Yeah, I remember the funeral . . . I remember seeing Mom's body. That was a big deal. I told Dad I didn't want to see it, and he said, "Well, I think it would be a good idea if you did because you can see that she's really dead." [Lynn can barely talk as she continues crying, choking the words out; the other family members are also crying]

(Framo: I thought Dad had done a wise thing by urging Lynn to see her mom's body.)

FRAMO: Dad wanted you to accept it.

LYNN: [just nods yes] And it was really difficult because I blocked a lot out. Like our pastor came over and read us a Bible verse, and I just wanted to tell him to get out of our house because I couldn't care less if he was there, reading a Bible verse to me . . . I just wanted him to leave. And it bothered me: all the people that came over. I just wanted them to leave me alone . . .

FRAMO: I hear you.

(Framo: When my sons died priests came to the house and recited what were, for me, empty phrases and platitudes like, "God acts in mysterious ways." Having been where this family was, I knew that there are no right words that can ease the pain. I remember not being able to wait for the clergy to leave.)

(Levine: This is where Jim's years of experience and comfort with his own unconscious process enable him to feel his own stuff without losing sight of the client's needs and process.)

LYNN: I was sick and tired of having people say, "Oh, you're so young. Your mom has just died." I wanted to say, "Shut up! I don't want to hear that!"

FRAMO: Uh huh.

LYNN: I just wanted to be around my family. One thing I can remember was the church was very large. It could seat a large number of people—what, seven hundred, eight hundred people?

DAD: No, no, no . . .

LYNN: Six hundred?

DAD. No. Three hundred and fifty.

LYNN: Well, anyway, we had chairs lined up in the back. People were standing, and chairs were on the side. And I suppose the one thing that just astounds me is that people could talk behind Mom's back right and left, but when her funeral came it was, "Oh, let's have everybody come to the funeral and pay our respects to this wonderful woman." If they had told her that before maybe she wouldn't have died.

(Framo: It is not uncommon after a parent's death for children to think magically, "If I had been good or had been nicer to Mom maybe she'd still be alive." Lynn may also be projecting her guilt, and it takes the form of anger at people who came to the funeral. It is customary after the death of a close one to feel that someone has to be blamed.

Another point that is relevant here is related to my work with family of origin. When I have adults meet with their parents and siblings, the adult children try to get their negative feelings out of the way so that they can express their love to their parents before they die. These children never had the opportunity to do so with Mom.)

FRAMO: Uh huh, uh huh. It's a sad thing to lose a mother of a family, isn't it? Makes me cry, too . . . Reminds me of the deaths in my own family . . . Ann, how was all of this for you?

ANN: (Ann is crying and wipes tears from her eyes) We were talking a
          little bit about this last night. You know how I was saying I never
          spoke up and said anything? I can remember this whole thing so
          clearly. It was the night before we were going to Katie's house for
          Christmas. This was one of the occasions I had stayed up all night
          with Mom because I just wanted to be with her; I just wanted to
          help her because I knew she was so tired. And so here I was, 15
          years old, and I stayed up all night. And in the morning I said,
          "Mom, I need to lay down a little bit. I'm real tired." And she
          started yelling at me. This was the first time I had ever spoken up
          against my mother, and this was the moment that she had her
          heart attack.

LYNN: You called her a bitch. [Lynn laughs, and Ann laughs with her]

FRAMO: Why, because she was yelling at you?

ANN: Uh huh.

LYNN: And we told her that we wished she would die. [Lynn laughs
          along with Ann] [Katie also laughs, but they are all crying as well]

(Framo: The laughter here by Lynn and Ann had no gaiety in it; it is
portentous of the secret about to be disclosed.)

FRAMO: You told her what?

LYNN: We told her . . . Ann and I went upstairs and told each other we
          wished she were dead . . . We told each other that.

ANN: Then we went down and Mom said, "Oh, my heart hurts." She
          had been sick before, and I said, "Mom, I'm tired of you playing
          games with us."

FRAMO: Ah, I see.

LYNN: We didn't believe her; we thought she was lying to us. [both Ann
          and Lynn are crying[

FRAMO: Uh huh, uh huh.

ANN: And, uh, she fell on the floor.

(Framo: This sequence of events—Ann expressing anger to Mom for the
first time, Ann and Lynn wishing Mom was dead, Mom saying, "My heart
hurts" and falling to the floor and later actually dying—sounds like a child's
worst fantasy come true: that if you get angry at your mother you can kill her.
This theme has appeared in fictionalized case histories, in plays, film, and nov-
els, but here it actually happened. Ann and Lynn have harbored this shared,
awful secret for a long time, and I wondered whether this was the first time the
rest of the family was hearing about it.)

FRAMO: [talking to Ann] You were there?

ANN: Yeah.

FRAMO: Was Lynn there, too?

LYNN: [nods yes]

FRAMO: What did you all do?

ANN: I did my "child." When I was little and used to get in trouble I used to hide. And here I was, 15 years old, and I hid behind the sofa because I was so scared. [she is laughing and crying at the same time]

FRAMO: Uh huh.

ANN: And I remember the ambulance coming [laughs] . . . And she had a dirty shirt on and—this is typical of Mom—she didn't want the ambulance people to see how dirty her shirt was, so she made me take it off of her and give her a new one.

FRAMO: [laughing lightly] Uh huh. Was she still conscious?

(Levine: Jim's slight laughter reminds us that there can be absurd/comic moments in the midst of crisis and tragedy.)

ANN: Yeah. She was still conscious.

FRAMO: You came out from behind the sofa?

ANN: No, not right away. They had to go and look for me. No one knew where I was. After I had gotten her shirt, I went behind the sofa and I was hiding. It was probably a couple of hours before I came out.

FRAMO: Well, who called the ambulance?

ANN: Dad did.

FRAMO: Oh, Dad was home?

ANN: Yeah.

DAD: I sure was!

ANN: And, uh, after that I was so sick, and I had a real high temperature. People said, "Do you want to go see your Mom?" I said, "No. I can't." And they started yelling at me, "You don't want to go and see your Mom? She's sick!" And after that my fever got even higher. I was ready to pass out. I was at my friend's house, and I couldn't sleep that whole night because I was sick.

FRAMO: Uh huh.

ANN: As soon as Dad walked in the door, and started crying and said that Mom was dead, the fever immediately left. It was all gone.

The pressure was all gone. I didn't have to worry about it any more. But boy did I feel guilty!

FRAMO: Are you afraid . . . Have you ever wondered, "Did I kill my mom?"

(Framo: I make explicit what was certainly implicit; I state openly the forbidden thought. I remember that Bowen did this sort of thing all the time. Even at the time I said this, however, I wondered if it was a bit strong.)

ANN: [shakes her head no] There was a time, a couple of weeks later—and this might sound strange to some people—but I was sleeping and I was praying, and I said, "God, you have to show me somehow that I didn't do this." I had a dream that night, and I saw my mom up in Heaven saying, "I'm not sick anymore. I don't hurt anymore." And she was singing in the choir there. There was a peace about me and, you know, the guilt was not there anymore. But, growing up, the guilt was there sometimes, but that dream took care of it, knowing that my mom was okay and in Heaven.

(Framo: Even though both Lynn and Ann had said to each other that they wished Mom were dead, for Ann the wish was equivalent to the deed. Some desperate measure for atonement was called for. Fortunately, her wish-fulfilling dream relieved the immediate guilt but, in the long-term effort to expiate guilt, I suspect her choice of a charismatic religion serves some redemptive function for her. This need takes precedence over her previous commitment to the family's Lutheran culture. Time does not always provide dispensation for certain guilts.)

FRAMO: Uh huh, and she was okay.

ANN: And she was happy there.

FRAMO: [nodding yes] Yes. [looking at Katie and Tim] Did you all know this, Katie and Tim?

TIM: Not the details like that.

FRAMO: Did you know this, Thomas?

THOMAS: A little bit about it.

FRAMO: Uh huh. May I ask, Thomas, how did you react to your mom's death?

THOMAS: I was upset and cried . . . I didn't cry. I was a little upset.

FRAMO: Were you home?

THOMAS: No . . . Dad called me on the phone and told me that Mom had passed away. He came and picked me up and brought me back home. [family members continue to cry as the conversation continues]

FRAMO: Oh, was it your dad who told you?

THOMAS: No. Someone from Good Shephard told me. Someone from Good Shephard told me . . . [Thomas speaks in quick, slurred speech, his stammering seems to stem from anxiety]

FRAMO: Did you go to the funeral? Your mom's funeral?

THOMAS: Yes, I did.

FRAMO: You didn't cry?

THOMAS: No, not too much.

FRAMO: Do you ever cry about her since then?

THOMAS: Once in a while. [speaking more clearly now]

FRAMO: You think about her?

THOMAS: Yes, I do.

FRAMO: Tim and Katie, did you know this story that Ann just told?

KATIE: Most of it.

FRAMO: You did?

KATIE: I think I knew the part where you [looking at Ann] were standing there and she fell. [Katie speaks very softly]

FRAMO: Did you, Tim?

TIM: Not a lot of it. I remember the part about her blouse being dirty . . .

FRAMO: You know what that reminds me of? You ever hear from your mother, "Wear clean underwear in case you get in an accident?" [family members, especially Ann, laugh]

(*Framo: I introduce a note of levity to reduce the tension, although, as I reflect on it, the joke seems incongruous and out of place. Only Whitaker could pull off this kind of humor. At the time, though, it felt perfectly appropriate. Besides, the statement did not seem to interfere with the process.*)

TIM: That's what it was . . . That's what it was . . . [family laughs] I was in Los Angeles when she died, and I was bothered for a long time by the fact that nobody called me.

FRAMO: How did you find out?

TIM: Katie called me.

FRAMO: How long after it happened did you find out?

TIM: Well, it was ten o'clock p.m. It was right before Christmas, and
           the family was supposed to be down at our house the next day.
           We were getting ready for them to come and my wife, Annie, and
           I went out to eat. We came home, and at about ten p.m. Katie
           called and told me that Mom had a 50–50 chance of
           living . . . And I . . .

FRAMO: Excuse me, Tim, for just a moment . . . Is there anyone who would
           like a drink of water?

*(Framo: I suppose I could read all sorts of things into my interrupting the
proceedings to get a glass of water, and give glasses of water to the family members, but the truth of the matter is that I was just thirsty. My mouth may have
been dry from my own inner tension. It is also possible that I wanted to give
something concrete to the family.)*

*(Levine: Since this is the second interruption within a few minutes, I think
Jim was expressing his own need and perhaps the family's need to take a break
from the intensity of the topic.)*

DAD: Sure. I'll take one.

FRAMO: Okay. [Dr. Framo pours a glass of water for Dad, and hands it to
           him]

DAD: Whenever there's a drink of water available I usually . . . [Dad
           gets out of his chair and goes over to Dr. Framo to get the glass of
           water] Thank you.

FRAMO: Anyone else?

THOMAS: No, thank you.

TIM: I'll take one.

FRAMO: [pours a glass of water and hands it across to Tim, who remains
           sitting]

TIM: Thanks.

FRAMO: [looking at Tim] So you found out how long after Mom had ac-
           tually died?

*(Levine: When we work as cotherapists I notice sometimes Jim seems to
divert the topic in sessions but then later on picks up the thread and goes back to
where we left off.)*

TIM: Well, she had not died yet. But she had been in the hospital since
           that morning. Katie called me and said that Mom had a fifty–
           fifty chance of living. She told me what happened. Dad was at
           the hospital at that point, and I wanted to call the airlines to get

up there. But it was late, and it was near Christmas, and all the flights were booked, and I couldn't get up. I remember being in a daze from ten to eleven to twelve. And then Dad called me up and said that she was in real serious condition, that she had improved during the day but now she was worsening . . .

FRAMO: So she lived for a while?

TIM: She lived throughout the whole day . . .

FRAMO: Uh huh.

TIM: And then he called me up at one a.m. [Tim looks at Dad] and said that she had died. [Tim's voice is shaking] And I remember being initially really angry that I didn't know in the morning, otherwise I would have done anything to get there.

FRAMO: Did you think of renting a car and driving up?

TIM: Oh, I wouldn't have made it. I could have gotten on a plane. I would have gone down there in the morning—to the airport—and I would have bumped somebody on this plane. You know, I would have done something to get up to Philadelphia, but it was so late at night that I just couldn't do anything . . . And I remember when Dad made that call before she died. I remember just telling him to stay in the room, talk to her, just image that her blood is going—get her blood going, just image it, keep pushing it. He told me that she had trouble breathing and she died. And he called me up and started talking about funeral arrangements right away, that we were going to have this funeral at Little Chapel of the Chimes, and I said, "That's ridiculous, Little Chapel of the Chimes!"

FRAMO: Why is that ridiculous?

(Framo: Before I had the chance to empathize with Tim's suffering over the loss of his mom, I got diverted by his expression of anger at Dad. As we saw with Lynn, after a death someone or something has to be at fault.)

DAD: [softly] Oh, gee.

TIM: Well, because this was the funeral home, and we're a family that operates out of the church, at least in terms of these events . . . [Tim looks at Dad] I know that you didn't believe me when I told you about this later, Dad, but . . .

DAD: I still don't believe you.

TIM: Right . . . It happened. You were talking about having this funeral at Little Chapel of the Chimes.

DAD: Oh. [in disbelief]

TIM: And I said, "That's absolutely ridiculous! We're going to have it at St. Michael's, and we're going to do this and this." And then I went outside and just walked around for a couple of hours . . . It was really hard to believe.

(Framo: Was Tim usurping Dad's role as head of the family? I sensed there were hidden meanings behind this interchange between Tim and Dad.)

(Levine: I agree. In Tim's eyes, Dad fell from grace. Tim seemed to be projecting his own guilt onto his father, about not appreciating and attending to Mom.)

FRAMO: Uh huh.

TIM: I remember just feeling very sad that I had not been able to be there with her.

FRAMO: I hear you.

TIM: I still think that maybe I could have done something, and I know that's partially ridiculous, but then I think . . .

DAD: No, but I think the realities are the following: She had the heart attack at nine o'clock in the morning, that is on the twenty-first. On the twenty-second [of December, 1978] at one o'clock in the morning she is dead. [Dad's voice begins to shake as he cries] [Dad takes a drink of water, and he cries and drinks water at the same time]

FRAMO: [leans toward Dad] I wonder, have you had a chance to talk about this very much with your family? [Dr. Framo looks toward Dad]

DAD: [as he continues to cry] We have . . .

FRAMO: Uh huh.

DAD: But the point was, when she was taken to the hospital, as you already heard, the nurse said nothing was wrong, the pulse was strong. When I got to the hospital the cardiologist said, "No problem; no problem." Edema, something like that . . .

TIM: Pulmonary edema.

DAD: Yeah, or mild heart attack. She was taken to the . . . [Dad weeps noticeably, and cannot continue speaking]

FRAMO: [again leans toward Dad, Dad is crying and wiping his tears] Have you cried much about this since then? Is this too painful to talk about now?

DAD: [leans forward toward Dr. Framo] It's very painful.

FRAMO: Sure. You know, tears are nothing to be ashamed of. [the rest of the family members are crying] [there is a pause without words as the family members are quietly crying]

(Framo: Father is undefended and I am quite moved by his grief as he becomes more emotionally open with his private self. Struggling to gain control of my own feelings, I temporarily become a member of this family and have to remind myself, "Hey, I'm the therapist!" My history with funerals briefly erased the boundary between us.)

(Levine: I'm reminded of Jim's self revealing article, "My Families, My Family," (Framo, 1968).)

DAD: [after pausing] The cardiologist said, "No problem. No need to call anybody . . . " [family members continue crying while Dad is talking] Still, when she was taken to intensive care I was there at her bedside . . . And she was saying, "Go on the vacation." And I said, "No way. We're not going."

FRAMO: Oh, she was talking?

DAD: Oh, yes. She was fully conscious all the way up to the end. The problem was the absence of breath, and she eventually, if you follow it through rationally, died of absence of breath. They put a balloon in her, attempting to rescue her at the end. [Dad's voice is shaking as he continues to talk] About, maybe, four o'clock in the afternoon another cardiologist comes and says, "Something has to be done." And I said, "Do whatever you can." [Dad weeps noticeably, and cannot continue talking] [the rest of the family members continue crying, this time including Thomas]

FRAMO: What happened next?

(Framo: As I resonated with the distress of this family as they mourned, I became aware of my caring for them. I think my caring came across to them, and provided some anesthesia for their pain. At this point, I deliberately asked factual questions, perhaps to contain my own feelings . . . I remember the line from The Godfather *movie, "All families have bad memories.")*

(Levine: By asking detailed questions about the events surrounding Mom's death, Jim facilitates discussion about their memories and feelings. This is an important technique in helping families, who have issues of unresolved mourning to come to terms with their loss.)

DAD: And then they called a surgeon to put the balloon in her because, he said, that's the one hope and that would rescue her. It was at this point, the first time, that I was aware of the fact that this was . . . [pause]

FRAMO: It was really serious?

DAD: Yes. There was no need, at that point, prior to that, four o'clock in the afternoon, to call anybody. After that we got busy and called people all over the place. If Tim wasn't reached it was probably because of an absence. But there were people there who were doing the calling. So there was no need . . . It was sort of late. By one o'clock she was dead. So you can see the sequence of events, enabling you to understand . . .

TIM: Yeah . . . I don't want to take it away from this, but I sometimes get angry [clears throat] at the hospital and the people there.

FRAMO: Do you think they misdiagnosed the situation?

TIM: I think they screwed it up.

DAD: Well, they did.

FRAMO: Uh huh.

TIM: I looked at the autopsy report, and I tried to figure out where something had gone wrong. I never talked to the doctors that had worked on her, but something happened there that went wrong.

(Framo: Tim shifted his anger from Dad to the hospital, clearly a displacement and triangulation, easing the tension that had come up between him and Dad around funeral arrangements. I did not think it appropriate to comment on the question of possible medical negligence in Mom's treatment.)

DAD: But the sequence of events, not just the individual reactions at the moment, is significant. It appears to me it wasn't a matter of neglect. And after that, then, of course, all hell broke loose, and anything that was done was an attempt to rescue the situation. When you look back at it you say, "Gee, why didn't I do this and that," as anybody would . . . In a situation like that.

FRAMO: Yes. [turning to Katie] Katie, how was this experience for you?

KATIE: Well, I think I felt the same way Tim did. I don't remember calling Tim, I just remember when Dad called me the first time. [Katie looks at Dad] Mom was in the hospital, but it wasn't that serious. And then the second time was ten o'clock at night, her blood pressure had dropped, and I guess I didn't take that as serious either except I knew we would try to get up there the next day. I didn't know it was a matter of dying. Then we got a phone call at one or two in the morning. As far as the relief the others felt, I was already out of the house . . . So, uh, I really feel sorry for Mom . . . Her life was so hard on her. [Katie chokes on her words as she cries] I wish she would have had time to enjoy it [Katie continues to cry as she talks] because I feel like she always had the bad . . . She always had a bad . . . The bad part of life . . . I can't remember her in the last years really having a good time and enjoying herself.

FRAMO: How do you know this? How do you know she didn't get pleasure out of her family, out of entertaining, out of giving all these parties? How do you know she didn't get pleasure from that?

(Framo: I challenge Katie's assumption about Mom's unhappiness and introduce a different point of view to the family. Parents experience their own lives in a way that is different from the way the children see them. I wanted to widen understanding of the multiple realities of Mom in order to relieve her guilt, and to reinforce the "good" Mom as a legacy for the family to incorporate.)

KATIE: She never talked to us about it. She was always sighing; there was always a sigh. I think her pleasure came from her preschool. She also taught preschool, with all that she had to do.

FRAMO: Uh huh.

KATIE: And that was her true pleasure. She enjoyed those kids, and that's where she had fun. At one point, I wondered whether she should teach because of all the things she had to do . . . And I'm glad that she had that at the end. My mother would have done anything for anyone else. I think if there was any job in her life it was giving.

LYNN: You know what is also ironic, too, is that when she taught I was a part of her preschool also.

FRAMO: You were in her class?

LYNN: Yeah. But she never got angry at the children. I was so jealous because I wished I had the relationship with her that she had with those little kids, 'cause she never got angry at them, she never yelled at them or hit them or screamed at them. When she came to me in front of those kids she wouldn't hesitate to shake me or things like that. I was so embarrassed about that. But Katie's right, teaching preschool was the one thing in her life that was her pleasure.

FRAMO: But don't you know it's always easier to be a parent to somebody else's kids than to your own? It *is*!

(Framo: Having been a parent, I could not resist imparting this bit of wisdom. The comment does not have much of an impact, and I wondered if I had invalidated Lynn's experience.)
(Levine: I think Jim was trying to balance the negative perceptions of Mom by helping to explain her behavior.)

Dad went on to say that Mom had had numerous health problems before her heart attack. She had a cancer of the breast removed, underwent radiation treatment, and had severe arthritis. When Dr. Framo asked whether Dad thought that these medical conditions made her so upset and angry he said he did think so, adding that she "lived on the edge of nerves."

DAD: She was a high-strung person, but very kind with it. But she had these other elements that the children are talking about. And it seems to me that, that she had to deal with additional things . . . [stumbling for words] With one of the children, you know . . . From the time the person was born . . . It's not easy.

FRAMO: You're talking about Thomas, the fact that Thomas is retarded, and this must have been very upsetting to her?

(Framo: Dad refers to Thomas in the third person, in Thomas's presence— a distancing mode which I short-circuit by making explicit what he is alluding to. I did believe that, consciously, Dad was trying to spare Thomas embarrassment. Yet I could not help but notice that he spoke about Thomas, in his presence, as if he was not there, thus impersonalizing him.)

DAD: Oh, yeah.

FRAMO: Is that a word that is not used in this family?

DAD: Right.

(Framo: I could tell that Dad was surprised or annoyed by my stance on this subject. I suspect I did not fit his concept of how a professional is supposed to treat this topic—that I was supposed to pussyfoot around Thomas's retardation the way everyone else does. Tim, I knew, wanted to deal openly with this subject, so Tim and I were in alliance here . . . Dad was also suggesting that Thomas was a considerable problem in the family. Apparently Thomas's condition went beyond retardation; Tim had reported that Thomas had behaved bizarrely at times. Both parents must have been under considerable stress, and were perhaps in conflict between their religious values and the hard and difficult realities of having a disturbed, retarded child who created turmoil in the family. I conjectured that the parents, especially Dad, like other parents of retarded children, could view Thomas as an irrational being whose very existence could be interpreted as a living example of the parents' failure.)

TIM: Well, last night I went up to Thomas and we talked about the retardation. Right? [Tim looks at Thomas]

THOMAS: Right.

TIM: I've had a problem seeing Thomas as a real person, and I want to do something about that. And I think one way to do it is to just talk about retardation because it shouldn't be embarrassing to talk about it, and . . . Thomas, you were really helpful to me last night. Because you came up to me and said, "Don't let it bother you." [Tim puts his arm on Thomas] Right?

(Framo: Tim dares to go against the family rules at this point, and I think his bringing up of this taboo topic will have beneficial effects later on. This is one place, perhaps, where his family therapy experience helped him work out stuff with his own family. I noted that the rest of the family ignored Tim's comments about Thomas. Was the brother connection something that the sisters could not relate to?)

THOMAS: Right.

TIM: And that was really good.

(Framo: I neglected to comment on this touching moment between brothers, perhaps because I wanted to stick with the topic of Mom at this time. I am reminded, however, of the films Rain Man *and* What's Eating Gilbert Grape? *as compelling illustrations of the pleasure-painful relationships that exist between nonretarded and retarded brothers.)*

FRAMO: So, you're saying that Thomas's condition was another stress on Elizabeth? [Dr. Framo looks at Dad]

DAD: [nods his head yes]

KATIE: One thing I should say about Mom is that we used her as a scapegoat, too. [Katie glances toward Dad] We would put all our problems on Mom. It was always her fault, and we kind of had alliances with one another against Mom.

FRAMO: Well, was Dad sort of looked upon as the good guy and she was the bad guy?

(Framo: Here I touched on a core issue in the family.)
(Levine: The anger at Dad was displaced onto other family members, like Tim or Mom.)

KATIE: Yeah. [Lynn is also nodding in agreement with Katie] I asked my mother how Dad sinned, because I could not think of a way that he sinned. [Katie looking at Dad]

FRAMO: What? How Dad what?

KATIE: Sinned.

FRAMO: Oh, sinned.

DAD: Oh, that I didn't know. [Dad laughs]

KATIE: I couldn't think of a way that my father sinned. You know, grow-
        ing up, he was the good guy.

FRAMO: Well, he's a human being, he had to have some faults.

DAD: [laughing as Dr. Framo talks]

KATIE: [laughing] Not *my* father!

FRAMO: Really? You saw your father as saintly?

KATIE: I think so; growing up I did.

DAD: [laughing as Katie talks]

FRAMO: You know it might be helpful to these kids sometime, Dad, if
        you would let them know some of your little peccadillos.

(*Framo: The intense ambivalence about Mom's negative and positive features had been well established. This intervention with Dad is my first attempt
to deal with the good–bad polarization of the parents by focusing on Dad's
shortcomings. I use this technique with clients who view one parent as the angel
and the other the devil; I search for the bad in the good one, and the good in the
bad one. This approach has implications for the effect on the children's intrapsychic conflicts. In this case, I did think that the perception of Dad as perfect was
not an unqualified benefit for his children. How can you be real with someone
who is so exemplary?*

*Defusing the myth of Dad as transcendent was a risky but necessary move.
Risky because one does not easily topple mythic saints, and I did not know Dad
well enough to know how he would take it. And necessary because if he set a
standard no one could live up to, then his children would always feel wanting
and flawed, and their attempts to resolve their conflicts about Mom would be
blocked. I was, here, creating the context for legitimizing disloyalty to Dad by
making it easier for the children to criticize him. These interventions did not
take effect until the second two hours. It was a good sign that Dad could laugh
with his kids about his saintliness.*)

DAD: [laughing[

KATIE: Now we know them all. [family laughs]

DAD: They know them now.

FRAMO: Oh, they know them all? [everyone is laughing]

DAD: They become informed as they grow older, you know. [laughter
        continues]

FRAMO: Like when you were a teenager, didn't you get into a little bit of
        trouble?

DAD: Sure.

FRAMO: Or didn't you ever do anything wrong?

DAD: Well, I possibly don't remember those incidents, but . . .

FRAMO: I think it would be helpful to these kids to step down off the pedestal, because they idealize you.

DAD: Right. Well, I know, but they shouldn't do that because I have feet of clay like everybody else.

FRAMO: Uh huh. But you were apparently looked upon as the good one of the family . . . The good parent.

DAD: Maybe so.

Dad went on to explain that during the children's growing-up years he was preoccupied with his duties as a college president. He indicated further that in those days there was a clear division in male and female roles—that men focused on their occupational performance and the woman was "looked upon as someone who was the expert in the home." He thought that that arrangement was "efficient from a time and motion standpoint." Dad did concede that gender roles have changed mightily since then. When he implied that, in effect, his wife had to deal with the day-to-day difficulties of raising the kids, disciplining them, and so forth, he was indirectly acknowledging that that could help explain why he was seen as the good guy. He said he was involved with the children, that this involvement took the form of tucking them in at night and singing them songs—the kind of fun things dads like to do with kids. He also said he helped to clean up the house.

FRAMO: Did you feel you didn't spend enough time at home because of your work?

DAD: In retrospect, well, I could have spent more time at home.

FRAMO: Do you also feel guilty about the death of your wife?

(Framo: I quickly realized I was too abrupt here. On the other hand, I was stating what everyone was thinking.)

DAD: Well, that's easy to work up—I'm sure that each of the kids here could work up a sense of guilt. From the perspective from which we come you don't spend a lot of time with guilt. All is forgiven, and you get on with the next step. Life is that way. You don't look at perfection, you goof, you do so many things which are wrong, you think about it—you try to make the correction and you get on with the next thing.

FRAMO: At the time of her illness and death, you must have felt that you had done the best that you could at the time.

DAD: Even at the time, there was more that could be done.

FRAMO: What could you have done?

DAD: I mentioned to Tim the other day: for a time, we should have gotten therapy.

(Framo: I should have asked, "Therapy for what, specifically?")

ANN: Some of the things that were going on inside of me . . . I finally went to a counselor and told the person what was going on and all the stresses. I remember his telling me, "You don't need to come in, your whole family needs to come in." That was a good idea, and I proposed that to my parents and they said, "Forget it. It's not allowed in this home." And I remember being so heartbroken. From that point on, I thought if I can't get help from my family where can I get it? I knew deep down in my heart, and this is real hard to say, it would be either me or my mom that would have gone soon because I was under so much pressure.

FRAMO: What do you mean that either you or your mom would have gone? What do you mean?

ANN: Suicide, whatever. I was under a lot of stress, and I could remember my body deteriorating. I'm a diabetic, and at those times I couldn't care less what was happening to me.

(Framo: Ann gives a clear indication of the great stress this family was under. Ann was perhaps the most vulnerable member of the family, the symptom bearer. Apparently, the family was established in its pattern of denial and did not take seriously enough her pleas for help. The question was raised in my mind as to whether a problem is not dealt with in this family unless it is life-threatening. Ann internalized the family's pain, and was the delegate sent out to get help for the family.)

FRAMO: Were you in poor control?

ANN: Yes.

FRAMO: So you thought there was a lot of conflict between you and Mom, or in the whole family?

ANN: Yes, in the whole family.

FRAMO: And when you suggested the whole family go for family therapy, you thought it was a great idea but your parents said, "No way."

ANN: Yes. No way.

FRAMO: Did you understand where they were coming from?

ANN: I did. They explained that it's just not done.

FRAMO: They came from a different generation where that idea seems very strange—of the whole family going.

ANN: Right. Things with me got taken care of, but it's been a long time running.

(Framo: I would guess that Ann's spiritual quest, the changing family circumstances, the passage of time, and Ann's own resilience resources enabled her to survive the crisis.)

(Levine: I've had insulin-dependent diabetes since age 15. I imagined how I would have talked to Ann about her diabetes (Levine, 1997). I wondered why Jim did not pursue this topic. My hunch is that his own countertransference feelings were operating since, as the husband of a diabetic, he worries about my health.)

FRAMO: Did you think of going for help just for yourself?

DAD: She did.

ANN: Yes, I did.

FRAMO: So you did go?

ANN: Those few times, but he said it's a family problem. It's not just you and how to deal with it, and not necessarily how my mom got into a fight or when my dad and mom got into a fight. It all went inside. It just got deeper and deeper so that I could hardly control myself.

FRAMO: What led you to the idea that either you or your mom had to die? Why just the two of you?

ANN: Because we were so much . . .

FRAMO: So much alike?

ANN: Because I could sympathize with my mom. I could follow just behind her heels.

FRAMO: Uh huh, uh huh. Tim, did you know about this?

TIM: No, not what Ann is talking about, but I remember her seeing a counselor. Was I in college at that time?

DAD: I think you were.

ANN: Uh huh.

FRAMO: Graduate school?

TIM: I know I would come home and she would talk to me about what the counselor was doing. Was that at the seminary or gradu-

ate school? You only went twice. We would talk a few times about
it.

ANN: Well, I called you because I was telling you what happened that
day—that I was going or wanted to go, and I wanted to know
what you thought because you wanted to be a psychologist.

TIM: Yeah. I was stupid enough not to do anything about it.

FRAMO: She was making a plea for help.

TIM: Uh huh.

FRAMO: Did you know that this thought was in her mind: that either she
or her mom had to die?

TIM: No, I didn't know about suicide. [turning to Ann] I don't know
whether you ever attempted suicide. [Ann nods yes] You did?
[turning to Katie] Did you know about this?

FRAMO: How did you try?

ANN: I stopped taking my insulin.

FRAMO: That will do it. And then what happened?

ANN: I got scared, and then started taking it again. I was in the hospital
and I really was scared, scared of dying because of what was going on. I was in the hospital when I first became diabetic. No
one had any inclination a lot was going on with me. Lynn and
my mom were visiting my grandmother and I was working, and
it was just me and my dad. Since they had no idea what was
going on they were very reluctant to say, "Yeah, you really need
to go to the hospital," and I barely made it there. Within a couple
of hours I would have been dead. And one other time after my
mom had died I almost died again.

*(Framo: I noted that no one in the family openly reacted to Ann's disclo-
sure of her suicide attempt, so I had to ask each one. I did wonder whether there
were some details about Ann's turmoil that the family knew but did not reveal.)*

FRAMO: Uh huh. Katie, did you know about this?

KATIE: Yes, after the fact.

ANN: It was like my mom, I don't know whether I was doing it for
dramatization or whether I was doing it to present the truth.

FRAMO: Did Mom ever threaten suicide?

KATIE: No, not suicide. But when Mom had her heart attack and she was
going to die they walked away because there was a lot of dramatization. So when Ann was in trouble with her diabetes we came
up right away. We really were concerned. We felt she was asking
for more attention.

ANN: No one ever knew about the suicide attempt except Lynn and me.

LYNN: I didn't know about the suicide attempt, but I do remember talking with Ann about an overdose of pills [considerable laughter] and I was going to do it, too.

(Framo: I did not think there was a serious suicide pact between Ann and Lynn. There seemed to be a histrionic quality to what was going on between them.)

FRAMO: Dad, did you know about this?

DAD: Not about the suicide, but I heard about it.

FRAMO: Do you remember the time when she asked if the whole family could go to therapy?

DAD: No, I don't remember. I purposely forgot that one. I was aware of the fact that she was going.

FRAMO: Did you know about all this, Thomas?

THOMAS: Yes I did.

FRAMO: What did you know?

THOMAS: I knew that Ann was a diabetic.

FRAMO: Did you ever worry about your sister?

THOMAS: Once in a while.

TIM: I do really regret not seeing some things earlier, and I'm still bothered by it.

FRAMO: Apparently Ann was sending out some S.O.S. signals.

TIM: Yes. And I think my mom was, also, for such a long time.

ANN: I knew what she was thinking. I knew what she was going through. I didn't understand how, or why, but because we were so similar I could understand what she was going through.

(Framo: This close identification between Ann and her mother was concerning to me, so I proceeded to help her differentiate from mother.)

FRAMO: I think, Ann, it's important for you to recognize why you feel you are like your mom in a lot of ways. Nonetheless, you are your own person.

ANN: I know that.

FRAMO: In a lot of ways I think you know that you are not like your mom.

DAD: Indeed, in many ways. She doesn't have those extremes.

FRAMO: But I think she is so closely identified with her mom that she overgeneralizes, and I want her to know she's her own person.

TIM: I've been a little concerned because Ann says that she is like Mom, and I know that's what Lynn has been thinking.

LYNN: Well, everybody, Dad especially, says, "You are so much like your mother."

FRAMO: So, Lynn, are you like your mother?

LYNN: I am. My mood changes. One minute I can be happy, and the next I can be in tears. Especially this year, I was under so much distress it was incredible for a number of reasons, and I would go absolutely berserk. You wouldn't want to be around me because I was so emotional, but I think I'm different from Mom. I'm glad that Tim and I had that talk because it bothers me. I do not want to end up dead at fifty-two.

FRAMO: Is that how old your mom was when she died?

TIM: Fifty-three. Her father died at fifty-three years old, the same age she died.

FRAMO: Your mother's father?

TIM: It was like an anniversary death. She died at the same age he did: at fifty-three.

FRAMO: Wow. That can't be an accident.

TIM: It bothers me. I'm in my thirties, and when I approach that time I'm going to need help.

(Framo: It was clear that these adult children were worried about their emotional stability and the possibility of dying young. Was mother's occasional irrationality and "programmed" death to be intergenerationally transmitted, a destined fate?)

FRAMO: But it's not an inevitable thing.

TIM: Not inevitable.

FRAMO: And it could be a coincidence.

TIM: It could be, but . . .

FRAMO: You are in a generation of people who are living longer now.

TIM: That's true.

DAD: He is exercising every day. He runs to the airport.

FRAMO: Lynn, do you think you are more like Mom? Ann thinks she is more like your mom.

LYNN: I think I'm much like Mom. I react like Mom in certain situations. Ann *felt* like Mom, but I *react* like her. Sometimes I don't think. I just go off.

FRAMO: Are you afraid you are going to die at fifty-two or fifty-three?

LYNN: No. The one thing that I have going for me is that I can verbalize myself a lot more. Mom kept a lot of things in when things bothered her, just like Ann does. But I'm the type of person that if something bothers me I'll talk it out with them. If I'm upset about something I'll say, "Let's sit down and talk." I can get angry about it and just let it out. I think Mom's problem was that she kept it all in. And she couldn't handle it anymore. And she directed her anger to other things. I'll do that, too, but then I'll deal with it a lot more than she did.

FRAMO: Uh huh.

(Framo: Lynn makes a healthy distinction here. She behaves like Mom, whereas Ann became Mom.)

FRAMO: What do you all know about your mom's family?

It is routine during family-of-origin sessions to inquire about the parents' backgrounds; such information makes the parents' attitudes and behaviors more understandable to their children. Dad said his wife told him that she felt different from the rest of her family. Tim said he was able to garner the following from his mom: She was the middle child who worked constantly in the home while her brother and sister went out to play; Tim said his mother reported having had an intense relationship with her father, who was unpredictably loving and punitive; Mom's mother was described as open, caring, and artistically creative; there was a suggestion that Mom felt sorry for her own mother because her father was distant and away a lot. Tim reported that his maternal grandfather was a minister, who baptized him and died three months later. Tim then jokingly wondered if he had killed his grandfather, bringing up again the murder theme from the preparation interview. Dad said his father-in-law was intense, demanding, and perfectionistic. Mom's history did offer clues about the roots of Mom's work compulsion, self-sacrifice, and angry-loving moods.

Tim reported that he, Dad, and Thomas were taking a trip soon to a distant state in order to attend a family reunion of his mom's family. He said he wants to find out more about Mom's family. It is likely that the plans for this trip were a direct outgrowth of these family meetings. Under usual circumstances father was not likely to have considered such a venture.

ANN: We all feel that we're a little bit like Mom, and maybe I feel, like, more like Mom than the others.

FRAMO: Do you mean in terms of, what, the mood swings?

ANN: Or, just, maybe a fear of dying early. You know, that's sort of coming out.

FRAMO: Oh?

ANN: We're so much like her. I know that's the first thing that went through my mind.

TIM: Well, the anger . . . I can get angry really quick. Out of nowhere sometimes . . . And I see that part of Mom. And when I see that happening to me . . .

ANN: . . . it scares you.

TIM: But, you know, it's really easy for me to miss the positive things about Mom. There's just so many great things about her.

FRAMO: That's the problem that everyone has about their parents. The natural feeling toward parents is one of ambivalence. You love them, and you hate them at times, and how you put that together is a task that everybody has to deal with.

(Framo: The internal representatives of Mom that these adult children carry around inside are at war with each other. My goal here was to help them integrate the conflicting introjects. I accented the perennial problem of living with confusion, irresolution, and opposing feelings about parents so one does not have to decide one way or other whether a parent was good or bad.

I digress to discuss a theoretical issue that is related to the clinical management of loss. It had become obvious to me that the central issue in this family was their difficulty in coming to terms with the loss of the mother. During the session intense guilt and fear of death permeated. An important publication, which offered two perspectives on dealing with loss, was helpful to me in understanding the dilemma that the family faced—the dilemma that everyone faces in dealing with the loss of a loved one (Strobe, Greene, Gergen, & Stroebe, 1992). The modern view of bereavement is that following the death of someone close one should, after a period of grief, gradually sever the bonds with the deceased and get on with one's life. As time goes by, memories of the departed one get dimmer and one has a new identity of which the lost relationship has no part. From this perspective, holding on to the past attachment is considered pathological.

Grief in other cultures, and in this culture a century ago, is expressed as a romanticist view of death, that of holding on to the departed loved one. From this perspective, breaking bonds would negate the significance of the relationship and would make a sham of the meaning of one's existence. From this point of view, there can never be closure, and pain can continue indefinitely, espe-

*cially when there are reminders (a song, a dream). Children who have lost
parents, and those who have lost partners, keep and hold close their connections
to the deceased, such as by talking to the dead loved one, visiting the grave,
dialoguing and making decisions with the departed, and so on. To be sure,
symptoms can result from extremes in both directions. There are those who live
almost exclusively in the past (e.g., make shrines out of the deceased's room)
and there are those with aborted mourning who deny the significance of the loss
and act as if the lost one never existed. They, too, pay a price. Parents who have
lost children are a special case. In truth, there are many ways of dealing with an
important loss. There is no prescribed series of phases one must go through.
There are many forms of expression of grief. My efforts with this family were to
help them to integrate the two parts of Mom and to balance the living of life
while retaining the connection with Mom.)*

*(Levine: Jim's family history of loss gives him a powerful window through
which to see, feel, and understand loss.)*

DAD: Yes.

FRAMO: And I can see you're all struggling with that, and what makes it
         especially difficult is the fact that she's gone. And there's no op-
         portunity right now to work out some of that positive and nega-
         tive stuff directly with her.

DAD: Yes. [softly]

FRAMO: That's what I see this family struggling with. But you know it can
         help talking about it like this, to some extent. You recognize that
         there were things about her you loved and admired, and there
         were other things about her that were difficult. But that's the way
         a lot of parents are. There are no saints [gestures toward Dad]
         except for Dad, of course.

DAD: No, no. [family laughs]

FRAMO: Our time is about up today. I just wanted to say that we are going
         to meet again tomorrow. I'm sure that we haven't touched on a
         lot of important things in the family. What I would suggest that
         you do between now and tomorrow is to give some thought to
         some other things that perhaps you'd like to deal with. We've
         talked a lot about Mom; I don't know if that's finished. If that's
         not finished maybe we'll talk about her some more tomorrow.
         Between now and then, think about what other issues you would
         like to deal with in the family. I'd also like you to give some
         thought to how you would like things to be better in this family.
         What would you like to change? How can the relationships be
         improved in this family—if they need improving? And some
         people don't think about this session at all in the night in be-

tween. Some people talk a lot. Sometimes only two people get together... Okay, folks. We'll meet again tomorrow morning. Try to give some thought about what you would like to deal with next time.

SOME IMPRESSIONS OF THE FAMILY DYNAMICS THUS FAR

Father's position as campus minister and university president meant that this family had an external base and was not handling its internal issues. In this situation, the kids were given the message, "Do unto others." Instead of taking care of themselves or each other, they were taking care of the world. Major themes of this family were: "work hard," "be frugal," "we don't really deal with our conflicts," "be careful about expressing emotions," and "don't be too happy." Father had a position to uphold and wanted his family to look good—thus the expectation of academic achievement and the minimization of problems. Mother participated in upholding father's status, which may have helped create strain in the marital relationship. From a development viewpoint, the family has had numerous crises (especially somatic) and losses. Mother had cancer before Lynn's birth, father had a brain tumor when Ann was three, a retarded son was born, there was Thomas's out-of-control behavior, and the mother died suddenly. One of the major goals of the therapy was to help this family to connect with each other, nurture each other, and to get some fun out of life. There were strengths in this family that enabled them to move in these directions: There was great caring, even if they couldn't show it; there was a commitment to make things better; they had survived their numerous crises; they all functioned well in the world and were accomplished; and they all had formed intimate relationships— the Achilles' Heel of everyone. Even Thomas had done well within his limitations.

In the following session, the next day, I anticipated the family would be dealing with the relationship between father and the children, and also with the sibling relationships.

Chapter 7

BETWEEN
THE MEETINGS
The System in Motion

TIMOTHY T. WEBER, PhD

AFTERSHOCKS

This first family session had been intense for me, leaving me drained, exhausted, and surprised. I surprised myself, and was surprised by my family. I anticipated that we could have discussed our family issues, coming to some understanding about what happened in our family and why. This kind of intellectual process would have been more typical for our German, Lutheran cognitive way of being in the world. But I did not expect us so quickly to touch the depth of powerful emotions that had been imprisoned within all of us. My family mythology was expanding to include a bigger picture of the family beyond the structured, intellectual picture of us I had always had with me.

There were many "firsts" in this moment. This had been the first time I had seen my father cry in public, only rarely seeing him with wet eyes in private. My "cool" father now displayed his most vulnerable side in a public forum. His courage was giving me courage, maybe permission to be different myself. Another "first" was the extended and deepening conversation about my mother's life and death. Never before had we gathered together to talk about her, and about our reactions to her, as we had done in this first consultation. I knew we had to address our memories of her, but I was surprised we moved in this direction so quickly and so emotionally. Another "first" was that this had been the first time that certain secrets had been revealed, such as the secret of Ann's suicide attempt. Many other "secrets" were made known, if "secret" is also defined as things known but not talked about. For example, we talked about the "secrets" of my anger with my father, my sisters' anger with my mother before she died, feelings of the pressure of success, longing for connections, respect for one another. We had not yet talked about the "secret" feelings about Thomas's retardation and his impact on all of us. Would this secret come to the surface tomorrow?

What had happened in this first meeting, and immediately thereafter, also helped me feel less "weird" in this family. I had always thought of my family as successful, but somewhat "weird." I was proud of our family's "outsides," but embarrassed by our "insides," the emotionally hidden parts that we kept private to the public. Thomas's "normal look" but his "hidden" retardation and potential for explosiveness almost any time contributed to my fear of our family being seen from the inside. And there were other experiences of criticism, anger, fighting, hurt, tears within our family's private life that made me feel like an impostor in public. I wondered how many families try to keep hidden the guts of their private life as if life is lived in two worlds—the world with others and the world within the family. This dichotomy had deeply troubled me, and I also had worked to maintain it for years.

During the interview, I noticed that Jim had cried at one point. Somehow, what we were experiencing in the family was touching something deep in another. I felt that the drama of our family was a drama about universal themes that could connect with many others. This movement from a sense of "weirdness" in the family to more of a sense of community in being linked with the stories of others was one of the most powerful benefits of this consultation.

I felt our business life—working too much, moving too frenetically through the days with rare moments of connectedness and reflection. I felt our struggle for esteem and the pain of striving for excellence—fearing failure, pressing on for acknowledgment, linking love and accomplishment. I experienced our anger and hurt in living with rigidly defined male–female role differences—women carrying the burden of domestic responsibility, men living out their lives away from the family; women feeling left and men feeling isolated. I felt our struggle of being children embroiled in the marital tension of their parents, children wanting to distance from the family because the emotionality in the family was too enormous and unpredictable. I felt our confusion of loving and hating the same person, feeling drawn by their love while also running away or attacking their anger. I could feel this deep yearning for parents and siblings that was unfed. The circle of our family's life was widening. I felt less "weird" and more connected with others in my family.

REFLECTIONS ON THE SESSION

I wanted to be alone during the lunch break, although I also wanted to be with my family. I needed to reflect on the emotional intensity of this first meeting, and I also needed to separate from others so that I could recoup some of the energy I had lost in those two hours.

I had experienced Jim's pacing to be on target for our family; there seemed to have been a right balance between challenging and creating a place of safety. He seemed to have been able to convey an overall respect for the family that says "I will honor your pacing, I will protect the boundaries, and I will also call forth in you strengths that you may not even have been aware of. To do this, I will have to challenge you." Jim's openness with his own humanity helped establish this respect for me. He was a "real person." Jim's coming forward as a person in his "naturalistic" manner was critical for me and for other family members who felt safe with someone who was willing to take personal risks himself.

This experience challenged me to reflect on my role in the family as the "distant hero." Could I continue to maintain a "hero" status if I got closer to my family? Part of being a hero is maintaining an illusion of a certain amount of invulnerability. I would jeopardize this status of "hero" if I got closer, but the sadness of this continuing isolation was mounting as I got older. I felt I had made some strides toward this other, more preferred direction of vulnerability. I also experienced this same movement with others in the family.

Yet, at the same time, I was also well aware of my fears, some that had dissipated somewhat, and others still present: the fear of destroying my father, the fear that my plea to my sisters for more connection with them would be ignored, the fear that all our rich conversation would result in little or no change in our lives after the consultation, the fear that I would be blamed for any problems or ill feelings resulting from these meetings, the fear that I would not change in my personal life and that I would continue to feel more emotionally imprisoned.

I reflected on my experience with Thomas in the session. Thomas seemed to be a separate entity as if there were three families among the siblings: Katie and myself, Ann and Lynn, and Thomas. The seating arrangements—with me, Katie, and my father on one side; Lynn and Ann on the other side; and Thomas in the middle—supported this "three-family" notion. Thomas didn't seem to be active in the session; I didn't know if he had the capacity to be more active or whether we as a family had the capacity and interest to include him more. Yet I also sensed that he had been very in tune with the family's emotionality, and in many ways he was the one family member most "inside" the family.

These reflections about Thomas accented a long and painful struggle within me. How do I include Thomas in my own life? I had always felt uneasy and irresponsible with Thomas, trying to include him but not knowing how to link his life with mine. It seemed that no matter how well intentioned and deliberate were my efforts to link with Thomas, there was always a wide gulf that separated me from him. These questions and this guilt haunted me. I felt I had to simply live with this problem. What could help was a family discussion, with Thomas present, about Thomas and our experience with him. But the family rule was "Don't bring up Thomas's retardation in front of him." Even without Thomas present, we had done little to talk together about his retardation and how our lives had been impacted. In the first family meeting, we had bypassed this conversation. Would we do the same tomorrow?

I also reflected on my mother, and Jim's questions around her symptoms and the possible underlying causes of those symptoms of depression, anger, reactive emotionality. I had thought about these questions before. Did she have any kind of biological or neurological disorder that could have contributed to her emotional ups and downs? Was she manic-depressive? These curiosities touched questions I had always had about my mother and, to some extent, also myself. Would I become like my mother in her emotional volatility? Was there some biological disorder we were both burdened with? The search for some biological "reason" was an effort to explain why she was so volatile, and to help us identify potential risks in our own development.

But this search also seemed like an effort to excuse myself and other family members from some of the responsibility. If we had acted differently, more lovingly, toward her there still might have been "X"—the biological condition. Her behavior, quite possibly, was beyond our control and hers. A biological diagnosis could provide some escape for our guilt. A "mental illness" diagnosis would have a different impact on me. I felt more embarrassed and also more vulnerable if she had some "mental disorder." A biological diagnosis could help me distance from her impairment. And yet, regardless of the diagnosis, my relationship with her had been shaken frequently by the earthquakes of her volatility, and by my angry and distancing responses to one who also could care so deeply for me. How could I put this together in a way that made sense?

One of the major leaps for me in the first family meeting was that I released my anger at my father about what happened the night my mother died. I experienced him more humanly as he described his struggle the day and night of her death. I heard his "confession" of the agony and pain he went through in trying to decide what to do and how to do it, his uncertainty of how best to support my mother, his confusion in following the changing medical information that came to him. His confession, protected from my interrogation and accusation during the structured family meeting, was critical in helping me to exonerate him of culpability in that day of her death. In being given this protected space of the family meeting, he not only reported the "facts" of the day as if he were trying to defend himself, but he told his story with tears and pain. He also said that he had other regrets at not having taken action sooner in the family to help remedy the pain in the family, especially my mother's pain. My father's confession about his struggle on the day of my mother's death was a "tissue sample" of his struggle with her throughout their life together, and now I saw his mistakes with more understanding, his absence with more compassion, and his love with more depth. And, in the midst of all these mistakes, some of which he even continued to make with us, I could be in the process of forgiving him as a struggling human.

The family consultation was essential in helping me to reappraise my resentments. In hearing the stories of others, in this simple art of listening without interrupting and jumping to my assumptions, I was beginning to adjust some long held beliefs about my father and mother. A part of the process for forgiveness is casting a new light on history. And as we integrate new stories into the one story we have constructed for ourselves, history changes. The facts of history were not changing for me, but I was crafting a different lens through which I could again reassess that same history. My father's story about himself, the stories I heard from my siblings, and my mother's story heard again in a different way helped widen the picture beyond the narrow story I had constructed for myself to help make sense of it all. Forgiveness was not "forgiving and forgetting," but "forgiving and remembering," and remembering in a different way based on conversation and an expanding consciousness.

I also thought it was becoming more possible for me to forgive my father as I was becoming more of a parent myself. My own fathering was rapidly teaching me how difficult it is to be a parent and how many countless opportunities there are to make many mistakes. Life experience and frailties in the task of parenting helped me forge this new path of father and mother forgiveness.

THE FAMILY REGATHERS AND REMEMBERS

After the family-of-origin session, I came home to the family, hoping to be seen more as a family member and not as a distant hero-psychologist son. Lynn was perky and pleased about the meeting. "Framo was like a psychologist," she said. "It seemed like his job was to get us to talk about things we don't want to talk about." She said she liked him, and also liked calling him by his first name (a symbol of budding adulthood). She liked the experience so much she began to see occupational possibilities, saying to me, "You're just like me. I want to help other families do this. It's wonderful!" Ann also began to remember some long-buried questions. She remembered that for years my father had put her to bed, and suddenly, one day he quit and she didn't know why.

Katie had said that coming home after the family meeting, my father had talked to her about some of his struggles in living, disclosing to her some things that he had not talked about before. She also began to reflect on her concern about having a second child. Katie said she had experienced great pain being the second child and having to follow the first. She did not want the second child to feel unaccepted because of the older sibling. Her revelation was more touching to me since she wasn't attacking me as much as simply describing her experience in the family in following an older sibling. Yet I also felt a twinge of responsibility in not having supported her as much as I could have, not being aware of her pain in following me, invalidating her feelings in her previous attempts to tell me how difficult it had been for her. Katie's reflections also illustrate the "bridging effect" that takes place in family consultations as members begin to build more of a consciousness from the experiences in their original family to experiences in the present, linking current impasses with old stories.

The next morning, before the second family meeting, Katie again said that she had not slept much the night before because there were so many issues to deal with. "How are we supposed to talk about all these things in such a short time?" she asked me. I too was concerned about the same thing, and was trying to be selective about what I wanted to address in the next few hours and what I was willing to let go, at least for now. I wish that we had scheduled at least six hours instead of four hours. I also began to think about a follow-up meeting with the family and Jim sometime next year. I was fearful about losing momentum, feeling that this new connectedness and openness was so tenuous, so easy to slip away.

Chapter 8

THE SECOND FAMILY MEETING
Father and Siblings

JAMES L. FRAMO, PhD

FRAMO: Good morning. We're going to be meeting for another two hours today. We can go in a number of directions. I'm going to leave it up to you as to what you want to discuss. So the ball is in your court, folks. What would you like to do?

KATIE: I had trouble sleeping last night; there was so much on my mind. I told Tim this morning, there's so much to think about and talk about. I just talked with Tim and the girls and Dad about unconditional love. I just read an article that the two people in your life that give you unconditional love are your parents and your grandparents, and those are the places you can go to feel that. I've been thinking about that, and my feeling is that we have had to earn appreciation, attention, and affection, and I don't think Dad was aware of that. I was thinking how Mom had to work all the time, she always had to please people. You always had to do something to please somebody, and I think my stress in growing up was that Tim, he made it! I haven't made it yet. [Katie cries] So I had to do a lot of things to earn that love and attention. Tim had the good grades and he was a sportsman.

FRAMO: Things came easily to him?

KATIE: I don't think he feels that way because he already had the attention and affection of the family. So it was my turn to make it. So what were the things I could do? I became competitive with the grades. [Katie cries and Dr. Framo offers some Kleenex] I think that my mom felt she had to earn affection and appreciation,

119

too. That was the atmosphere of the family. And then I look at my sisters and maybe they had to go through that, too.

FRAMO: Do you think there was a male–female difference in the family? That the boys were given some favorite treatment and the females were not?

KATIE: I think in the chores there were. In talking with Tim, he doesn't feel that way at all.

TIM: I think you overestimate the attention that I got. I can remember playing many games, and Dad and Mom were busy. I graduated from college, and Mom and Dad weren't there.

DAD: She was there.

TIM: No, Mom wasn't there for college. She was there for the seminary graduation.

DAD: For your seminary graduation?

TIM: [to Katie] Mom and Nana were there. I think that you think I got a lot more than I really did.

FRAMO: Let's hear what the rest of you think. Dad, what do you think about what Katie is saying?

DAD: I'm not too sure whether I can plug into that frequency. I'm sure there is something there.

FRAMO: She feels that she got short-changed.

DAD: Yes, that's something that surfaced later on after she became an adult. Then I reflected on it. I think there is some credence to what she's been saying, an unwitting kind of . . .

FRAMO: If it were so, do you have a sense of how that came about?

DAD: I think in the natural flow of things, because Tim was pulled out of the family by virtue of his athletic competitions in basketball, baseball, and football, and there were those obligations. Perhaps that's a scary word for it, but those obligations pulled him away when Katie did not have those commitments; and having none, therefore, being at home, she got assignments which Tim never got.

(Framo: The simmering competition between Katie and Tim, mentioned previously by Tim in the preparation interview, surfaces here. I wondered whether Katie had ever previously told her family about her pain. I noted here, also, that Dad could not see the distinction between Tim engaging in sports, which he called obligations rather than fun, and Katie being stuck with household tasks and child care. To be sure, in his generation gender roles were clearly defined in this way.)

FRAMO: Not only assignments, but she was responsible for raising these two girls.

(Levine: Note Jim's succinct language in response to Dad's earlier comment.)

DAD: Yes, yes.

FRAMO: As she said yesterday.

DAD: But there was no effort, as I review my mind and if I reviewed the mind of Elizabeth, of discrimination.

FRAMO: Although the oldest child has more burdens placed on them, they are usually the more responsible ones. What was your birth order in your family? [addressing Dad]

(Framo: The transition seems abrupt here, but in family-of-origin sessions I wait for the opportunity to learn some things about parents' families of origin. Knowing more about what shaped the parents makes their behavior in the present family more understandable.)

DAD: I'm in the middle of eight.

FRAMO: You're the middle child?

DAD: Uh huh. I got all the benefits from both sides.

FRAMO: Who was the oldest in your family?

DAD: Fred. In his instance, Fred was pulled out of the family in his first year of high school. He went away from my family, from my family of origin.

FRAMO: Who took the responsible child position in your family?

DAD: My older sister.

FRAMO: Your sister did?

DAD: My older sister.

FRAMO: Did she feel overburdened?

DAD: Yes.

FRAMO: Uh huh. So she was the functional oldest?

DAD: Correct; yes.

TIM: Well, in your family, your sisters stayed home in order that the boys could go away to college.

FRAMO: So, from the family from which you came, apparently the women did not have careers, but they got married and had babies and the men had careers. Is that correct? It was a very traditional family?

DAD: Right, right.

FRAMO: Do you understand that, Katie? That your father's attitudes were largely based on his experiences in his own family? [Katie is silent] . . . That doesn't seem to make a difference for you, does it?

(Framo: I tried to diminish Katie's torment by trying to explain that Dad's attitudes were consistent with his own background. It didn't work. The force of her feelings was too intense.)

(Levine: It is a fine line between being sensitive to gender role unfairness and appreciating the burdens and limitations of the past. Jim tries to acknowledge the historical and current unfairness of being a female in this family, while acknowledging Dad's traditional upbringing. Boszormenyi-Nagy calls this multidirected partiality [Boszormenyi-Nagy & Krasner, 1986].)

KATIE: I still think this family functions under the lack of unconditional love. I really do.

FRAMO: You know, the only time in this world you are entitled to unconditional love is when you're an infant. That's the only time in this world. Otherwise, there are always conditions. But little babies are the only ones entitled to unconditional love without question. Do you agree with that?

(Framo: By giving this gratuitous speech I invalidated Katie here in my biggest mistake of the session.)

(Levine: I agree. Jim should have asked Katie what she meant by "unconditional love," which for her encapsulates feelings about being judged, criticized, and pressured to achieve.)

KATIE: No. I should think, as a family, we would want to be together and call each other on the phone. We would just want to be together and not worry about how you appear. When Tim called about this meeting I thought, okay. I thought of things in order: um . . . my husband needs a job; how's my book going?; how is my life?; am I fat, am I thin?; do I look good? All those things go through my mind when I meet with this family.

FRAMO: You're talking about *now*!

KATIE: Yes, I'm talking about now.

TIM: You're talking about who you have to impress, like me?

KATIE: You! Dad! Everybody! What can we talk about that's real?

FRAMO: You mean, you've got to show them that you have accomplished something in life?

KATIE: Uh huh.

FRAMO: Let's hear from the rest of you. Did you know that Katie felt this way? [pause] Lynn, you're crying again.

LYNN: Oh, I always cry. Yeah, I feel the same way. I think it was easier for me of all the kids because I got a lot of attention because I'm the youngest.

FRAMO: Uh huh.

LYNN: Because I'm the youngest, it's real easy for me to get attention because I'm a very affectionate person. So if nobody gives me attention I'll go to them. I don't hesitate to do that.

FRAMO: Do you think Katie should do that?

LYNN: I don't think it's her personality. She does it with me, but I don't think she does it with Dad, or with Tim, or Ann. Like, if I want affection from Tim I'll go up and give him a hug; or if I want affection from Dad I'll do the same thing; or with Ann. But I think some people have barriers around them.

FRAMO: Well, are you aware of whether Dad ever calls up Katie and says, "How are you doing? I really miss you. I'd love to see you"?

(Framo: I was indirectly giving a suggestion to Dad here, seeding his unconscious. I couldn't tell whether he was picking up my message. I figured I would find that out later.)

LYNN: No. That never happens.

FRAMO: It never happens?

LYNN: It never happens. Once in a while—especially at college this year— Dad calls me.

FRAMO: When Dad sees Katie, does he ever hug her?

LYNN: There's a difference between a hug and a meaningful hug. I mean, you can hug somebody because you see them, and greet them. That's a way of greeting people. No, I don't think there's a lot of affection at all.

FRAMO: Who do you think Katie wants it from the most?

LYNN: I think she wants affection from me. I think she knows that.

FRAMO: And she has it from Thomas?

LYNN: Yeah, yeah.

FRAMO: Okay.

LYNN: And I think she needs to be reassured when it comes to Dad.

FRAMO: Dad? How about Tim? Does she need it from Tim?

LYNN: Yeah, yeah; from the older members of the family.

FRAMO: So from Tim and Dad? Is that correct, Katie?

KATIE: I've lost touch with Ann.

FRAMO: With Ann?

KATIE: Yes, with Ann, too.

FRAMO: Ann, do you have any thoughts about this?

ANN: I feel the same as Katie. We sort of see ourselves as the only ones needing this attention. We think we're the only ones who have this need. And at the same time everyone else is hurting and not knowing it; because when I come home I feel this way.

FRAMO: You have similar feelings, Ann, that you have to earn your attention somehow?

ANN: You always have to have something interesting to say: how am I looking, how am I feeling, how am I doing. It's as if you always have to be in competition to show that you are capable, that you can handle it, that you can be the hard-core person who doesn't have any problems. It's one of the reasons why I have a hard time telling other people about the struggles in my life unless things get serious. Like, Lynn and I had a different type of relationship, and with everybody else it was different because they have been the older set of the family . . . I was telling Dad last night that even though I'm twenty-three and married I still need the father's love.

FRAMO: Uh huh, uh huh. You never get to the point where you don't need that. I sort of get the sense that—in this family—it's the males in this family that the females are longing for. Am I picking this up wrong?

ANN: A little bit. I think of the males as parent figures.

FRAMO: Are you more eager to get something from Dad than from Tim?

LYNN: Uh huh.

ANN: Uh huh.

FRAMO: Okay, Dad, the ball is in your court. [considerable amount of laughter from Dad] How are you going to deal with this?

DAD: Well, it depends upon the supply of love . . . You have to distribute it all around in equal quantities, so I really don't know.

FRAMO: I got the impression that you have been a very concerned father, very responsible father, that you tucked the children in at night and sang them songs. Gee, there's a lot of people who never get that; but something's obviously missing.

DAD: Right, right. [with some chuckle]

FRAMO: I would suggest, Dad, that you address your children.

TIM: Well, it might not just be to the males and the females—I don't know how much you can really give, Dad. You're really like the only parent in this family now. Sometimes I think I'm really pushing you too much by talking to you about some things, but I don't think it's just you and the girls—it's me, too.

(Framo: Tim rides the back of his sisters' pleas by advancing his own planned agenda about what he wants from Dad. He wants what his sisters want, but did the females again fade into the background? Tim, having observed me pushing Dad to get more emotionally involved, perhaps saw me as doing what his mother did to Dad. It will be recalled that Tim tried to protect Dad from Mom.)

DAD: It's between myself and you.

FRAMO: Do you feel some of that, Tim, that the girls are talking about?

TIM: Yeah, in a lot of ways. I remember when I had this great football game. I ran a hundred and fifty yards or something when I was in high school, a great day on Saturday. The coach came over and congratulated me. The first thing you said, Dad, was, "Don't get a big head."

DAD: [begins to chuckle]

TIM: I hadn't even gotten a head at that point. It just had happened, and you said, "Don't get a big head." That is one thing I always remember. It's like whenever there's something to celebrate, it's like watch, watch that you don't get over enthusiastic about it; keep it toned down; don't get too happy about it.

FRAMO: Could there be some explanation for that, Dad? What's your philosophy about that? [Dad leans forward] I'm glad to see you lean forward. Now you're getting involved.

(Framo: I should never have used the word "philosophy." I am making more personal remarks to Dad in order to help close the distance between us.)
(Levine: On the other hand, by using Dad's intellectual language, Jim was tracking and joining with Dad.)

DAD: [chuckles] Well . . . Aristotle's Via Media—the middle way. As soon as you find yourself in a mood of overrejoicing or happiness, invariably you've got to come down from the high because the realities of a life dictate that there's going to be some pain at the other end. And the object is, in my situation, they don't call it the head of the family anymore. But I'm the principle tutor of the family, and you attempt somehow to be sure that the children have some understanding as to what life really is.

FRAMO: So you're trying to save them from pain?

(Framo: In my reframe, here, I give Dad credit for his good intentions. I deliberately couch my language in everyday, concrete terms in order to attenuate his depersonalized intellectualizations.)

DAD: From pain by virtue of the fact that they got these highs and the lows, which is not uncharacteristic of the Weber personality.

FRAMO: But Tim saw it as a dampening of enthusiasm.

DAD: I understand. I understand. And today, if I were to relive that situation, I would relive it differently.

FRAMO: Could you tell Tim that instead of me?

(Framo: One of the most difficult, yet eventually rewarding, things for family members to do in family-of-origin sessions is to talk directly, face to face, to other family members about emotionally charged matters. It is much easier for the family member to address the therapist.)

DAD: Oh, sure; sure.

FRAMO: Go ahead.

DAD: Tim, if I were in that situation today I really would commend you, and I think in the last ten years of my life I've begun to see the need of the personality on this point. [looks at Dr. Framo] Maybe the philosophy assumptions that one brings to a given situation should play a lesser role . . . in meeting a situation of commending people.

(Framo: This statement of Dad's is as close as he could get to making an apology—a therapeutic step. At this point in the interview I could see how difficult it must have been for Dad to come to these sessions, much less to stick with the process. At the same time, for this family to come to terms with its demons, there had to be an honest, open exchange of experiences and feelings that had long been avoided or suppressed or expressed through symptoms. Dad hardly knew what had been going on inside his children. This session gave him the first opportunity to find out.)

FRAMO: Excuse me, Dad, you're back talking to me again. [pointing to Tim] Talk to your son.

TIM: Well, Dad, I'll tell you where it affects me. It affects me not only in dealing with you now, because there's some things I really feel good about—I think you're changing a little bit in some things. But when I think about how I am with Annie, Ty, and Stacy, like you, I'm always taking this role of "Let's not get too happy about what's going on." If we go out someplace we're always talking about how much it will cost. Annie criticizes me, and I think she's right because I go to the restaurant and we enjoy a meal, but I say it could have been better, or the food wasn't great and we should have gone to that other restaurant—and I'm always looking at what wasn't right. That's a problem for me. And I have trouble saying it was really great and I enjoyed it. It's really affecting me now, and I really need to do something different about that.

DAD: Well, I think as you review the total situation, you're going to come closer to reality. There are some religious factors which play a role here which may, in this instance, serve in a negative way. As soon as you're a religious personality, from the perspective from which we come, you get to be ultracritical of a given situation. Critical of a given situation which is a kind of prophetic role that the Christians should play: being critical, but at the same time take on the positive approach instead of the negative approach, and that is to look at the good of a situation and celebrate that. I expect that in the last ten or fifteen years the celebration aspect of it became more of my personality, more of a response to people than it did before.

FRAMO: I was wondering if Katie and Ann knew that Tim had similar feelings about Dad?

KATIE: I think that Tim and I share two things in dealing with life: that is, looking negatively at things that are even happening positively; the other part is not being able to relax. In a social situation, I can't go to a party without wanting to make an impression.

FRAMO: You're concerned about what other people think?

KATIE: I think I am. I can't have fun.

TIM: I have that problem, too.

FRAMO: Ann, you too?

ANN: Yes. I've had a hard time slowing down and just being satisfied with what I'm doing. It's got to be a conscious effort in being the best I can. Don't worry about it. There's something in me that pushes me to do more than that. Now I see that we have something to talk about—something to get together to talk about because I see it's something we have in common.

FRAMO: Did you know that Tim had difficulties of this nature?

ANN: No, no.

FRAMO: How does this make you feel to know that?

ANN: Better.

FRAMO: Why?

ANN: To make me feel that I'm not . . .

FRAMO: Not so different?

ANN: Yes, that I'm not the only one. We have similar personalities in a sense, and we can share this now with somebody else, or vice versa.

(Framo: My aim here was to take Tim down from the pedestal his sisters had put him on and reduce their envy of his role in the family. The siblings were beginning to coalesce.)

FRAMO: Are you learning something from this, Paul? About how your kids feel?

DAD: Well, I suppose in a sense, but I think that I've learned it already. It's not that this is something new, merely that it's being underscored and italicized for me. But what is being said is something I would have said to myself ten, fifteen years ago, where maybe, given a little more time, I could articulate a little better. But it is where one looks at life in terms of perfection, not consciously, but unconsciously. You want that sort of perfection on the part of yourself. I'm pretty hard on myself.

FRAMO: I bet.

DAD: Yes and, therefore, apparently I've been hard on the kids in this respect.

FRAMO: In what respect?

DAD: In demanding perfection and expecting perfection according to the norms which I have for myself and, therefore, the reluctance to freely celebrate the virtues, the excellencies, the good things that are there. And what I have learned is that the celebration of the virtues is significant, and that, therefore, people need to be commended. And to be commended is not necessarily to subtract from somebody else, but rather to enable that person to be what that person really should be, with all the time and talents that person has. Am I making myself clear?

(Framo: Again, Dad is apologizing in his own way. I have found that it is healing for adult children to hear from parents the errors they [the parents]

made. I thought this statement was a difficult admission for this prideful man to make.)

FRAMO: Yes, Paul, I have a very concrete suggestion I'd like to make to you, and see what you think of it. You know, often we don't tell people the positive things about them; we figure that they should know, or it's understood, or you don't have to put it into words. I think it would be very helpful if you would turn to each of your children and tell each of them what are the different things about each of them you really like. Do you think you could do that, Paul?

(Framo: I have found this intervention to be very productive, particularly when the family-of-origin consultation has been characterized by considerable expressed anger among the family members. As typically used, I have each family member tell every other family member what they most like or admire about that person. Such positive messages are almost always received with surprise, relief, and pleasure, often leading to changes in long-held beliefs and attitudes, as well as self-esteem. In this case Dad was not ready to do this, certainly not on my terms.)

DAD: Now the way you put it, my impression is that I have done that. Not maybe to the extent that I maybe should have, but I have really done that.

FRAMO: Each one is a different individual.

DAD: Each one around here has gotten that kind of comment from me from time to time. Such as, you do this thing very well, or something like that, or my thanks to them for something they have done.

FRAMO: Do you all agree with this, what Dad's saying?

KATIE: I think so. I think, occasionally, I've heard thanks for the way I've done a certain thing.

LYNN: But the thanks come when you do something extraordinary. It's like you have to do something absolutely extraordinary to get any recognition whatsoever. I know what you've said—in the last ten or fifteen years you've changed, you've noticed. *Have* you noticed? But I'm nineteen now, and was four when you changed. I can remember volleyball games, too. I know you didn't have a lot of time, but it was a big effort for one of you to come to one of our basketball games to see me cheerleading or to see me playing volleyball. When I got all those awards at graduation, I just feel like this family expects you to do something extraordinary to surpass somebody else. If we get good grades it's expected of us, or if we graduate from college with honors, or if we get this great scholarship, then maybe we will get recognized.

KATIE: The other part of it is that it's not just Dad to us, it's one another to each other. We treat each other the same way. Part of it is that we don't know each other personally. What is Tim like? We don't know. And does he know what we're like? And does he know what Ann's like? [crying] Has anyone asked, "What did you do this summer?" I don't think anybody's asked. What would a normal situation be like when you get together for a family reunion?

(Framo: Katie introduces the topic of the sibling relationships, indicating the sense of nonrelatedness among some of the siblings.)
(Levine: I wonder if Katie's focusing on the sibling issues at this point reflects some guilt about the criticism father has been receiving.)

FRAMO: But don't forget, now, he organized this session, so obviously he does want something to change in this family.

KATIE: I don't mean just him, I mean each other. I don't think we've talked about Ann and me—our relationship. Lynn and I talk quite a bit.

FRAMO: You don't feel that you know each other very well?

KATIE: Oh, no. Personally, no.

FRAMO: Don't you think that could change?

LYNN: I feel differently. With Tim I feel that way, like you [Tim] said, "Why don't you ever call me?" That really never occurred to me. Why don't I call you? But I feel so detached from you that I just feel there is no hope because we're eighteen years apart. You have your family and your kids, and you're not interested in my entire life. With Katie, I guess I call Katie. I get on the phone and say, "Well, what's going on?" Maybe I don't do that enough, like writing letters, things like that. With Ann, she calls me from work every once in a while, and we just sit there and talk. Among the four of us, I feel I have a bit more contact than the rest of you do.

FRAMO: Do any of you feel as if you know Thomas very well?

(Framo: Like the rest of the family, I found it was very easy to ignore Thomas, so from time to time I brought him into the conversation.)

TIM: I don't know. Sometimes, Thomas, when you call me, I don't think I spend enough time with you on the phone trying to find out what's going on. You say what's happening, and sometimes I just want to get off the phone. I feel bad about that.

FRAMO: Do any of you ever call up Thomas?

KATIE: Yes.

FRAMO: How about Lynn and Ann?

LYNN: No.

FRAMO: You never call up Thomas?

LYNN: No.

FRAMO: Why not?

LYNN: Because I feel like I don't know him very well. When I was born he was out of the house, and the only contact I've had with him is when he comes home for vacations and visits. That's terrible because I feel that I'm kind of ignoring the situation.

FRAMO: How about you, Ann?

ANN: The same.

FRAMO: But Thomas apparently is the one who calls others.

LYNN: Yeah.

FRAMO: So he wants to be included more as part of the family.

TIM: Do you? [turning to Thomas]

THOMAS: Yes, I do.

TIM: Do you feel that I ignore you?

THOMAS: Sometimes; but I wish you could do better.

TIM: You wish I could do better?

THOMAS: Yes.

TIM: Like doing what?

THOMAS: Calling me more often on the phone.

TIM: Do you think I send you enough things?

THOMAS: Yes, you do.

FRAMO: Thomas, would you like to hear from your sisters more?

THOMAS: From Lynn and Ann I would.

FRAMO: Maybe they can do something about that.

TIM: I know that sometimes, Thomas, you ask a question over and over again. Like when are you going to come for a visit, and presents, and sometimes it's just so much. You know, I think Dad feels that way because you call Dad a lot.

THOMAS: Yes.

TIM: You keep asking the same question again and again, and you do
           that to me sometimes over the phone. I don't have a chance to
           ask you a lot of questions because we're always dealing with your
           questions as to when are you going to come home.

THOMAS: Yes.

TIM: You understand?

FRAMO: Paul, what are your thoughts about this?

DAD: There are a lot of factors in all this which cannot be revealed
           because of a variety of reasons. Thomas is on Melaril and
           Stelazine. Those two drugs play a tremendous role in his life, and
           what Tim is talking about is ideational paranoia. I don't know
           how much to articulate at this point. There are other factors that
           play a role here. Therefore, you expect that kind of thing, given
           the situation that you have. It isn't the most comfortable situa-
           tion that you would like to be in. Tim thinks he has a problem
           [with Thomas] and should multiply that by fifty, and then find
           out what kind of a problem I have.

*(Framo: Dad hesitantly talks about Thomas's psychoticlike behavior, which
apparently at times created havoc in the family. Dad makes clear that he is the
one who had to carry this burden and responsibility, as had his wife before her
death. Dad is holding back about his frustrations in dealing with Thomas.*

*On a deeper level, Thomas was an embarrassment and source of shame to
this public family. He did not fit in. Although well cared for, he was isolated
despite his efforts to push himself into the family via frequent phone calls. Tim
follows through on his agenda by raising the topic of Thomas's retardation with
the family.)*

*(Levine: Father's restraint also reflects his sensitivity to Thomas and his
concern that Thomas would become upset and disruptive.)*

TIM: You know, we have never sat in a room like this and talked about
           Thomas's retardation and his influence on all of us because we're
           too afraid. I've been too afraid to talk about it. We've never sat
           down as a family and talked about Thomas's retardation, or Tho-
           mas as a person. Sometimes I think we put Thomas on the side
           here, and maybe that's one of the reasons why we don't know
           each other, because that's been sort of a habit.

FRAMO: Well, I sort of slipped into that myself asking why the four of you
           don't get along, and I realize there's five of you.

TIM: Yes. Maybe that's happened to all of us. Maybe we've just started
           to put people away—we put each other away.

KATIE: [crying] I know when we have conversations at dinner Thomas is ignored. It bothers me a lot. We ignore him. He eats dinner there, and we never talk to him—rarely—and maybe Dad will try to bring up something. He'll try, but there's nothing there. And you have to feel that, don't you Thomas?

THOMAS: Once in a while.

FRAMO: Is part of the reason, though, that it's hard to have a conversation with Thomas because there's not a give and take?

KATIE: Yes. But there is a little bit at dinnertime; yes, there is. Not to say one word to a person . . . We don't do that to the company that comes over!

DAD: [whispers] No, it's a little different though.

FRAMO: Where would you all like to go with this? Would you like to include Thomas in conversations? Call him up on occasion, see how he feels? What would you like, Thomas?

THOMAS: I'd like for all of them to call me up, and I'll call them and they can call me up.

FRAMO: You'd like for them to call you up? Okay, well, that's settled. We can have that happen. Would you like for people to talk with you more often at dinnertime?

THOMAS: Yes.

FRAMO: Okay. So that's settled. We can have that happen. [there's a bit of a chuckle by Dr. Framo]

(Framo: I should have let the family negotiate on this.)
(Levine: By discussing Thomas as if he was the same as everyone else, Jim is trying to counterbalance the family's tendency to make Thomas invisible. Dad's whisper about how differently Thomas is treated goes unacknowledged. I think Jim, in his eagerness to resolve this, reflected his own anxiety.)

TIM: I've enjoyed the times Thomas came to visit me. We like that—when you want to come visit us. We want to keep that up, but I get the sense that whenever we talk about Thomas it's hard to talk. It's like we want to do something to Thomas where we're going to blow him away; that he is too fragile or something. I don't think that's true.

FRAMO: Where do you think this message is coming from?

TIM: It's been all our life, as far as I can remember. I don't remember what it was like when Thomas was born and Mom and Dad discovered that he was retarded. I remember being a little kid, and I don't know what happened to me in those first few years when I was alive. Here I was an only child, the center of all the attention, and all of a sudden Thomas is born and something happens in this family and everybody's worried about Thomas. I don't know what happened to me. Something happened to me. (voice raises) All of a sudden, one night the attention stops. In a matter of a week or a month it's like something happened. Poof—gone!

FRAMO: You know, one of the things we haven't talked about, Paul: Your kids seem to be saying they want more love and affection from you, as corny as it sounds. Even when you grow older you still don't want to ever give that up. But I'm wondering what things happened to you personally in your life. You've had a lot of tough things happen in your life: You lost your wife, you are getting older, you have a son who is retarded that you've been concerned about—you've worried about through the years—you've had your profession to think of, and I don't know what other things you have been struggling with. I think it would be helpful to your children if they could hear some of the things that you personally had to struggle with.

DAD: Well . . . My first response is that I am very happy with the family that I have, in spite of the struggles.

FRAMO: I know that.

DAD: There are some slippery words one can use. Burdens are turned into bridges, crosses are turned into crowns.

FRAMO: Lemons into lemonade.

DAD: Right.

FRAMO: You've learned that one.

DAD: But, no, the fact that adversity doth best discover virtue, prosperity doth best discover vice. That's Bacon.

(Framo: Dad again avoids feelings by retreating behind abstract sayings that were out of place in this context. But I don't give up on trying to reach him.)

(Levine: Jim's care and concern about parents in family-of-origin sessions is a hallmark of his style. He continues to try to touch distant parents to help them to become more emotionally available to their families.)

FRAMO: Paul, if you could just not quote philosophers and just tell me, as a person, some of the tragedies of your life that you've had to struggle with.

DAD: [hesitating] Well . . . Well, it's tough for me to do that because I've already turned those around for my own purposes. I've listed, and you have listed, some of them. Well, I've had a brain tumor in 1966 . . .

FRAMO: Oh, you did?

DAD: Yes. [chuckles] That might tell you . . .

FRAMO: What effect did that have on you, Paul?

DAD: Nothing.

FRAMO: You recovered from it?

DAD: It was a plastoma mengeoma, one of the five percent that was totally operable.

FRAMO: You were lucky.

DAD: Yes, very fortunate.

FRAMO: Were you frightened about facing death at that time?

DAD: No, no I wasn't.

FRAMO: You weren't?

DAD: Obviously that was a possibility. In fact, the prognosis was that.

FRAMO: Uh huh. [turning to the family] Do you all remember this—when Dad had the tumor? [there's general assent] How did you all re-act to it?

DAD: I didn't get any love then. [he begins to chuckle and laugh]

(Framo: This was a curious remark Dad just made. I should have followed up on it.)

FRAMO: You didn't? Didn't they all gather around you and hug you?

KATIE: Mom was pregnant with Lynn at the time. A terrible year actu-ally.

DAD: Yeah, right.

TIM: Yes, it was a terrible year.

KATIE: And I remember it just happened so quickly with Dad. There was no indication it was happening until the week before. It was the morning of surgery when we all had to go in and pray around the bed.

FRAMO: How did he know he had something wrong? What were the symp-toms?

TIM: One night my mom came running into my bedroom and said, "Your dad's dying." I'd always feared that—that something like that would happen. So I ran into the bedroom and saw him there on the bed with blood coming out of his mouth.

DAD: It's the first time I have heard that.

KATIE: Strawberry ice cream it turned out to be, though.

FRAMO: So it was strawberry ice cream? [everybody begins to laugh]

TIM: The story is better with blood. Mom said that this was blood . . . And I didn't know that it was strawberry ice cream.

FRAMO: What were the symptoms? Could he speak?

KATIE: Yes.

TIM: Nobody knew that this was happening until it happened, and then he went to the hospital.

KATIE: They thought he had a stroke. Is that what they thought? [looks at Dad]

DAD: You're telling me things that I don't know.

TIM: You mean we didn't tell you this? When I ran over to my football coach's house in the middle of the night, it was raining. I pounded on all the windows to get them out of bed. He was big, and I thought he could handle the situation [the entire group begins to laugh], so I kept knocking on the windows and the doors. He got up, and then we ran over to the house. But before that, I had called the neighbors to get an ambulance. They got an ambulance, and by the time we got there he was being wheeled off. You, Dad, were awake and you said, "What happened?"

DAD: I didn't want to go to the hospital. I remember that.

TIM: So they went to the hospital. And what I remember is that, when you were in the hospital, the hardest moments for me was coming into your room before surgery and you couldn't talk. [tearful]

DAD: Right.

TIM: You were just struggling, you know, just trying to say a word.

DAD: Right. But the operation was relatively minor—in light of the diagnosis. It could have been major if the diagnosis had been different.

TIM: Bit I think what you do is downplay the effect it had on other people. Now, you may have handled all of these things well in your own way . . .

FRAMO: But you were all scared?

KATIE: We were told he wasn't going to make it.

FRAMO: And you all got around the hospital bed and prayed?

KATIE: The morning of the surgery, we had to go to school. We were all forced to go to school that day, and Mom was pregnant with Lynn. That was really tough on her.

FRAMO: Lynn, what are your thoughts on all this? Come on, there were some intrauterine thoughts.

LYNN: It's all interesting. I'm just sitting here listening—it's like we have totally different lives—and sitting here listening to all these things I don't know. I didn't realize Tim and Katie were old enough to realize what was going on. I hear all these stories that Dad had a brain tumor, and all these things were going on, and they say, "It's the best Thanksgiving we've ever had, and little Lynn needed a father."

FRAMO: How old were you, Ann?

ANN: Four.

FRAMO: Four. You don't remember this, Ann?

ANN: The only thing I remember is Dad being wheeled out.

FRAMO: How did you feel about it, Thomas?

THOMAS: Someone told me, I think.

FRAMO: Were you upset?

THOMAS: A little bit.

FRAMO: How old are you, Paul?

DAD: Sixty-eight.

FRAMO: How does it make you feel to hear your children say they want more from you?

DAD: Well, yes, very nice. I accept it, and I think, as I've indicated before, there has been a shift in my own perspective.

FRAMO: From what to what?

DAD: From the fact that they need this kind of affection, and the positive strokes that we are talking about. Not accept them as part of the reality.

FRAMO: Do you remember positive strokes as you were growing up?

DAD: Not particularly, no. I suspect if there is one virtue that has been underscored in my life that was the aspect of humility. That is what underscores a lot of the things we have been talking about here. When one looks at life theologically, it's that God gets the glory.

(Framo: Dad makes clear that humility plays a key role in his life. Nonetheless, I keep pursuing Dad. By asking specific questions about his own family I try to get him to come down to earth.)

FRAMO: Was your father a minister?

DAD: No, he was a teacher.

FRAMO: Were you close to him?

DAD: Yes. With eight kids, I was close to him I would say.

FRAMO: Was he very affectionate to you?

DAD: No, no.

FRAMO: Not very demonstrative?

DAD: No, no.

FRAMO: Was your mom more so?

DAD: No, no.

FRAMO: Neither one was?

DAD: No.

FRAMO: Where did you get it from?

KATIE: His sisters.

FRAMO: His sisters?

KATIE: They idolized him.

DAD: Get what, what are we talking about? Get what?

FRAMO: Affection, love, caring.

DAD: Apparently I don't have as much as I thought I had. [chuckles]

FRAMO: You just grew up without it?

DAD: Grew up without it?

FRAMO: Apparently you didn't feel the need for it.

DAD: I'd have to reflect on that a bit. My own recollection is that I need
        in my life recognition—if that's what you're talking about. I would
        say that I need that, and I suspect I got that in my life, not neces-
        sarily from my immediate family, but from those people who
        are around me. Because like Tim, back in those days when they
        used peach baskets for basketball, I played a considerable amount
        of basketball. There was a goodly amount of return for that kind
        of performance. If that's what you're talking about, I got a goodly
        amount of it.

FRAMO: No. What I'm talking about is the feeling that dad's going to say,
        "Boy, you've done a terrific job."

DAD: Yes, no . . . That's the same kind of reaction that Tim has against
        my reaction to him. My father was not that kind of a person that
        would go up to someone and slap you on the back and say, "That
        was a great, great job."

FRAMO: And you don't remember longing for that?

DAD: No. The facts that I mentioned might indicate that I somewhat missed it, but it was not at the point where there was a void in my life.

FRAMO: Uh huh.

DAD: So I suspect that I missed something of that, and I suspect that I miss it more right now than I did in those earlier years.

FRAMO: That's interesting. How about your mom, what was she like?

DAD: With eight children and little help from the outside, she was busy.

FRAMO: She was busy?

DAD: Very, very, very busy. And in those days you didn't buy things canned; they all had to be made from scratch. So she was eternally in that kitchen and serving other people and this sort of thing.

FRAMO: Did she ever hug and kiss you?

DAD: On rare occasions.

FRAMO: Like when you would leave home to go to school?

DAD: Yeah, that's right.

FRAMO: Did she tuck you in and sing you songs?

DAD: No.

FRAMO: Where did you learn that?

DAD: Along the way—I don't know.

FRAMO: Did you get some affection from your sisters? One of your sisters?

DAD: Yes, I got a goodly amount of affection from them, from two of the sisters.

FRAMO: Another thing you seem to be saying, though, is while these kids of yours are all saying that they want something from you, you're also saying, by gosh, you're not too old to want something from them.

DAD: [laughs] No.

FRAMO: Why not? Katie, what do you think about that? Your father wants some affection.

DAD: [protesting] No. They're all very good. I don't even want to put myself into that cast. I appreciate the kids.

FRAMO: Oh, I still like affection. Hell, nobody can ever give me enough. You never get to a point in life where you don't need that. Ever.

(Framo: It is very difficult for this man to express his needs. I self-disclose in order to facilitate Dad's awareness of his neediness.)

DAD: Well, I realize that you need something of that, but there are, you
         know . . . Life consists of more than exchanging love epithets and
         comments and gestures with one another.

FRAMO: Of course. We've got to get on with our lives, we've got work to
         do, careers. But, nonetheless, it does smooth the way a little bit.

DAD: That is true. If it's a means to accomplish a greater end. This is
         my philosophical judgment: if it's going to make them more full
         personalities. Because in my judgment, the full object of every
         life is servanthood to humanity.

FRAMO: Is what?

DAD: Servanthood. To humanity. Servanthood.

FRAMO: I don't know that word.

DAD: Oh. Where you live to serve other people. It's called love, in the
         best sense of that word. If you want to get into the Greek, it's
         agape. It's love, even for the enemy.

FRAMO: But, I personally believe that charity begins at home.

(*Framo: This direct challenge to Dad's belief system was one of my best
comments of the session.*)

DAD: Well, if . . .

FRAMO: I'd rather love my family than the world.

DAD: Well, that's true. We're using some catchy phrases here. I don't
         think there would be any principal disagreement here at this
         point. But it does mean that we are here not as ends in ourselves.
         That is a slippery term, too.

(*Framo: Dad's use of the words "catchy phrases" and "slippery" suggests he
is annoyed and feels somewhat tricked by questions that use a concrete, different language, threatening his characteristic way of thinking. I'm really trying to
get him to take in the pleas of his children. On the other hand, I should have
recognized the altruistic nature of his belief system.*)
(*Levine: It is tricky business to respect this father's religious and spiritual
beliefs while challenging use of these beliefs in his defenses against intimacy.*)

TIM: Dad, just wait a minute. This isn't a discussion about philoso-
         phy. I get uncomfortable because I do this, too—I do what you're
         doing right now.

DAD: You mean retreat into philosophy?

TIM: Yeah.

LYNN: You have to have a vocabulary to do that. This is how our family has always dealt with things. Can you imagine being twelve years old and having to listen to him say this? That's how he deals with us, sometimes in a philosophical manner. I'm not one of his colleagues—I'm his daughter! I don't want to be treated as a colleague like you should love the world and all these things. I don't want to be treated that way.

(Framo: It was a sign of family strength that Tim and Lynn could question Dad's academic approach to his personal relationships.)

FRAMO: What do you think would happen if you all tucked Dad in at night and sang him songs? Do you think he might change?

(Framo: This apparently incongruous intervention, a playful, role-reversal suggestion, was my attempt to shift the context to Dad's unexpressed needs for nurturance. When I said it, I could feel Carl Whitaker looking over my shoulder.)

LYNN: I don't think you can teach an old dog new tricks. [there is general laughter throughout the entire group, especially on the part of Paul]

FRAMO: Oh sure you can, sure you can.

LYNN: Like last night, I went in to see Dad and we talked for an hour, until one or two o'clock in the morning. And I just sat there and we talked. It's all fine, Dad, that you need a certain amount of love, but I think that out of all the kids I've hit it; I know what makes you tick. I know that you love when I come up to you and cuddle with you at night, and when I hug you and hold you, or tell you how much I love you. I take the initiative. I think that some of the kids are holding back a little bit.

FRAMO: So with you he's not a philosopher?

LYNN: Oh, he is. But I think with me there's a little more touching, and a little more opening up. Dad can be his philosophical person all he wants to, but I don't put up with it.

FRAMO: You don't have to listen to him and his ministerial lecture?

LYNN: I hate it! I hate it! He can tell me all those philosophical things about how we should love the world, but we're dealing with a family here. I think that is what's important here.

(Framo: Here I was legitimizing disloyalty and giving permission for Lynn to break the family rules. She takes full advantage of this opportunity to express a long-held feeling. Lynn is open and real.)

FRAMO: You take the initiative in reaching out and touching Dad?

LYNN: Yes.

FRAMO: What do you think would happen if Katie did that?

KATIE: By the time Lynn came around Dad had changed a little bit. She
         had a different relationship with Dad than any of us did. It was
         like a grandfather to a grandchild rather than as a father to a
         child.

FRAMO: Yeah, but what stops you from doing with Dad what Lynn does?

KATIE: I don't think Dad wants it from me.

FRAMO: I don't know. Is it true, Dad, you don't want it?

DAD: [chuckling, pats Katie on the back] No. [still chuckling]

KATIE: I don't think he cares to change. [crying] It's not important to
         him. We have a relationship and he's comfortable with it. I don't
         think he's uncomfortable with our relationship.

FRAMO: Let's give Dad a chance to reply. What do you say to Katie at this
         point?

DAD: I don't have an immediate comment.

   (Framo: Katie's aching longing for acceptance and love from Dad was so
apparent here. I quickly realized that my effort to get Dad to declare his caring
for Katie was premature. I did not yet understand the meaning he ascribed to
intimacy between fathers and daughters.)

FRAMO: What would happen if Katie were to do to you what Lynn does?
         Would you like it? [there is considerable silence]

DAD: I really don't know. I guess I would like it. I would like it, but it
         can be done in a variety of ways. She wouldn't have to come as
         Lynn does. She somehow comes in at one o'clock in the morn-
         ing and we talk until two o'clock in the morning.

FRAMO: Why not?

DAD: Well it's a different role. She's a married lady, and Lynn is unmar-
         ried. I don't know if that plays even a role.

   (Framo: For Dad it is okay to be affectionate with Lynn because she is
unmarried. He makes a clear distinction and boundary between him and his
married daughter. That is, being affectionate with grown daughters can have
sexual implications, and sex can only happen in the context of marriage. I felt I
had to handle this sensitive topic carefully. The rest of the family disputes his
logic. I do believe that the affection expressed between Lynn and Dad was quite
innocent.)

TIM: I don't understand what the difference is. She's married and Lynn's unmarried, and that somehow doesn't make it possible for Katie to come in at one o'clock in the morning?

LYNN: Like Ann said, just because she's married doesn't mean to say she doesn't need affection anymore.

DAD: No, but . . .

ANN: I think Dad doesn't realize that it's not only that Dad gives us something, but our fulfillment goes two ways, not just one way.

FRAMO: You mean you'd like to give to him, too?

ANN: Uh huh, uh huh.

FRAMO: Do you think he would have trouble accepting it, but he would take it from Lynn?

ANN: [nods yes]

FRAMO: You do.

ANN: Well, she's got the availability since we are not at home.

FRAMO: But when you are together, what's to stop you from going into Dad's room at one o'clock in the morning?

ANN: I did.

KATIE: She felt uncomfortable doing it.

ANN: Uh huh.

FRAMO: Did you talk with Dad last night?

DAD: No, the night before.

ANN: Yes. But I think the change started, I don't know, probably after Mom died.

FRAMO: What change took place?

ANN: Dad needs affection, too, 'cause Mom wasn't there to give him that reassurance, and he was more willing to receive it then from his kids. At that time I was fourteen, and sort of on my way, and Lynn was still a child. That was the reason the relationship developed that way.

DAD: It seems to me, since Elizabeth died there is obviously a certain amount of affection that everyone needs.

FRAMO: You grant that?

DAD: Indeed. I need a certain amount. If it's overdone then I think I would resist.

FRAMO: Oh, I see.

DAD: But with Lynn, she had no one to bring affection to her life. No husband or no wife to bring it.

LYNN: I had Ann.

DAD: But Ann was married, and she had her husband.

LYNN: No she didn't.

DAD: Well, yes, I know, but when she did marry . . . I suspect before that she was off to college.

FRAMO: You see, the assumption your Dad is operating from is that after you get married you should get that sort of thing from your spouse. You don't need it from your parents anymore. That's not so.

DAD: [protesting] No, no. Not anymore. Not in the type of way it was given. Not in the manner in which it was given beforehand. There are ways by which you can communicate your love and concern for each other other than the manner in which I am dealing with—with Lynn.

ANN: Do you feel uncomfortable when I hug you?

DAD: No. No, I don't.

ANN: Did you feel uncomfortable when I went in to say goodnight to you?

DAD: I don't know. I guess I didn't have any reaction. I guess it would be interesting. You don't want to turn it up for popular vote . . . How many married daughters in the country today come into the bedroom of their father and lie with him in order to show affection to him? [everyone laughs]

FRAMO: I hear what you are saying. Most fathers, as their daughters become teenagers, get uncomfortable and start pulling back because of the sexual implications . . . Ann, do you and your dad talk on the phone? Does he ever call you up and ask you how you are?

ANN: I do the calling. There are times I call to ask him how he is doing.

FRAMO: Does Dad call you just to ask how you are?

(Levine: Jim acknowledges Dad's anxiety about sexuality, but then changes the subject.)

ANN: No. Maybe once, and I was shocked when he did it.

FRAMO: For an emergency?

ANN: Just business-type stuff.

FRAMO: Would you like him to call more often?

ANN: Well, yeah.

FRAMO: Do you hear that, Paul?

DAD: Yeah, right.

TIM: Well, a lot of the things that other people have been talking to you about I have problems with, too, so I'm trying to understand how I can do it differently. I'm not attacking you, but I notice the similarities—you started laughing when Ann was talking to you seriously. I think you told me [looking at Ann] when Dad talks to you . . . You told me the other day, when you say something serious Dad laughs, and I sometimes feel I have the same problem, but I don't hear what somebody else wants—like with Annie, Ty, and Stacy. I'm not just listening, either it's important or it doesn't make any difference.

DAD: Now, you're going to smile at this because I'm the penny pincher in the family . . . I'm on a limited budget; I'm a retired person. If I should be calling you as often as you would like or suggest I could never afford it. Our bill is now $225 a month.

(Framo: Tim compares himself to Dad, saying that, like Dad, he mini-mizes other people's feelings and needs. Tim, here, continues his search for an identity separate from Dad. Dad does not hear this message, and instead justi-fies why he does not call his children more often.)

(Levine: Although the family is worrying that Dad feels criticized, he is still engaged. I think it is a mark of this family's healthy functioning that they could begin to express their longings for appreciation and affection.)

LYNN: I remember when you called me at school that time. I hated it when you made a list: how was the money situation, how are the grades, are you going to church. Then it would come, "How are you doing?" It was categorized: A, B, C, and D. Sometimes I'd like you just to say, "Hey, how is it going?" And you did that this year. You did call me up and say, "Hey, how is it going?" Or when I was upset about a paper and I would call you and you would call me back. I remember every Saturday there was a designated time when I would call you, and that made me very happy.

FRAMO: The sense I get is you are more comfortable about how Dad feels about you. I don't think your brothers and sisters are. For ex-ample, how often does Dad call you, Katie, and say, "How are you?"

THOMAS: Dad and I have a hard time communicating with each other. We should communicate better.

FRAMO: What's that? You and Dad?

THOMAS: Dad and I have a hard time communicating with each other. Tim and Katie communicate better. Dad and I don't communicate very good.

FRAMO: He doesn't?

THOMAS: No.

FRAMO: What's missing for you, Thomas?

THOMAS: He doesn't let me finish a sentence. He doesn't listen to me.

FRAMO: Gee, Dad's really getting it today.

TIM: I feel somewhat concerned about Dad right now.

DAD: Why?

TIM: I wonder how you're feeling being dumped on like this? Do you
         all feel any concern about Dad right now? I don't want him to
         die or to get depressed or go into a hole now. [Ann seems to be
         wanting to break in as Tim is talking]

   (Framo: As Dad is criticized by his children, an old dread is reactivated for
Tim: that Dad could be killed by negative feelings. In my next intervention, I
reframe the criticisms of Dad by indicating that he could get something from his
children's complaints. I also indirectly give him an assignment.)

FRAMO: But that's not why we're talking about this. I think the reason
         this is coming up is to bring about some change, and I think Dad
         is learning some things that he didn't know. I think he's becom-
         ing more aware of how much his kids want to hear from him,
         and I think that this will change. I wager, when you write to me
         in a couple of months [he points at Tim], you'll tell me that Dad
         is more in touch with his kids and he's going to feel better about
         himself, and they're going to feel better about him.

TIM: What I'm worried about right now is this protection. I feel, right
         now, that I don't want to say anything more about Dad because I
         don't want to keep piling it on. And I'm just wondering . . . See, I
         have trouble doing that with a lot of people. When I want to say
         things to people, like if I want to say things to you, I might not
         do that because I'm afraid of piling it on, of hurting someone.
         Right now, anything that you all say to Dad I want to say . . .

FRAMO: You want to protect him?

TIM: I want to protect him because I think he's too fragile.

DAD: [laughs]

TIM: Right there, laugh, not serious. [points to Dad]

FRAMO: How fragile are you, Paul?

DAD: [laughs]

FRAMO: Are you going to fall to pieces?

DAD: [chuckles again] No, no.

FRAMO: I think your Dad has many resources—more than you think he does.

TIM: Then how come . . . [addressing Ann and Lynn] I would be curious as to why both of you were saying, "Yes, we're dumping too much on Dad." You were nodding when I said we are dumping too much on Dad, and I don't think he can take it.

ANN: It's not so much that he can't take it, it's just that...

FRAMO: It's not fair?

ANN: No. It's just being courteous that when you have a negative there should be a positive.

FRAMO: Then why don't you tell your Dad some of the good things you got from him. What good things?

(Framo: In family-of-origin sessions, particularly those characterized by negative feelings, I routinely make it a point to ask the adult children what positive things they have gotten from each parent. Thomas, however, takes advantage of the opportunity to join in the criticizing of Dad. I make a decision not to deal with Thomas's comment because it is likely to be unproductive. I wonder if that decision was a mistake.)

(Levine: I suppose Jim could have asked Thomas to elaborate. However, he was moving toward closing the session on a positive note so I think he made the right decision.)

THOMAS: Dad teases me a lot. I don't want him to tease me anymore. He teases me. I don't like to be teased. I get angry.

FRAMO: Everybody teases you?

THOMAS: Not everybody. Some people do it. Dad does it all the time.

FRAMO: How do they do it, Thomas?

THOMAS: It's hard to explain. I just don't like it.

FRAMO: I understand that. [pause] Ann, tell your dad some of the good things you got from him.

ANN: Sensitivity to other people. There's positive parts about being meticulous and being thorough.

FRAMO: Being perfectionistic?

ANN: But there's also the balance to it, too. We're always go-getters. Everybody's working at their job, and has done well because Dad was always a go-getter, and he was an example of good working.

FRAMO: He set a model of working hard?

ANN: Uh huh.

FRAMO: And that's good for you.

ANN: To a certain degree. In everyone's life there needs to be a balance.

FRAMO: Katie, what do you think you got that was good from your dad?

DAD: Not much.

(Levine: Is this defensive in that he is identifying with some anticipated criticism or is he uncomfortable about receiving too much praise?)

KATIE: Not his nose at least. [laughs] I think the ability to forgive. And affection. And always striving to do your best.

FRAMO: That was a good thing for you.

KATIE: It is now, in my career.

FRAMO: What is your career?

KATIE: I'm a teacher.

FRAMO: Did I hear you talk about a book?

KATIE: I worked on a book, and I went to a couple of school districts to get it published.

FRAMO: How is that going?

KATIE: It's for use in the classroom.

FRAMO: Uh huh. Had Dad helped you with that?

KATIE: No, no. But I think the drive to do it . . .

FRAMO: Does he praise you for the book?

KATIE: I think he asked about it.

FRAMO: He does show interest?

KATIE: It hasn't been published yet.

FRAMO: Uh huh.

KATIE: I think my sense of humor comes from Dad.

FRAMO: Uh huh. Tim, what did you get from Dad that was good?

TIM: I really admire his thinking, his ability to think and the ability to use his mind. And his ability to deal with people in public situations has been really good. You've given me good advice about how to deal with my career—how to have both careers cooking at the same time. That's been the best advice I ever got.

FRAMO: What both careers?

TIM: Instead of just stopping after the seminary, going on to graduate school and keeping a number of things alive. That's been very helpful advice, and I think I would have been a much different person if I had just gone to the seminary and then quit at that time.

FRAMO: So he set a model, then, for intellectual achievement for you?

TIM: And diversifying, really encouraging me to diversify. And basically, he also has not interfered with my life. [turning to Dad] You really have not told me to do anything about anything unless I ask. You haven't said, "This is the way you should have handled your family and your marriage or your life." You just have given an opinion here and there, but basically laid off it.

FRAMO: I also get a sense you got from your dad something I'm picking up: a sense of integrity.

TIM: Yeah. I don't think I have as much integrity as he does, but he's very well respected by many, many people.

FRAMO: Let me ask Thomas. Thomas, what good things does your dad do?

(Levine: Since Thomas is so responsive to the affective tone of the family, Jim gives Thomas another chance to respond, this time in a more positive manner.)

THOMAS: Well, he comes out and picks me up and takes care of my clothes. He gives me love, and he's happy to see me.

FRAMO: He's happy to see you?

THOMAS: Yes.

FRAMO: You feel good about that?

THOMAS: Yes.

FRAMO: Uh huh. Okay. How about you, Lynn? What did you get that was good from your dad, besides those nice philosophical lectures?

DAD: [laughs]

(Framo: I had gotten to the point where I could kid with Dad, knowing he would not be offended. I did notice that, as the session progressed, Dad's language became more direct and to the point. All along, I deliberately used everyday colloquial terms.)

LYNN: I think the way I deal with people. Dad was a really caring person who taught us that people make a difference. You make outsiders feel very comfortable, and you are very personable, and your values of Christianity are very important. You know how God enters your life, and that's very important. [addressing Dad] You have been an example in that respect, because whenever there's a problem you go to God first. I think that all of us have based our belief in Christ on that, and that's very important.

ANN: There's one thing I want to add: Probably the most memorable times about growing up were that Dad didn't tell us fairy tales; he read the Bible to us, and I appreciated it. A lot of the time he made Jesus as being important. Those are the things that, when you look at your parents, you ask what you want to do with your kids and what you don't want to do. That's what I want to continue because that's very important.

LYNN: [addressing Dad] Last night when we were talking, you said that when I told you that you were important to me it made you sparkle. [crying] That was the neatest thing you could possibly say. You said something that was most important to me, and I told you that you were so important in my life. I love you so much, and hearing that made you so happy. I think what we're saying is very important to you, but you may be laughing at it right now. You're saying that it's not that important, but really deep down inside I really think that you appreciate what we're saying. [everyone crying]

FRAMO: Is she right, Paul?

LYNN: [to Dad] Don't smile.

DAD: No. I suspect that part of my laughter is always to counter some other response you might be bringing to the scene. And you want to change your own attitudes so as you can respond more positively to the situations. It isn't the kind of situation where you don't want to listen to someone because you laugh, it's because you want to change the mood. What Lynn is saying I could not have said fifteen years ago.

(Framo: Dad insightfully acknowledges that his laughter stems from embarrassment in dealing with feelings—his own or others'.)

FRAMO: So you have mellowed?

DAD: As I have said, the last fifteen years I suspect it was true of my father, and it was true of a goodly number of other people.

FRAMO: Your dad mellowed, too, in the later years of his life?

DAD: Yes.

LYNN: What I don't understand is why you can't just stay there and say, "I really appreciate what you guys are doing." It's like you have to explain everything. Why can't you just say, "I feel this way"?

DAD: Permit me to have a couple of warts in my life. Maybe this is one that I will have to bear for the rest of my life.

TIM: Dad, you really don't have to talk.

(Levine: Tim and his sisters are in conflict between confronting Dad about his lack of emotional expressiveness and protecting Dad from their anger. In addition to feeling guilty about their anger, I believe they share an unconscious fantasy that strong emotion—especially anger—is powerful and catastrophic. Here, Tim functions as an agent of the sibling system, but Jim does not feed the fantasy by going along with their protectiveness.)

FRAMO: Actually, Tim, yesterday after the meeting you said you saw your father in a different way than you've ever seen him before.

TIM: Yep.

FRAMO: What was different?

TIM: Well, I didn't think he'd come here for one. So when I called up and asked . . . The two people who I really had to call first were Dad and Katie, because I thought if they would come everybody else would come. So just being here . . . I really appreciate your saying yes. [Dad moves to speak] Don't intellectualize it, okay? I have a great deal of respect for you as a professional person. As a human being, your being here was very important to me. Your willingness to risk yourself is something I haven't seen, and that's really hopeful.

FRAMO: Well, I do get a sense . . . I assume that Dad's really going to hear what you guys are saying. Don't be surprised if you get a letter or telephone call on occasion, not with a list of things to talk about, on business matters, but a call from Dad saying, "How are you doing?" "How are you feeling these days?" Somehow I feel that is going to happen . . . Now what about among you five kids; what do you still have to work out with each other? I call you kids; sorry, you're adults.

(Framo: I shift to the sibling subsystem.)
(Levine: Both Jim and I dislike the term "adult child," but we have not found a comfortable replacement. We revert back to hierarchical role descriptions in family sessions, referring to parents and kids even though the kids are now adults.)

KATIE: I think Tim and I should get to know each other, but I still think Tim approaches situations intellectualizing. [crying]

DAD: A chip off the old block.

(Framo: Dad feels comfortable enough now to use humor.)

KATIE: And as frustrating as it is . . .

FRAMO: [apparently observing Thomas's raised hand] Just a minute, Thomas.

KATIE: Even though I think he wants to—we took a vacation together last summer. When Tim talks with me he blocks. He always goes into an eight-year-old behavior, and he can't deal with me as a sister and as an adult.

FRAMO: What's a typical kind of interaction?

KATIE: "Oh, Katie, how are you?" [quoting Tim] It's so forced. We're starting to try, but it's forced, it's intellectual. I don't think you know even about my teaching. I don't think you know anything about me personally or socially, or anything I do.

FRAMO: Do you think he's uncomfortable with you?

KATIE: Oh, yeah. I definitely do. I am uncomfortable with him.

FRAMO: Is there competition between the two of you?

KATIE: I admire him a lot. I don't know if I feel competition.

TIM: Well, when I am with you there are these digs. I feel I'm being ganged up on.

KATIE: That's probably true. That's the way I jokingly relate to you.

TIM: When you and Annie and you and Ann and Lynn are together, I feel I'm being ganged up on.

FRAMO: What do you mean? By the three of them?

TIM: Yeah.

FRAMO: How about when just you and Katie are talking with each other?

TIM: I feel a bit more comfortable, because there's no one for Katie to gang up on me. Do you know what I'm talking about? [looking at Katie]

KATIE: I know what you're talking about.

FRAMO: How do they do it, Tim?

TIM: Well . . . [turns to Katie] What are you thinking about now?

KATIE: I don't want to say it. [Katie is chuckling] Like last summer when I said you were getting too much like Dad—you hated that. The fact that you ignore it or don't listen. The whole world could revolve around and, Tim, you're not aware of it. And I dig and dig and dig at you. Maybe that's just me, in order to get my point across. I don't know how else to relate to you. I don't think you accept me.

TIM: Well, I do accept you. Annie has helped me in this area, and I do more than I did in the past because we fought a lot, we scratched each other.

FRAMO: Tim, she says you don't know her.

TIM: I don't think I do that much. I don't think I work at it hard enough.

FRAMO: Excuse me, Tim. Thomas has been trying to say something.

THOMAS: We got to try to get along.

FRAMO: Yes.

THOMAS: In the family.

FRAMO: You mean everybody has to try to get along?

THOMAS: Yes.

FRAMO: I agree with you, and that's what we're working on now.

(Framo: Thomas is anxious about the dispute between his brother and sisters.)

TIM: I think I just need to spend more time . . .

FRAMO: Tim, do you ever ask any questions about her, her work, her person, what she does?

TIM: I'm very bad at that. I'm not very good at that. I'm terrible at it.

FRAMO: Why did you get insulted? Why did you get angry when she said you were just like Dad?

TIM: There's a part of Dad that I'm glad I'm like. There's parts of Dad that I have a problem with. But the way you were saying it, I wasn't paying attention. I was ignoring it. [turning to Katie] Right? That's what you were saying?

KATIE: Right. That's the part of Dad. I will dig at Tim; I'll tease him back for all those years of neglect. It's my way of communicating with him. It really is. I want him to admire me like I admire him.

FRAMO: Do you hear her, Tim?

TIM: Yeah. [there's a lengthy silence; Katie is sniffling in the background]

FRAMO: How can this change?

KATIE: Again, I feel I have to earn it like I had to earn it with Dad.

FRAMO: How would you go about earning it? Write another book?

KATIE: Oh, perhaps what I do. Maybe that's the only topic that might be brought up. How I look.

FRAMO: It must be a terrible thing for you that you always feel you are on trial, that you have to prove yourself. What's wrong with just relaxing and being you, and if people don't like it to hell with them.

KATIE: I just wasn't brought up that way.

FRAMO: *I'm* bringing it up that way. [there's general laughter throughout the group]

(Framo: I challenge the family rule and Katie's belief system.)

KATIE: I'm trying. I really am. But we're involved in the Christian Ethics. We never say to hell with anybody. We always have to think of the other person.

FRAMO: Do other people have to come first?

KATIE: Definitely.

FRAMO: I personally believe that your first obligation is to yourself.

KATIE: I am trying . . . As I grow older I think I'm wiser.

TIM: Katie, you don't really know how I'm looking at you. I don't judge you. I really don't approach you that way—in my own mind. But the problem that I have is that I don't have a lot of practice at being close to people. I'm bad at that. I'm not good at that. You know, it's not that I'm good at it with some people and not good at it with you. I'm not good at it with anybody, and so I really have to work on that.

FRAMO: What can you two do about this situation?

KATIE: Probably spend more time together? Get together.

TIM: I think more time. I think we have been doing more in the last few years about taking vacations together. We need to continue to do that. Calling on the phone, you know, is really important. And then when we get together, we need to talk about how it's going because sometimes I think we get into doing whatever we're doing instead of just sitting down and saying how's it going between us. I think we need to know what's working, what seems to be right, and I think we need to talk about it.

KATIE: Maybe a time away from the kids and the spouses, because whenever we're together there is the family.

(Framo: This conversation between Tim and Katie is probably the most honest one they have ever had. They are really struggling to understand each other, to meet on another level.)

FRAMO: Paul, do you have any thoughts about this conversation that your son and daughter are having? Do you have any suggestions for them?

DAD: Well, I guess not.

FRAMO: Did you know they had this difficulty with each other?

DAD: Peripherally, yes. But the extent of it, even as I review it in my mind . . . I understood that they have had difficulties all the way back. Tim was out there being celebrated in his role, and Katie was obligated to stay home and do the work. And that's when it began, no doubt, and has developed over the years.

FRAMO: Evidently, Katie feels she needs some recognition in this family, and she deserves it. Lynn, do you agree?

LYNN: Yes, yes. [Lynn in tears]

FRAMO: You seem to be the in-house counsel with this family.

LYNN: It's obvious that Katie has lacked any recognition from any one of us, and I told her just last night that I idolize her. I do, and I want her to know that.

FRAMO: [to Katie] Did you know that?

KATIE: Lynn and I have a special relationship, and I know that from Lynn.

FRAMO: [to Lynn] Did you appreciate the mothering you got from her?

LYNN: I don't remember it, because I was too young. I was probably a brat, ignored it a lot. I just think she is absolutely exceptional, an excellent person, and I also want to say something to you, Ann, because you're looking like . . .

(Levine: Lynn is exquisitely tuned in to the emotional temperature of the family. Jim tracks Lynn's concerns about how Ann is experiencing her conversation with Katie.)

FRAMO: And I'd like to hear Ann's diagnosis of this situation, too. Between Tim and Katie . . . Why Katie feels she got short-changed in this family for recognition. But you said that you felt similarly. Do you have any thoughts about what those two can do? [points to Tim and Katie]

ANN: I think it helps to understand where each other is coming from, to be open in order to build relationships, and not being afraid that you will be hurt again. If the hurt comes it can be healed up because the communication is there. The sooner the communication starts the better. You know that no matter who you are you can be accepted by yourself and by the other people around you.

FRAMO: Ann, how is your relationship with Katie?

(Levine: As with Dad, Jim deliberately asks Ann a simply worded question to model direct communication.)

ANN: Well, during the last couple of years we have been so busy and stuff like that; so I've been pretty much on my own. But there are times when, growing up, she would be the first one I'd call to talk to and to get advice from.

FRAMO: Do you call each other in recent years? Do you talk to each other?

ANN: No, not as much.

FRAMO: How come?

ANN: I don't know.

KATIE: I'm thinking back when Ann felt the loss of affection. I really feel close to these two girls, but what's new to me is that they don't remember it. But I remember when my parents went to the Philippines, I was in charge of a one-year-old and a four-year-old for weeks, and I just loved it. It was a very positive experience for me. But I think when Ann came down to visit us, when we were married, she withdrew herself so much so that when we would come home Ann walked away. I feel like I really tried, but maybe I didn't. You were a little girl, but all of a sudden you were this adult who internalized everything and would not share with me, and that was really hard. I think it is still that way. [begins to cry]

FRAMO: Well, what, then, could make it change? Why can't you two be in touch with each other now? [long silence] What are you struggling with right now, Ann?

ANN: I think it's still a front that I put up . . . [Ann bursts into tears and others are quietly weeping] Because yesterday the three of us went out and I withdrew again.

KATIE: It bothers me a lot. What do we do?

ANN: I want to be a part, but I don't know how. Because I see the relationship that you have been able to carry on . . .

FRAMO: You mean between Katie and Lynn?

ANN: Uh huh.

FRAMO: You'd like to be a part of that?

LYNN: Ann, I thought that we went out of our way to include you. Ann, you and I have a special relationship.

ANN: I know, I know.

LYNN: It felt like we went out of our way to include you, and all you do was walk away. You walked twenty paces ahead of us all the time.

FRAMO: But she says she wants to be in, but she doesn't know how.

LYNN: But I don't know what we can do.

ANN: But I feel so different from the two of them.

KATIE: Do you think that part of the difference is when you became involved with your church group? All of a sudden I was excluded, and that feels like a difference between us.

ANN: No, not at all.

KATIE: Well, I wanted to talk to you about this issue.

FRAMO: What is she involved in?

ANN: It's not part of the Lutheran church. It's a different denomination.

FRAMO: Of what nature?

ANN: Charismatic.

FRAMO: Do you feel that this alienates you from the family?

ANN: No.

FRAMO: Does Dad have negative feelings about it?

ANN: I don't know. When Dad said the Lutheran church does this and this, I needed something more. Because of all the things that were going on, I needed something that would make Christianity more personal.

FRAMO: This fills your needs more?

ANN: Uh huh.

FRAMO: I see. But I gather that you don't think that that stands between you and Katie.

ANN: No, not as far as I'm concerned.

KATIE: But you've made a comment to me that your church friends are now your family. You've said that to me! They are your closest family. You said to me one time, "You do not understand." I felt okay about it, but then you walked away.

FRAMO: Well, then maybe when this family gets closer, as I suspect you're going to, there might be less need of that. Maybe her family will be her friends. You think? [addressing Ann]

ANN: I don't know whether it's true. I don't know why, but I think out of everybody I needed something more than what was given to me growing up.

(Framo: Ann apparently needed a hands-on, palpable religion that, from her perspective, was more intimate. Her choice of religion may have been her way out from the family stress; she joined a new family home. Still, by moving away from the family Lutheran tradition, she may feel disloyal. That guilt, perhaps also associated with the circumstances surrounding Mom's death, may help explain her sense of isolation and differentness in the family.)

(Levine: I also think that Ann's diabetes adds to her feeling that she is different from her family. I am also curious about how Ann, as a child and now as an adult, makes meaning of her diabetes [Williamson, 1997].)

FRAMO: I wonder whether Dad would care to comment on this.

DAD: Yes, it's true. Again, I don't want to wax philosophical at this point or I'll tread on someone else's territory. So I wouldn't want to comment.

FRAMO: You don't have any negative feelings about the religious direction she's gone?

DAD: No.

FRAMO: You don't?

DAD: No, I don't. No. Essentially not.

(Framo: I knew Dad had negative feelings about Ann's choice of a religion, but here I felt he was being protective of Ann.)

FRAMO: Do you hear that, Ann?

ANN: I don't feel there was any tension between Dad and me. I know there was between Katie and me. I know that I'm still learning, but I now have a better grip on accepting myself because, as a Christian, I'm first accepted by Jesus. That's the one important thing. From then on, I could be myself, but they don't understand that part of me.

FRAMO: How about you and Tim, Ann?

ANN: What do you mean?

FRAMO: What's this relationship like?

ANN: Well, we're really trying. We're really trying, but the availability isn't there.

FRAMO: Tim, would you like to comment?

TIM: Ann, how come you didn't call me all last year? I know I didn't call you, and that's a problem; but I'm wondering how come you didn't call me?

ANN: Because you're older.

TIM: Because I'm older you didn't call me?

ANN: Uh huh.

TIM: What does that have to do with it?

ANN: It might be wrong thinking, but you being able to say something to me is important. Because in my whole life I'm always trying to reach out this way, and I just got tired of doing that.

FRAMO: Would you like it to change?

ANN: I think I need to reevaluate where I am at, too.

FRAMO: In this family?

ANN: Yeah.

FRAMO: Would you like to hear from Tim more?

ANN: I think we both need to do it, and that's not to say that it's either my fault or his fault.

(*Levine: Jim's inclusion of siblings in these sessions is unique to his family-of-origin approach. Not only do sons and daughters renegotiate the family hierarchy with parents, but they do so with each other. Here, Ann and Tim are trying to move their childhood relationship into one of adulthood.*)

TIM: I think we're more alike than I thought, because I think we both withdraw. [Ann chuckles in agreement] I might not walk twenty feet ahead of people, but I think that both of us kind of shut down. I hadn't thought about it before, but I think there might be some similarity between us, more than I think.

FRAMO: Do you think that the two of you will keep more in touch with each other?

TIM: Well, yes, because we have to deal with these two. [pointing to Katie and Lynn]

FRAMO: How about you, Tim? You and Lynn?

(*Framo: Throughout the interview, I attempted to foster more emotional and physical connectedness among the family members.*)

LYNN: You were saying, "Why didn't we call you," but I was thinking that you have never been part of my life. You were always the visitor. You've never been a real part of my life. I always thought why would you ever want to be? It's true, we do talk on the phone, like at Christmas and things like that, but it's very uncomfortable. I think that you feel the same way, too. It's small talk. It's like, "Oh, how's it going?" Or, when I go up and hug you, Tim, and you pat me or you don't embrace me hard or it's like real quick, and it bothers me.

TIM: We'll have a long embrace this afternoon. [everybody laughs] We'll make up for lost time.

LYNN: I think the neatest thing would be if we could all be "best friends."

FRAMO: Could all be what?

LYNN: I guess it would be quite hard, because of the age difference. I'm not married, I don't have kids, I can't talk about all those wonderful things that you guys can talk about; but I would suggest that we be just like best friends.

TIM: I admire a lot in Lynn. I think that Lynn is a cheerleader—you know, a really lively person—and I admire your ability to be a brat because that's not something I've ever been able to do. I've just been very good.

FRAMO: Too good?

TIM: Yes, too good. Lynn, you are ready to handle anything that comes your way. You don't hold much back, I don't think. I really like that. [turning to Ann] The thing I like about you, Ann, is your commitment to what you have done with your career, and also your church.

FRAMO: What is it that you like about Katie? Go on, tell her.

TIM: I think you are a very caring person, Katie. Very caring. What you've been able to do with your job, too, and your book, you know. I think that's wonderful, and you are so creative . . . This has been wonderful—without our spouses being here. [bursts into tears]

FRAMO: Tim, what are you struggling with right now? [there is considerable silence, and Tim continues to weep] Try to put it in words.

TIM: Oh, it's just something that I don't do.

FRAMO: Katie, would you give him this. [handing Katie a few Kleenex] Why do you all think your brother is crying right now? What do you think, Thomas?

THOMAS: Because of the relationship with Katie, and their problems. Because Katie doesn't know Tim very well.

FRAMO: That's true. But I get a sense that he's crying about something else. Is it gratefulness that everyone came together for this meeting?

TIM: It's really hard for me to tell people that I appreciate them in my life.

FRAMO: Are you embarrassed at the idea of saying nice things to Katie?

TIM: Yes. I like Katie a lot. That's very hard for me to . . .

FRAMO: It's hard to tell her that?

TIM: I can do a lot of things well. It's very hard to do this well. I don't spend much time doing this. I spend most of my time just . . . This is really hard.

(Framo: Tim's weeping here took me by surprise. He ascribed it to his difficulty expressing caring and appreciation. I wondered, since the session was coming to an end, if Tim was overwhelmed by the session's proceedings. Was he more aware of his personal shortcomings, or was his weeping due to relief that the emotional life of his family had at last been dealt with?)

FRAMO: Well, I think Dad has some of that, too. It's a little difficult for him to say positive things. He can more easily say it to Lynn than anyone else. [pause] We're going to start pulling this together now, and I want you all to know that I'm glad that I met this family. I think that we've started a process here that I really think you're quite capable of continuing on your own . . . And watch the videotapes of these sessions. You'll get a great deal out of it when you do. You will notice things that you didn't notice at the time. I think we've started something here. I asked Tim to write me in a few months to let me know what's happening with this family. I really do want to know. There may be more conversation within this family. I have a sense that you all will be more in touch with each other. You may make the telephone company a little richer, but the family's going to be happier . . . [chuckling in the background] I want to personally thank you all. I really enjoyed meeting with you all and, by the way, my door is always open should any of you want to come down to San Diego for a follow-up meeting.

DAD: Let me express my appreciation—if there's such a thing like the head of the house today. I suppose I shouldn't be speaking for all of them, but we appreciate meeting with you, too.

FURTHER IMPRESSIONS OF FAMILY DYNAMICS: END OF SECOND TWO HOURS—FATHER AND SIBLINGS

In the preparation interview, Tim described his family as "tightly controlled, bound, contained, and careful." During emergencies this family style was breached, with either eruptions of feelings or somatic disorders developing. When the family was contained, the main emphasis was on accomplishing or doing tasks. This was a stressed, conflict avoiding family, so when emotional outbursts occurred around critical events, they were very dramatic.

Among my therapeutic goals were: to loosen the constraints, to challenge the rigid family rules, to offer the family alternatives, and to establish emotional connections among the family members (i.e., helping them get to know each other better). In order to put these goals into effect, I had to acknowledge the father's strengths, challenge his intellectualizing and isolating defenses, humanize him in the eyes of the children, and lead him into the emotional life of his children, which had been hidden from him. In order to close the distance between Dad and me, I introduced some fun and kidding in my exchanges with him; I felt he did warm to our jousting.

Each sibling in this family presented his or her own unique difficulty. Katie longed for recognition and appreciation. Ann was isolated from the family, wanted back in, but didn't know how. Lynn, the most open one, tried to be the family healer; she would say what others did not say. Thomas wanted to be more a part of the family, but felt disregarded. Tim—who took the initiative in bringing his family together so change could take place—wanted so much for the family members to understand and come to terms with each other. He came to recognize his close identification with Dad, and wanted to change that.

My presence and interventions allowed these adult children to confront Dad and each other in a safe setting. They affirmed love for Dad, their remaining parent, but they also brought up his shortcomings, especially his difficulty with expressing feelings. I aided the adult children in trying to make Dad more grounded and real. For the first time, Dad heard what had been going on inside his kids over the years, as witnessed by his language change as the session progressed.

The siblings, most of them distanced over the years, became more connected.

On a personal note, I had been moved by this family and the difficulties they had struggled with. I appreciated that they had allowed me entrance into the heart of their family.

Chapter 9

RESPONSES TO THE INITIAL FAMILY CONSULTATION
Aftershocks and Reflections

TIMOTHY T. WEBER, PhD

IMMEDIATE REACTIONS

In the final moments of this family consultation, I had cried openly and embarrassingly, unable to attach words to my tears. I didn't understand why I was crying, what had triggered my emotions. I just cried, and slowly felt words of gratitude and respect for what my family had given me in bringing themselves to this experience—and, more so, what we had given ourselves. I was proud of us as one unit. It was one of those rare moments in my memory when the joy and pride of being in this family as a whole were more important than any individual matter. I also felt relieved that we spoke the unspoken. And I was grateful that in the process of talking our secrets, the deep desire for love and connection and concern for each other was made known and felt. I felt like a huge weight was being lifted off my shoulders, and now the crafting of a new story of our family history, not just my history, was more possible than it had ever been before.

Finally we had dealt with the taboo topics that had been pushed away within the family: the life and death of my mother, Thomas's retardation, my feelings of distance from my sisters, my anger toward my father, hunger to be known and seen as a human being and not as an achiever, permission to be fragile and not accomplished. As long as I had kept all these things within myself, I had felt blocked and strained in relating to others in my family. I sometimes felt as if we were walking ghosts going through the routines of being family. Now there was some

163

real substance. Our family's stiff formality was shifting to more fluidity and openness. I also felt more complete as I had listened to the family tales. There was much that I hadn't known about my family history, not only missing information about what happened but obliviousness to the experience of others. I think sometimes people survive in families by engaging in long-term self-hypnosis: numbing themselves to their experience, forgetting their memories. I believe I had been able to make it by living in a fog and focusing most all of me on being better in a very narrow range of tasks—academics and sports—even during the entire course of my training to be a pastor and clinical psychologist. Now I was catching up to myself, the person I had left far behind. My history felt less confusing. Family relationships felt more clean. My awareness of myself and others in the family was less incomplete like some poorly drawn dot-to-dot picture, and was becoming more filled with substance.

I especially had a much clearer picture of my mother, and felt less anger toward her and much more understanding. I had gotten to know her more completely through our family conversation, and was beginning to have more respect for her, particularly her strength and determination. She had an enormous load in dealing with all of us together, somehow holding us in some kind of connected form, managing Thomas and his retardation, trying to link with my busy father, doing all the necessary things to keep five children alive. While we bemoaned living under the shackles of this "achieving" mandate in the family, at least we achieved with a good deal of success. I was appreciating now, for the first time, how my mother held all this together and made it happen. My anger and confusion with her before made it difficult for me to feel her strength and love. I felt sad that she was not with me now; I deeply wanted to say all this to her face to face.

I now could be more reflective on the session that had just concluded. I was grateful that there seemed to have been more direct interaction in this second session, especially among the siblings. In the first two hours more attention had been focused on my parents, first my mother and then my father. This kind of process was an absolutely necessary step—first the parents, then the siblings. The presence of parents defines the life of the family, and as sons and daughters assume adulthood they need to examine, question, test, challenge the parents' lives and definitions of the family in order to move on with authority and their own self-definition. We were doing just that as the sons and daughters of our parents. And we also were making room for other adults in our family besides our two parents. These conversations were not simply for our benefit as maturing adults, but for the benefit of the family's resiliency and strength. In a culture of conversation such as ours, family-of-origin consultation becomes the authentic initiation ritual and the rite of passage into adulthood.

We siblings talked more to each other and about each other in this second meeting. Even Thomas seemed to be more engaged and animated in the meeting. We sons and daughters also had unfinished business with each other. There was the disconnection between me and my sisters that was awkwardly painful for me. Why should I be bothered by this? Why should my sufficient self need them? But I did want them, and had a hard time admitting my need. I stated my need rather perversely by talking about my paranoia, my fear that they were talking behind my back, my desire for them to talk directly to me instead of gossiping about me with each other. They downplayed this notion, almost laughing at me for having the idea that I was that important to even talk about. But now I was beginning to understand how my paranoia was more than simple self-aggrandizement. It was a perverse way of connecting, of staying in touch, of holding my sisters deeply within my consciousness where it was safe instead of talking about my desire to have them in my life. Instead of talking about how important they were to me, I was obsessing about how important I was to them. I was cleaning up my intimacy inhibition by being more direct rather than indirect. It was still too early to know how they would respond.

I wondered about the damage that could be done to me and others, especially my father. In reaching out to my sisters, they could turn away from me or could profess their love for me and not follow through. I was concerned with how I could be hurt, but focused my consciousness instead on my father and how he could have been hurt in the sessions. Over the years in our family, I had frequently come to the defense of my father, especially as he was being challenged by my strong mother. Somehow I got the idea that he couldn't handle himself and needed me to be some emotional bodyguard. I had been enacting this history in our family sessions, often coming to his defense, interrupting some pressure on my father and deflecting attention to myself. During the conversations, I was sometimes aware of this automatic reaction to protect him, and often I would move in to protect him from emotional intensity without any consciousness of what I was doing.

In these family consultations there can be widely differing interests. People can go into these consultations with a kind of "parent-bashing" stance, where the goal is to lay on the parents all the past grievances that have accumulated over the years. Another kind of goal is "parent protection," where there is a great sensitivity toward hurting the parents and a deep desire to protect them from further harm, even if it means continuing family secrets and truncating the truth. Neither of these stances would work for me in these conversations. Both stances would result in no change and no personal responsibility.

I had to deal with my father honestly and with care—the tightrope of all family conversations—taking personal responsibility to collaborate with him in creating a different future for our relationship. I could not expect him to do this job alone. But to do the work of the future, I had to get clear about the past. I had to address the specific grievances I had toward him, and the legacy that he had passed down to me: his emotional guardedness, his intellectualizing, his formality, his turning conversation into a preaching opportunity, his love of work and marginalization of the family. Once I had cleared my grievances in a mutual conversation with him, I could more generously and authentically affirm his gifts to me: a strong religious foundation, a caring model of leadership, attention to and curiosity about the wider world, a critical embracing of issues, a commitment to values.

I wanted to approach him more as a human being, grasping the fuller complexities of his personality rather than continuing to oversimplify him. These family conversations were helping me to see not only my father, but also my mother and siblings with more complexity, more substance, more layers to their mystery. The capacities of childhood and the stress of growing up tend to force us to construct simplistic views of each other—good and bad, right and wrong, intellectual and emotional, leader and follower, strong and weak. Without these family consultations, family members can remain one-dimensional and overly simple, cast in a biased light so that they can be more easily managed in the mind. The "truth" about others in the family was becoming more ambiguous, less certain, and certainly more imaginative.

NEW STORIES BETWEEN DAD AND ME

I was becoming aware of the emerging new stories in my relationship with my father. These new stories were not profound diversions from the way we had been with each other. Rather, there were small changes in the lines, the familiar script between us. Small but noticeable new ways of being with each other were being woven into the old patterns. In all these stories, what seemed to be new was what I would call "the spirit of inquiry." I noticed in my father new questions, more research into his history and relationships, more reflection and conversation with me about those reflections, more openness to other viewpoints. Maybe I was also more open to him, more willing to hear him now that I was beginning to shed my grievances. I want to describe three incidents that happened within a few days and weeks following the family consultation.

In the family meetings my siblings and I had expressed our irritation at my father's tendency to engage in intellectual monologues, cutting off the other and offering his own wisdom. I believe my father was generally unaware of this process. When faced with this feedback, in the family meetings and at home, he responded in the more typical fashion of try-ing to explain or defend his way of being in the world. This was "old Dad" at work. But after the last family meeting at his home we had been discussing some of our reactions to the session. My father then surprised me with a question: "Do you think I really am this way? Lecturing to others and going on and on?" He seemed to inquire with genuine curios-ity. This was an opening I had rarely seen in him, especially around one of his most cherished behaviors of turning conversations into preaching opportunities. I remember this incident because our conversations took a different course. He truly was interested in my feedback, and even ex-panded the question to include more interest in how I generally experi-enced him. He wanted to know, not defend.

A few days later another small and remarkable event occurred be-tween me and my father in his back yard. My father began reflecting on a 25-year-old memory when his father had come to visit him. He remem-bered he had been preoccupied with his own business and the many demands of his job, unavailable for his own father, who stayed at his home tending to the rock garden and pruning the rose bushes. My father cried softly as he told this story, confessing that he had not been attentive to his father's need for companionship. Through his tears, he regretfully recalled how he didn't take time off, not realizing that his father might have been lonely. He and his father never talked about this; they did not have that kind of relationship with each other.

His sharing of this memory with me, and his tears, felt like a confes-sion, one that he could have made to his father were he alive. Now my father needed intergenerational absolution from me. The true absolution was that both of us were now, in that moment, changing the intergenerational story. We were there, together, in the rose garden: nei-ther of us in that moment too busy to be with each other. I also heard my father saying behind his words, "Tim, don't forget me as I forgot my own father. I want to live our father–son life differently. Stay close to me, take days off, and thanks for taking time off to be with me now." To hear my father's story and to recognize that he had taken time to be with me in these family meetings was in fact the intergenerational absolution. In my role as the grandson of my father's father I could absolve my father. In correcting intergenerational errors, parents often look to their children for absolution and compensation. This was one of those moments.

The third incident was a trip my father, Thomas, and I took, several weeks after the family meeting. We had planned this trip before the fam-ily meeting, but how we took the trip was different than it would have been without the family meetings. The three of us visited the homelands of both my father and mother in the Midwest and Pennsylvania, staying at the homes of my father's and mother's siblings along the way. One night, at the home of one of my father's older sisters, my father and his sister exchanged stories from their childhood, hearing some different and contrasting memories from each other for the first time. They were particularly interested in talking about their experiences with their parents. My aunt had a much harsher and more painful experience in the home than had my father. He seemed to have been more detached, more honored, more protected, less exploited (similar to my role in my family?). Days later, my father was on a mission to northern Wisconsin to visit his older and younger brothers who were in a feud with each other. My father was attempting to bring about some understanding between the two in this effort of "shuttle diplomacy." The actual outcome seemed to have been rather insignificant, but what mattered to me was my father's initiative in his family, his attentiveness to pain within the family, and his commitment to work toward healing. I viewed this attempt as a spreading effect of our family consultation.

We journeyed east to Pennsylvania to join a family reunion of my mother's side of the family. I felt sad that my mother was not alive to be with her family, and yet felt that I wanted to honor her after our family sessions. We took some small detours, through the little town in Pennsylvania where my mother's parents were buried. My mother's father also had grown up in this town. I felt like a detective with my father as we visited the grave sites, and then attempted to get into the church nearby where the records of birth, baptism, confirmation, marriage, and death were located. The doors to the church were locked, and the pastor was on vacation. We then made our way through the town, asking for people who may have known my grandfather. We visited one old gentleman who had known him. He was very hard of hearing, and his memory was not that good. But we were able to fill in some of the gaps and recover some distant, faint memories.

My father was a partner with me in this research as I continued to feel less of a distant and hierarchical relationship with him. We were becoming more peerlike as we journeyed together in this mission of inquiry and discovery. As we listened to all these stories of family life, we talked about historical patterns, how they were showing up in him and in our family, how these patterns were shaping our beliefs and behaviors, and how we were challenged to change. We were talking about ourselves in a wider frame of reference, as members in a huge historical drama that was ongoing and ever developing. There was this new thing happening between me and my dad—more free-wheeling, more open, more peerlike. But there was also more to us than us. We were more a part of the whole, more appreciative of the extended family that surrounded us, and the families that preceded us.

RUMBLINGS IN THE FALL

I was encouraged by my father's reflections, and what seemed to be more openness between us. When I returned from the Midwest trip, however, Katie phoned me and raised some concerns about the family consultations. She said, worriedly, "I'm concerned about Dad. He's been so quiet lately. I think he was hurt by those family talks." She believed that Dad had been "turned off" by the family meetings, and she was so concerned about his quietness that Katie visited Ann and expressed similar concerns. She did not talk directly with our father. Maybe she was projecting her own discomfort on our father? I told her that I saw things differently, "Dad not only seemed to value the family consultation, but he was using it in our talks and visits to other family members." She seemed unpersuaded by my report. I also had been talking with my father, who was especially concerned about Katie and Ann. He said to me, "They would not do this over again if they knew what they were getting into." Was he now speaking for himself or for them? Everyone seemed to be worried about everyone else's fragility. And it looked like I was the culprit who had gotten everyone into this family mess. I knew that I could not base my impression on the reports of what others were thinking and feeling. I had to go directly to each family member.

My father was due to visit our home, and this visit was about to test the strength of our growing intimacy. He was eager to talk about the family meetings now that he had reviewed the videotapes. He said that he and his wife, Linda, recently had stayed up through the middle of the night watching the tape. They were the only family members, besides Ann and her husband, Mark, who watched the tapes after the consultation. Why did I avoid watching the tapes in spite of the profound impact of the meetings? Was I too busy? Did I want to preserve my memory of the family meetings, fearing that watching the tapes would taint the memories that maybe I had distorted? Did I not want Annie to watch the tapes since she could catch me in a lie or hold me accountable to what I said I would do? Was I embarrassed at myself—my vulnerability, my tears, my pain?

At any rate, my father met me and began to talk about his reaction to the tape. He surprised me as he launched into interrogation regarding my one-to-one interview with Jim prior to the entire family meeting. When Jim had interviewed me in the preparation session, I had forgotten that I was being taped. It was a forgetting that I think helped me focus more on my experience and less on how family members would react to what I was saying. During that interview I had expressed to Jim my concerns and sense of dismay about our family process and life together. Even though my experience was now in the process of shifting significantly, my father listened to this interview as if what I had said then was indicative of how I felt now. I also had shared some old and painful memories that still felt significant. But as my father again heard those old memories he was irritated.

My father had been particularly saddened and angry that I had not included more positive references to the family, and to his contributions as a father. What struck him more, however, were my comments to Jim about how I had once perceived the shakiness of my parents' marriage, and how worried I had become at that point. I had also talked with Jim about my experience of anger in the family, and my fantasies of death, and my fear that people would die. My father was repulsed, disgusted, and angry that I would ever talk about my family experience in this way. Even in our family consultations with Jim, my sisters had talked about wanting my mother dead and, in fact, she then died. Angry and murderous fantasies, I believe, are a part of the texture of family life. They are more likely to lose their actual power when expressed, and more likely to grow monstrous when left hidden. In thinking about my family, I was reminded of what Carl Whitaker once said about surviving and community, and the necessity to have a place where we can "hate safely." I had to embrace and own completely all these ambiguous and unacceptable feelings for me to feel whole.

My father and I fought about my perceptions, and about what I said and did not say. But there seemed to be a new freedom in our conflict. I was less protective of him, more focused on my beliefs than on my worries, more attentive to his point of view, but not willing to accommodate to him because he was my father. I pushed back in protest: "Don't lift out this section of the tape from the whole tape. Don't make this section of the tape determine the whole context!" I wanted him to see the whole meeting in its entirety. I wanted him to see me in my wholeness, with all the mixed feelings together. As we argued back and forth, we did not necessarily use great communication skills. But we seemed healthier, more resilient, more respectful. There was more flexibility in our relationship and, in that sense, I had more of an experience of being a peer with my father.

Yet my relationship with him was not a relationship of peers and, in my mind, would never be. He would always be "father" to me, and I his "son." I experienced a distinct difference between two types of hierarchies. Before I had felt more distant, critical, angry, formal, and cut off emotionally from my father in what might be called a "hierarchy of power." Now there was more mutuality and respect between us within this father–son hierarchy in what might be called a "hierarchy of respect." There is no need to demolish the hierarchy to achieve authority. I felt my authority while holding onto the respect I wanted to acknowledge to my father as my father.

A consequence of this more mutual openness with my father was my effort to gossip less about him with my sisters. Instead of talking to my sisters about Dad (a habit that reinforces the hierarchy of power and intimidation), I found myself more ready to go to Dad, trusting both myself and him to stay connected within the conflict. The principle of speaking directly was also spreading to other family members. I noticed more one-on-one conversations.

One opportunity for deepening one-to-one relationships in the family came when Ann attended a conference near my home several weeks after the family consultations. Ann spent a good deal of time talking with me and Annie about her reactions to the family meetings. She said she had mixed feelings about the consultation. She sensed Dad, Lynn, and Katie were distancing from her more since the meetings. She asked the question with a sad expression: "What really has changed?" She continued, "Dad still hasn't come down to see me. He hasn't even called to ask me how I'm doing."

I could feel Ann's sadness and longing for Dad. I wanted to listen to her and also encourage her. "Ann," I said, "It seems to me that this family consultation is beginning—taking care of some unfinished business, helping us get clear, opening up opportunities. I think it's going to take a lot of ongoing work to make a real difference." What seemed ironic about this conversation is that we were talking about no change in the midst of change ourselves, crafting a different way of being with each other, embracing and talking about distress rather than pushing it away and pretending something different.

Ann was also concerned that Lynn had not talked with her in weeks since the consultation. Lynn also had lived with Katie during the previous summer, while she was on a school internship. The longstanding alliance between Ann and Lynn seemed to be shifting slightly. Ann, using her "understanding" response, acknowledged that Lynn probably was at a point in her life where her interests were shifting more toward school, career, and her boyfriend. We talked about Ann talking directly to Lynn about her current perceptions and feelings, although the experience we had in sharing our perceptions with each other was new enough. We were in "consultation," not in "gossip" with each other. My job now was to gently nudge her back toward direct conversation with Lynn while staying open to whatever she wanted to share with me in this moment. I was enjoying one of my sisters coming to me, and felt an opening toward an alliance with Ann, less of a "me–them" split within the siblings.

Ann took a great risk in our conversation as the discussion continued. She thought I had not really shared my feelings in the family consultation, and that I had remained distant. Now we were pressing the envelope of our relationship, and talking less about "them" and more about "us." This is the direction of intimacy. I acknowledged to her that I had built up distance all my life, and that I did feel somewhat constrained and tight during the family consultation, careful about what I said in the midst of taking risks in what I said. I told her I was trying to break through my more impersonal style, trying to weave in my feelings. Annie was there in that moment, and added, "He's that way everywhere . . . that's just him." Annie wanted more of me as well.

Ann told me that viewing the tape had helped Mark better understand our family, but he also had felt not liked. By whom? Who had said what in those meetings that led Mark to conclude that he was not liked? Ann couldn't provide any further details, and I knew that to ask questions without asking Mark would likely confuse me even more. I liked Mark, but I wondered whether he really knew I liked him. I had not talked with him directly about our relationship, and now wanted to follow up on at least connecting more with Mark. We ended our visit with each other, feeling more gratified that we had talked.

Lynn also called me about the family consultation; she was somewhat confused. She said, "I don't know. If we had been living together I would have felt differently. But we all live in different parts of the country, and rarely see each other; we build up emotion, and then leave." She talked about missing the deeper connections she had made with family members. Following a family pattern, she was particularly worried about how Dad was doing, and how he had been impacted by the family consultation. We always seemed to direct our sibling talks back to some concern about our father, as if we didn't want to neglect him and his distress as we had done with our mother. It seemed that we were giving our father more of this concern for his welfare and health. In any event, the challenge to have one-to-one talks with each other without bringing in Dad or anyone else was ever present.

In this conversation with Lynn, I began to think more seriously about a follow-up family consultation. I wanted to keep building momentum and was worried, in a similar way as Lynn, that the progress toward building emotional connections in our family would fade. I knew that I did not want to try to recreate the first family meeting, nor did I yearn for some continuing emotional intensity between all of us. I wanted to dig deeper, especially around the relationships between the siblings, because the first meeting had focused more on our parents. I did have some concern about all these worries about my father. Was I missing something? I didn't seem to be as concerned as my sisters. I wanted to examine these concerns at another meeting.

For now, I developed a habit of calling my father when I heard worries about him, saying to him, "Dad, I just heard from X that X is worried about you. And I'm confused as to why X is worried. Can you help me?" This question often would generate some laughter, some defense, a statement of surprise, perhaps some explanation—but overall a clear minimization of the worry. I decided to listen to my father's description and base my worry on whether he thought I should worry about anything. Even then, I might not worry. But I wanted to go directly to him for information, and inform him of the gossip within the family. I had some concern about how my sisters might respond to my going directly to my father. But I had a greater interest in promoting more direct conversations, my father's personal responsibility in speaking for himself, and my own health and wellness. I began to hear less about "father worries" from my sisters, although we continued to talk about our relationships. Still, there were enough rumblings in the family to warrant a family follow-up meeting.

CONSOLIDATIONS

As the months progressed, I was consolidating even more learnings from the previous family consultation. I was encouraged that these learnings were spreading to other parts of my life beyond my family of origin. Annie observed that I had been changing since the consultation. She saw me as more self-reflective and less reactive. She sensed in me a much deeper desire to connect with my family, and also with her and our children. I believed I always would struggle with this close connection with others; I was going counter to all that I had learned and the temperament that was deep within me. But now at least I was seeing openings toward intimacy, and was more mindful of taking initiative and risks in that direction. Intimacy was more of a struggle for me, rather than something I was not mindful of and didn't care about. Being conscious about the struggle was hopeful. Having had the experience of closeness in the family meetings provided a direction.

I was encouraged by Annie's observations. It seemed that the immediate wave of positive feelings that family members had experienced after the family consultation was dissipating. There were more comments around concerns, worry, confusion, even though there was a noticeable increase in risky disclosures and substantive conversations about relationships. Our family system seemed to be much more open and fluid while we continued to talk about our worries. Maybe we just had trouble having fun, and felt more authentic or responsible when we were worried about each other. I knew that if this family consultation were to continue to influence my own development I had to move back from wanting to have something different happen in my family. I needed to refocus my attention on my own personal learnings, and on building relationships between me and others in the family that were more open, direct, and deep.

In the months that followed, I noticed within myself a greater awareness of relationships in all aspects of my life—marriage, children, work, friendships. I seemed to have a greater consciousness for connection and disconnection, conflict, unfinished business. I seemed to be more alert to relationships that were not "clean," and seemed to be more deliberate and intentional about speaking my "truth" in those relationships. The family consultation had helped me build courage. If I could talk about all the untouchable topics in the family meeting, risking emotional death with the people I cared about, and still survive while building even greater intimacy, surely I could carry this courage into many other relationships. Impasses and snags with other people seemed less of a "big deal" once I had "passed the test" of the much "bigger deal": the family meetings. I also experienced having more of myself available in other relationships. It seemed I had freed up some emotional energy within myself. Less energy was spent on managing my emotional strife, anger, worries, unfinished business, sorrow with my family. More energy was available for my "now."

I was experiencing some change in Thomas's behavior as I talked with him and other family members. He seemed less agitated, less frantic, less paranoid about others in his group home for the mentally retarded. This news was heartening, and made me wonder about what I had studied—how the apparently bizarre or irrational behavior of one family member is closely tied to the ongoing life of the family system. If we in the family system (and Thomas was a full member of that system) were in the process of dealing with long-held secrets, cutoffs with each other, grievances and resentments, our family feelings of paranoia and intimidation (not just individual symptoms within Thomas), might this open conversation have something to do with the lessening of Thomas's distress and paranoia? Perhaps Thomas had the role in the family of holding all of our pathologies most dramatically. The rest of us struggled to "look good," polishing our public presentations and our private struggles with competency. With our historically massive efforts to do well in life, had the family unwittingly assigned Thomas to the role of the collector of our collective pathology? Now I was experiencing the converse; as we claimed our individual and collective pathologies with more responsibility and began to work them out with each other, was Thomas being freed? This was a stunning question for me, linking personal responsibility and family pathology.

I noticed other shifts in our family connectedness. Katie also began to call me more frequently about problems with her students, and asked me for my opinion. I felt wanted and valued by her. I wondered whether I desired and valued her opinions for anything going on in my life. It had always been difficult for me to ask for help, to express my neediness in some way. I was a model of painful self-sufficiency—looking not-needy externally while feeling deep desire for help internally. What did I need from Katie? I needed a relationship with her, and what was most apparent to me was the striving and distress of my internal world. More and more I began to express parts of this internal world with Katie, sometimes becoming more dramatic in my obsession with death. Sharing my episodic fantasies about dying with Katie unwittingly put Katie in a more competent role and put me in a more needy position where I needed some support and reassurance.

In one of our phone conversations, I moved toward her with my distress as I said, "Katie, there have been so many times recently I have felt like crying for absolutely no reason. I might be sitting at home, driving in the car, usually by myself, and I want to cry." Katie seemed surprised to hear "big brother" have little rational explanation for his feelings. She stated that she, too, had experienced moments like this in her life. She was happy to hear about this new self-emergence, and couldn't help making some jokes about my aging and loss of control.

But could Katie offer me more than reassurance and emotional support? Did I value her intellect, her wisdom, her professional competency, her creativity? We began to have some conversations about the book she was working on, and her associated entrepreneurial skills. This kind of conversation did move us more toward being collaborative peers. In the spring of that year, I asked Katie and her husband to be sponsors at the baptism of our new child, David. They agreed and flew out for the baptism. This was an important moment of connection for me, and an honoring of Katie.

My marriage was growing, and I was becoming a more active part of the growing. Annie had always taken the lead in attending to the quality of our relationship. I had sometimes been a willing participant and often a reluctant partner, burying myself in the work life outside the marriage. I clearly was not abandoning my passion for work; I believed I always would embrace work with passion and creativity. The shift was more in re-sorting priorities and becoming more mindful and attentive to my own emotional process and our relationship. Consciousness about Annie and the family was more central than peripheral. And our conversations took on more depth, more mutuality, more inquisitiveness about our life. I think maturing marriages have the quality of "co-researching," where the partners are more curious about their own individual lives, their life together, and their histories. This kind of curiosity was becoming more integrated into our conversations. We still experienced strife with one another in all of its colorful forms, such as criticism, judgment, unfairness, reactivity, and cutoff. This is the ongoing texture of marriage. But now we had additional resources, other dimensions we could access to build intimacy and to lessen the impact of strife.

PREPARATIONS FOR OUR FOLLOW-UP CONSULTATION

I began to develop plans for a follow-up family consultation. There was more to do, especially between us siblings. I also wondered about the possibility of expanding the system to include the spouses. There were other issues to address, such as our relationship to Linda as stepmother and her experience of being in the family. This was another "secret" that begged for exposure but had gone unmentioned in any family group conversation. I also wondered about Mark and Ann, Ann's continuing feelings of "distance" from the family, and Ann's sense about Mark not feeling liked in the family. I wanted to strengthen my alignment with Mark. I also wanted more closeness with my sisters and wanted to be less on the outside. I didn't know what I wanted from Thomas. I continued to feel disconnected from him, while also wanting him to be more included in the family. Perhaps this was the primary change for me and Thomas: I had a stronger intentionality about including him as a family member. I had the sense that we siblings in the family would go "easier" on my father if we were to meet. I did not really have anything primary that I needed to work on with him. But I sensed in conversations over the months with my siblings that they had been worried about Dad and wanted to shift their focus elsewhere.

Preparations were made to link a family consultation with a vacation. Bribes were still useful. We all planned to stay at the same hotel, mixing the vacation with the meeting. I offered to pay for the hotel expenses to make the trip more affordable for others, and to express some gratitude for what the family had given me. At this time, I also had the most money of all the family members, and felt some obligation to share this with the others. I was partly bothered by my role in providing money to the family. I had some fantasy about having parents who grew old, had money, and would bring their sons and daughters and their families together for reunions. My father had worked for the church, made little in his life, didn't think too much about investing, had little money to give us during his working years, and had even less to give us now. The roles seemed reversed to me as I gave to him and the family. What helped me to proceed with more graciousness was my belief that he had not squandered money or been irresponsible. He had worked "for peanuts," and worked for the church—a meagerly paying institution. I also had chosen a profession that helped me generate more income. I had been fortunate in my investments, and now I wanted to give back to the family. I also saw this as a good investment in building my own health and my family's health. I'd rather pay for the hotel than for doctor's bills.

I had been talking with Jim about the follow-up family. He was glad to help, and suggested that his wife, Dr. Felise Levine, join him as a co-consultant in the follow-up session. Jim and Felise had previous experience conducting together numerous family-of-origin sessions. I supported this co-consultation idea, believing that a female consultant might be able to forge a greater connection with my sisters and also might be more aware of Linda's experience. In a sense, Felise was coming in like a step-consultant, similar to Linda's role in the family system as a stepparent. I wanted Linda to feel supported.

The plan was to spend two hours with members of the original family, and to invite spouses in for the second two hours in the afternoon. I worked hard to get the proper audio and video equipment for the meeting. I wanted to preserve our experience for review and learning. And it wasn't just another family experience. How many times would we all come together for an extended period of time with a consultant to talk about our experience with each other? I believed that this experience might not ever happen again. It was monumental to me, like some of the major nodal events in family life: birth, marriage, death. I had to record this event.

As the time for the family meeting drew closer, crises began to surface, disappointing crises that both saddened and angered me. After all these preparations and building hopes, defections rolled in. First, I heard about Mark, who decided not to attend because of "work problems." I had wanted to build my connection with him especially; now he wasn't coming. I was sad, but also irritated. He always had had work problems. Would this ever change? Wasn't this event important enough for him?

Then Linda canceled her trip. She had an ovarian cyst, and needed treatment. Again, I felt more sad than angry. Medical problems seemed more excusable than work problems. But I also wondered how Linda's body might be "cooperating" with any emotional reluctance she may have had. Was she concerned about where the family conversation might lead were we to focus on her role in the family and our relationships with her? We had not talked about the agendas for the family meeting, but I'm sure she sensed what could be coming.

Another possible absence was reported. Katie called me one night and said that Steve might not be able to come. Katie wondered if the spousal sessions still would be held. I was angry, and told Katie, "I absolutely want the spousal session to continue. It would be unfair to Annie, and ultimately to all of us, if we canceled now. We planned it and it will happen!" My sympathy for her plight was low. This third defection was pushing my patience. I began to wonder whether inviting the spouses was a good idea anyway. Maybe all these happenings led to a message: Don't bring in the extended family. The one strange possibility that emerged in all of these conversations was the possibility that Lynn's boyfriend might attend the meeting! Katie called back a few days later and said that Steve now was able to attend. I was relieved; at least Annie wouldn't be alone.

We all arrived, and when I saw Ann at the hotel I realized that, with Linda absent from this meeting, Ann had had new opportunities to connect with my father in their long trip. Ann told me that they had driven many miles together and had talked extensively, deepening their relationship. She said she had never had this kind of openness before, which led her to feel more hopeful about my father and her relationship with other family members.

Other connections had been building. Lynn had been living with Katie and Steve during the summer, working on her internship in business. Ann had visited all of them during that time. These connections were evolving, sometimes more slowly than I had wanted. They were connections that did not come naturally or easily, but demanded intention and decision. Family life will evolve on its own. But the richness and depth of family life evolves only with mindfulness and decision. We were about to enter another one of those moments in family life when opportunities are ripe.

PART III

THE FOLLOW-UP FAMILY CONSULTATION

Chapter 10

THE FIRST
FOLLOW-UP
FAMILY MEETING
Assessing Change

JAMES L. FRAMO, PhD
FELISE B. LEVINE, PhD

The follow-up session was held a year after the first consultation. Tim, who had the onerous task of organizing the session and making travel and hotel arrangements for eight people, had suggested to his family members that they watch the videotapes of the first consultation before this meeting.

Ordinarily, when we organize family-of-origin sessions, the spouses of clients are not included, primarily because the paramount goal is the working out of issues with the parents and siblings, not with the spouse. Under the present circumstances, however, because this consultation was a follow-up session, we wanted to get feedback from the spouses. We were interested in hearing their perceptions of that first consultation as well as whether they had noticed any changes in the family over the last year. Furthermore, because spouses were to be included in part of the follow-up meeting, I invited Felise Levine, a psychologist-family therapist, as a cotherapist for this second consultation. My wife and I had previously conducted together numerous family-of-origin sessions. Similar to the first consultation, the second one was four hours long, divided into two two-hour segments, with a lunch break in between. In the first two hours we saw the family, and in the second two-hour segment two spouses of the adult children were included.

FRAMO: It's good to see you all again. I'd like you to meet Dr. Felise Levine, my wife. As you know, she will be joining us today as cotherapist. We have worked together previously, and she has watched the tapes of the previous session so she is familiar with this family. I want to thank you all for coming back. It must have been quite a logistical thing to get everybody here.

TIM: Oh yes!

FRAMO: I suppose all of you watched the tapes of the last session?

DAD: A few months ago, when we received the tape, Linda and I watched it until two-thirty in the morning.

KATIE: Lynn and I watched it the night before we came here.

FRAMO: And when did you see it, Ann?

ANN: Last December.

FRAMO: Thomas, did you get a chance to see it?

THOMAS: No, I didn't.

TIM: The other night Annie and I looked at the tapes for the first time. I really wasn't conscious of the fact, at the time, that the family would see this tape of my individual interview with you. I knew, and yet I didn't know.

FRAMO: You said some things in that first hour that did not come up in the family session at all.

TIM: I said some things that I should not have said. For me, it was an interesting process. I should have been aware of that.

ANN: You said a lot! I think your perception of us is totally wrong.

TIM: Of who?

KATIE: I don't know how you got there, but I thought you thought Lynn and I idolized you.

LEVINE: You mean he's not the family hero?

ANN: Not particularly.

LYNN: You said a lot of things, and Dr. Framo had never met us before. I think when we came in here Dr. Framo had one conception of what all of us were like.

(Framo: The preparation session held with the initiating person, before the family-of-origin comes in, has its own unique characteristics and consequences. The "prep" session is somewhat like an individual therapy session, where the individual relates his or her own perceptions and experiences without having to be immediately concerned about the effects of their views on other family members. *People are much more open and unguarded in "prep" sessions, and are usually embarrassed when they listen to the session later and realize how family members might react to it. When Tim did the "prep" session, telling the story of his family on videotape, he did not know whether his family would ever see the tape of that interview. In his words, "I knew, and yet didn't know." It is obvious here that some family members were offended by the way Tim described them. Tim had told us that Dad, in particular, was shocked at some of Tim's views of family members and events.*

I have used this dynamic process to motivate reluctant family members to come in for family-of-origin sessions. For example, when a client is not able to get his or her family to come in, I sometimes suggest that the family listen to the tape of the "prep" session. When the family members hear the story of the family, as seen through the client's eyes, they are persuaded to come in—if for no other reason than to correct the record. To be sure, some families, upon listening to the tape, become aware of the pain in the client's life and they come in because they want to help.)

(Levine: We are also very aware that these "prep" sessions reflect only one family member's perception so we are careful not to form conclusions about the family. In addition, the emphasis of the "prep" session is to help the client to organize and prepare an agenda, not to give a full family history.)

FRAMO: I was quite aware of the fact that this was from Tim's perspective only. I was, therefore, anxious to meet the entire family to see what they were really like. [turning to Tim] Tim, I remember that first hour, and Felise and I notice that you used the words "murder," "suicide," and "death" frequently. We've had some thoughts about that. This family has, indeed, had many losses, and not just Mom. You have had a lot of crises in this family, and you've had to struggle with quite a bit. I think these crises have something to do with your preoccupation with death: There was Thomas's retardation, Dad's brain tumor, Mom's cancer, Ann's diabetes, Mom's death. There was a whole series of medical crises in this family.

(Framo: I was too abrupt, here, when I shifted to Tim's preoccupation with death. I should have explored more the family members' resentment about how they were characterized by Tim. Tim's comment—that he said some things that he should not have said—suggests he felt disloyal because he had broken the family's rule about privacy. I noticed that Dad did not voice his objections to what Tim described in that first interview, but I knew that he had some strong negative feelings about it. I should have given the family members further opportunity to dispute or agree with Tim's perceptions.)

TIM: I feel we were walking time bombs, fearing what's going to go up next.

ANN: I don't think it's that bad when we compare ourselves to other families; some of them have had it worse. But the way that Tim describes it, he's afraid of what's going to happen to him, and being a psychologist I would think he wouldn't want to let those things out of his mouth.

TIM: Are you referring to my recent headaches?

ANN: Uh huh.

TIM: As I was telling you, I may have a brain tumor. I have had these headaches for the past three weeks. I did go in and there was a sinus infection that was discovered, and I've been on antibiotics.

FRAMO: And your fantasy was . . .

TIM: A brain tumor, brain cancer, or an aneurysm.

DAD: Preoccupation.

LYNN: Tim and I always talk like that, even though we've never had anything major.

TIM: I don't know what's going to happen.

LEVINE: So you two share that concern, like "Oh, is it going to happen to me?"

LYNN: Yeah. More so when I was younger, because what's going to happen is going to happen.

TIM: I remember once when Katie and I were talking, Katie said, "Nothing's happened to you." Remember when you said that to me? It was almost like saying, "Something *should* happen to you."

KATIE: [laughing] Remember when I said I was going to wear black to these sessions? I have a sense of humor that you don't relate to. I tend to say things in a sarcastic way, and you have to know how to deal with me. Jennifer looks at things the same way.

TIM: I have a sense of humor, too. I can be very sarcastic. I have a great sense of humor. But that comment about me not having anything wrong with me . . .

LYNN: I think we are all too sensitive.

FRAMO: I want to comment on two things before we go on. When you, Ann, said that he was a psychologist and should know better, no one is immune to personal problems whether he or she is a psychologist or psychiatrist. When you're dealing with your own personal stuff you are like anybody else.

ANN: I know, I know. Tim wouldn't be here otherwise.

FRAMO: Your psychology knowledge does not help you. The other thing I want to comment on is that although this family has been through a lot of crises, I have a sense of a strong feeling of family cohesion, and I have a sense of a lot of healthy features in this family.

LEVINE: A lot of strengths in this family.

(Levine: Cotherapists can differ or agree and amplify each other's comments. Here I amplify Jim's comment in order to counter the family's negative perceptions of themselves and their concern that we may have negative perceptions of them as well.)

FRAMO: You all still have a sense of humor, despite what you've been through. That's quite an accomplishment. Okay, now we can get back to this other stuff about Tim and Katie.

TIM: Anyway, Katie, as I was saying, I have felt somehow that I must have something physically wrong with me to identify with this family.

LYNN: You have to have something wrong with you to identify with our family?

TIM: I think I've come through pretty cleanly throughout life. Basically things are going along well in so many ways.

FRAMO: Do you sense that something awful has to happen?

TIM: I don't know. Actually, I've had these headaches, and I've been trying to figure out what's gone wrong with my head.

FRAMO: Have you been checked out?

TIM: I've been checked out. I sometimes feel like Woody Allen in "Hannah and Her Sisters." You know, how he ran from doctor to doctor.

ANN: He stresses real easy.

TIM: In my profession there's a lot of stress. I always thought that I could do anything as much as I want, and I'm beginning to think that's not true. I'm beginning to take a look at my limitations.

FRAMO: Tim, have you been in individual therapy at all?

TIM: No, I have not.

FRAMO: It might be something you might want to look into. [general laughter]

ANN: I think there's a little fear of it.

TIM: It might be something to look into. It might be a good idea to consult with someone.

FRAMO: Some of this catastrophic thinking may be family related. What we're doing now is a brief procedure, so you might want to go into your stuff more intensely in individual therapy.

TIM: I might do that.

FRAMO: Some of your preoccupation with death is related to what has happened in this family.

TIM: I can make a lot of jokes about death, but every time I leave my office my secretary and I carry on a little game about life insurance and airplane crashes. We really do talk about death a lot.

FRAMO: Does anyone else in your family share this worry?

DAD: I do not share this worry myself. When Tim's daughter, Stacy, was ill with nephritis about three months ago immediately he thought in terms of her death. Immediately he converts that to some death symbol. I suspect that some other members of the family might have some comment on that.

FRAMO: Does anyone else have any thoughts on Tim's preoccupation with death? Thomas, do you think about dying?

THOMAS: Yes. I'm afraid to die.

FRAMO: We all are. But do you think of it a lot?

THOMAS: I do a little bit.

LYNN: I think Tim is obsessed with it. When Mom died he brought out a tape recorder and we were all asked how we felt about it. Whenever he comes to visit he asks, "Do you ever think of Mom?" He's the one in the family who brings it up the most, and it scares me because two people I knew died in a span of three weeks. I think it's natural that when you get older you think of how you want to do all these things. You have all these plans, and you are looking forward to your career, your entire life, and you worry, "What if something should happen?" But with Tim, whenever we go to Mom's grave he asks us, "How do you feel about this?" and that's too much.

(*Levine: Tim's asking to discuss Mom's death may be an attempt not only to alleviate his catastrophe fears, but to emotionally engage the family through a shared experience.*)

TIM: Oh, it's not all that much. And we don't go too much to Mom's grave.

LYNN: But of all the children, you're the one that mentions Mom's death the most.

TIM: I do think about it. I feel a lot more fragile.

DAD: And insecure?

FRAMO: Do you think about it, Paul?

DAD: Death? I get myself occupied with life, and if death comes [pause] it comes. If it comes at thirty-five it comes at thirty-five. I think that's my attitude toward all of life. Life is a risky business, and having the religious faith that I have, and we have, there is nothing to fear.

(Framo: I noted the contrast between Tim's open expression of his fears and Dad's denial of any anxiety about death. Was Tim expressing Dad's fears for him? On the other hand, one could view Dad's attitude about death not as denial but as one based on his strong religious beliefs. It is curious that Tim regards himself as the most fragile one of the family.)

LEVINE: Ann, when did you get diabetes? How old were you?

ANN: Thirteen.

LEVINE: Has the family ever talked about that?

ANN: Dad does whenever I see him. Whenever I see Dad he asks me how I'm doing.

(Levine: I try to move from an intellectual discussion to one about the actual medical illness or problems in the family; I hope to give Ann an opportunity to talk more openly with her family about her diabetes. I also struggled with whether to disclose my own diabetes but felt I wanted to join the family in another way.)

FRAMO: You've never discussed your diabetes with the whole family?

ANN: Have we? I don't know whether it's been their concern.

TIM: Whenever I come across an article on diabetes I think of Ann and calling her on the phone.

FRAMO: Ann, do you wish that people would mention it more?

LEVINE: Or just act as if it's not there?

(Levine: We voice both sides of the conflict that patients with chronic diseases feel. On the one hand they want family members to understand and be involved in their care; on the other hand they want to be in charge of their own experience and keep family members distant. I know this conflict well.)

ANN: I don't know. I don't think I want people to feel sorry for me. Definitely not.

FRAMO: You read about what could happen to you?

ANN: Yes and no. Mainly I think of having children. I think that's where the main concern is, because being pregnant I couldn't work. In talking to my doctor, I would have to be monitoring myself so much that it would be a full-time job just being pregnant. That would take a lot of time and effort.

FRAMO: Katie, do you have any thoughts about her diabetes?

KATIE: Well, when she became diabetic I know she was very, very sick, and we drove straight to the hospital. She seems to be concerned about the kinds of foods and shots, about how things are going. But we don't really talk about it. Ann doesn't want to talk about it, so I don't want to bring it up.

ANN: It's not something that I really want to ignore, but I appreciate it when people like Tim read something and bring it to my attention.

FRAMO: How about you, Lynn? What are your thoughts about it?

LYNN: The only concern I have is when we go somewhere and Ann eats sweets. I always watch what she eats, and she doesn't know it.

LEVINE: Now she does! [laughter]

LYNN: When we went to Disneyland, I remember I coaxed her to have a piece of chocolate, but not a lot, so we shared it. I noticed that she went to the bag and ate the rest of it.

ANN: I had to have it. I didn't have enough to eat for lunch, as I told you.

LYNN: And then you had a chocolate banana, too.

ANN: Because I needed it.

LYNN: I'm always aware of what she eats. When we got out someplace, I'm aware of how much sugar she eats. She knows how much sugar she needs.

FRAMO: Ann, so you're quite aware of your food—what you need and what you do not need?

ANN: Uh huh.

FRAMO: How often do you worry about future complications?

(Framo: To be honest, this comment also reflected my personal concern about complications arising from Felise's diabetes.)

ANN: Um, I don't make a habit of thinking about it. As I say, it's a matter of having children. I think about it, but I'm not overly concerned about it.

FRAMO: What about your husband, Mark? What's Mark's attitude?

ANN: He does not know much about it, actually. He's the opposite. He's hypoglycemic. We know that each other's blood sugar is different levels, but he doesn't know much about diabetes.

LEVINE: Is that by your choice or his?

ANN: He's never asked. He's not here today, so we won't get to talk about it in this group.

(*Levine: The spouse's knowledge of a chronic illness is very important in managing the impact of the disease on the relationship. Over the years I have found that gender plays an important role; for example, wives almost always are informed about, and are actively involved in, the day-to-day care of their husband's illness, whereas husbands, unless there is a medical emergency, are less informed and less involved in their wife's daily care.*)

Ann was disappointed that her husband, Mark, would not be there for the afternoon session with the spouses, and at the same time she excused his absence by indicating that he was very busy with a project he was working on. Tim wondered whether Mark was avoiding coming to the session because both Ann and Mark felt outside this family. Ann mentioned that Mark was not Lutheran, and came from a different background, but stated that was not why he wasn't there.

TIM: What I'm concerned about . . . I don't want Ann and Mark to drift outside the family.

ANN: You don't have to worry about that.

TIM: What I'd be concerned about is that we be together at family reunions, or family meetings. I don't want Mark and Ann to feel they're only marginally a part of this family. I don't want that to happen, and I wanted to bring that up because sometimes I think that you feel you are only marginally a part of this family.

ANN: I was talking with Dad on the trip down here—and this might be only my perception of things—but being close and having family ties and stuff like that is important. You know Lynn and Mark get along famously. They hit it off very well. We went skiing during March, and he came along and felt part of the family. Wouldn't you say so, Lynn? [Lynn nods yes]

LEVINE: When I watched the tapes of the last session, it seemed like you felt you were an outsider and you felt different because you chose a different religious affiliation.

ANN: I think that, because of their concern about my church, there is a problem. That's what has put up a mental block between us. It's in their thinking, not mine. I made it a point last year while Lynn was in school to write, call, and send packages. Because of how busy she was, responses did not come. Because of relationships we've had in the past, I made it a point to keep that going because it's so important that families keep close.

(Framo: Ann is in a dilemma here, arising out of a loyalty conflict. She has made a religious choice that does not conform to the family tradition. At the same time, she longs for family acceptance, and more family "togetherness." Here, I neglect to pursue my inner speculation that Ann's experiences around her mother's death were related to her singular religious choice, as well as her yearning to be back in the family.)

LEVINE: So you've been initiating more?

FRAMO: Do you feel more connected with the family since last year?

ANN: I think the results aren't there, but the effort is there.

LEVINE: How about with Katie?

ANN: In a sense, not so much contact. It's not that I don't want to, because I really do, but because of how busy our families are and stuff in our individual lives. Things get so complicated. Then nothing happens until we get together, like this, and even this is not as natural as it could be. What we did yesterday was fun because the family was together. I wish we could do that more, like at Christmas. With Mark's family it's just the opposite because his family is in the same city, and when we go up there it's like a family reunion. We visit his family, there's a cohesiveness there that's not even vocal, it's in the manner they react with each other. That's something this family could do. I see it as an example—how it *can* work—but it's so difficult to bring it about.

(Levine: Ann acknowledges that Mark has the kind of family she wished she had, saying in effect, "If I can't be born into it, I'll marry the family I want and need." This is not an unusual marital contract.)

DAD: And we're so far apart geographically.

ANN: That has something to do with it.

FRAMO: It's true. A lot of American families are geographically separated. Your dad said that the two of you drove down from Oregon.

ANN: Right.

FRAMO: Did that give you the opportunity to get to know each other?

ANN: I don't know whether the word "know" is the word to use, because I've always known my dad and that's not a problem.

DAD: Yes.

FRAMO: What was the occasion for the trip?

TIM: We went to the reunion of my mother's side of the family in Pennsylvania; so we traveled from Chicago to Pennsylvania, and we had a lot of time to talk.

(Framo: One of the frequent consequences of family-of-origin consultations is that the family members often develop improved relationships with other family members who were not present in the session. For example, the adult children from time to time report a better relationship with their spouses even though the spouses were never seen. I call this "marital therapy by proxy." Or, a parent decides to reconnect with a cut-off sibling. I call these the "spreading effects" of family-of-origin consultations. In this case, I felt that the impetus for the trip Dad, Tim, and Thomas took to visit Mom's family on the East Coast was an example of this sort of indirect growth of the family consultation.)

FRAMO: Thomas, you were present?

THOMAS: Uh huh.

TIM: Yes, I think it was really a good trip. And when you, Ann, said that you just came down with Dad, I think that's a marvelous opportunity.

ANN: We did get to talk.

DAD: Ann unveiled her past, I don't know what you call it, late blooming. I don't think it's unnatural for a person going through those times of mental and emotional changes. She felt that she had finally found herself as an individual person.

ANN: I don't know when that issue was brought up.

DAD: Remember, when you mentioned you felt more natural or at ease with yourself, more harmonious with your own inner feelings, and more harmonious with the people around you. At one time you were reluctant to expose your feelings or vent them because you were confused over what to say, confused inside.

ANN: Uh huh.

DAD: So we talked about things like that.

(Framo: I wondered whether this personal conversation between Ann and Dad could have taken place prior to the previous family session. It seemed to be a departure from their usual pattern of avoiding openness. I also felt that Dad really "heard" what Ann was trying to say. I noted, too, that Dad's style of communication had become much clearer since the earlier sessions.)

FRAMO: Paul, what were your reactions to the sessions we had last year?

DAD: I think, generally favorable. I didn't know how the girls felt, and their reactions to their mother. I always thought it was a more harmonious relationship than what they felt. I felt at times they might have overreacted—at least from my perspective. I understand where they were coming from.

(Framo: I puzzled over how Dad could have been so unaware of the effects of his wife's erratic behavior on his daughters. Why didn't the daughters go to him for help? Did Dad handle things by avoidance? These are questions I should have asked in the very first session, when the focus was on Mom.)

FRAMO: During the last half of our previous session Mom wasn't mentioned. I got the feeling they were looking for more closeness with you, and I sort of made the prediction, at the time, that you would be calling them more often. Did it happen?

DAD: Let's see, how shall one put it . . . I think I mentioned first of all, yes, they called more often.

(Framo: I had asked Dad whether he called, and he turned it around to say they [the children] called more often.)

FRAMO: It wasn't a question of making more phone calls.

DAD: It was a matter of dollars.

LEVINE: It was a question of touching each other.

(Levine: I was trying to shift Dad's thinking to the intimacy issue.)

FRAMO: When you did call, instead of going through a list of topics you were first of all to ask them how they were getting along.

(Framo: I felt a little uncomfortable here, because I was sounding like a teacher rebuking a student.)

DAD: That's what I've done; I've done it very methodically. Instead, now I say, "Now, be sure to ask them how they are," "Be sure to ask how they are before you go into your list."

FRAMO: [turning to the family] How about Dad's calls? Were they any different? Lynn, you're shaking your head no.

LEVINE: Lynn, have things been changing in the past year?

LYNN: I guess, from watching last year's tape, I'm much more quiet this year. But I think bringing us together is really a neat idea. What's changed for me is that I'm more involved with people at school, and the person I'm going out with. I notice how close families are, especially in the Midwest where they make a point of doing things together. They get together for birthdays, family reunions, and they make big productions of these events, and I think that's wonderful. Also, I lived with Katie this summer.

(Levine: Lynn sounds like she has some regrets about being so open in last year's session.)

FRAMO: You did?

LYNN: Yes. I lived with her for three months, and we talked about the family—not in a negative sense. We shared our perceptions of people and what we thought. We became very, very close. I think that we saw ourselves as kind of distanced, but when we came together, like this summer, I think that we can be close. When Dad would call, I remember Ann's comment that, "The efforts were there, but the results were not."

FRAMO: I think Dad said that he is making an effort.

LYNN: I haven't seen Dad since February. Now we've got these couple days together in July, then I have to go back to school and I won't see him again until December. It's really hard for me not to be his little girl any more, and I told him that. I always have to ask him, "Aren't you going to ask me how I'm doing?" I have to tell him about my job or school before he asks. When he does ask how am I doing . . . I don't think that this family will ever change. We've been in this pattern for so long.

TIM: What pattern?

LYNN: I think we ask, "How're you doing?" but it's like we have to, not like we want to. But the one person who asks about my life is Annie.

TIM: That's wrong because I ask you how you are doing, and how is
         William. I don't think that it's something I have to do, because I
         really want to know.

LYNN: Then my perception is probably wrong.

LEVINE: Sounds like you're feeling a little discouraged.

LYNN: Well, yeah. [tearfully]

*(Levine: The effects of family-of-origin consultations vary across time. Some-
times the short-term effect is relief and elation followed by disappointment when
raised hopes were not met. I think Lynn is also feeling the natural disappointment and loss that comes with adolescent de-idealization of parents and family.)*

FRAMO: Something is bothering you. Let's hear what's bothering you. [as
         Lynn continues to cry] You want more closeness with the family.
         You feel that the family is not close enough yet, and you feel that
         people are not showing enough personal concern for each other,
         that things won't change; is that what it's all about?

LYNN: [nodding agreement] I was just thinking, if we hadn't come down
         for this session, I would not have gotten to see Dad before I went
         back to school.

FRAMO: So there has to be a functional reason, there has to be a purpose
         in getting together.

LYNN: Yes. Everything has to be business. We go out to dinner, but it's
         never spontaneous like, "I really miss you. Let's come down and
         see each other." Living with Katie this summer was the best thing
         that happened to me. She cared for me, personally, when I needed
         someone to talk to, and needed one hundred percent attention.
         People just assume that I'm okay, and that because I just turned
         twenty I can do everything on my own. That's not true. But maybe
         being the youngest that's how it is. Even though I'm a big girl
         and have this career and these big ideas, I still need a lot of caring
         and cuddling.

FRAMO: I hear you.

*(Framo: I had long ago acquired Bowen's understated way of being em-
pathic.)*

LEVINE: You got that from Katie this summer: She was not only your big
         sister, she was like a mom.

LYNN: Yes. [smiling appreciatively at Katie]

FRAMO: Katie, what are your thoughts about what Lynn is saying?

KATIE: We had a great summer. It was great to be with her. Tim and I have gotten together for vacations for the past two or three years— not because of an obligation, but because we thought it was fun. Dad visited us, and Thomas and I talked about his coming down. Ann is the one who has not had a lot of time with us. We don't get to her city, and Ann can't come to us. Also, we have obligations to my husband's family, and there are a lot of people involved in that. We're at the point where our house is like a vacation motel.

FRAMO: Last session you said you didn't get enough recognition in this family. You said you weren't getting recognized as a person. Now, this year, Lynn's talking that way and you're not. Do you feel differently now than you did in our last meeting?

KATIE: Well, I understand, now, where Dad is coming from, and I understand his perspective. Tim's interview alone—that I heard on the tape—was his perspective of the family, and I couldn't believe it. His perspective of the family was different from how I viewed it.

FRAMO: If I would have interviewed you an hour beforehand, you would have told a different story than Tim?

KATIE: Yes. In sessions, we found out where people were coming from, so I can understand Tim maybe a little bit more, as well as Dad and Ann.

FRAMO: But you don't seem to be as troubled as you were last year.

DAD: You had a couple of works published last year. How many were there? Six?

LEVINE: And now you've become a successful author.

(Levine: I want to model acknowledgment of Katie's accomplishments because, in this family praise is difficult to express.)

DAD: Yes.

KATIE: I have a different perception than what I had in our last session.

FRAMO: Of your family members?

KATIE: Yes.

TIM: How do you see me now, Katie?

KATIE: See you?

DAD: As a tyrant?

TIM: You keep things secret. I think there should be some secrets, but
           I think that I'm gossiped about instead of being told things di-
           rectly. One reason why you think I don't share a lot of myself is
           that you block me out. I think that you put me into a corner. I
           think that all three of you females do that. Lynn was to come to
           our place last Thanksgiving, and we made all these plans, but
           they didn't come off. Katie has never come to our house during
           the four years we've been in another city.

*(Framo: In the previous sessions Tim's sisters perceived him as having a
privileged position in the family, and as not being needful like them. What is
being revealed here is Tim's loneliness and sense of isolation from the rest of the
family—probably a factor in motivating him to request the family-of-origin consultation, and follow up.)*

LYNN: The reason I didn't come was because of money.

TIM: It's always some reason—money or schedules.

FRAMO: You'd like them to visit more?

TIM: Oh, yes. I really appreciate Ann coming. Yeah, money gets in the
           way of a lot. Katie and Steve have never been to our house in four
           years.

KATIE: You've been at our house three or four times.

TIM: That's right—that's the reason we keep coming. We will do that.

KATIE: But your family travels more than any other people in the world,
           more than any I know of.

TIM: But you've never been to our house. Lynn, we made those plans
           for Thanksgiving and they didn't come off. That pissed me off. I
           want to make a point here. I feel, at times, that I'm being ganged
           up on. I feel like there's talk between you all that I'm excluded
           from.

FRAMO: I don't think you mean that you're being ganged up on, but I
           think you mean that you're being rejected.

TIM: I haven't thought about that, but maybe I do feel rejected.

LEVINE: What do you think they're saying about you?

TIM: I think they're saying various things about me like I'm distant,
           that I'm not interested in them, that I'm such a big ass, that I
           don't care about them. I feel put down a lot.

*(Levine: Tim feels like an outsider in the triangle of himself–Katie–Lynn,
which is similar to Ann's experience. In fact, Tim feels like an outsider in all of
the triangles in the family. He also is concerned that as the alliance between*

Katie and Lynn strengthens they will continue to scapegoat him. Keeping Tim in the outsider position also strengthens the dyad between Katie and Lynn.)

KATIE: I'm hesitant to talk to you because you said, in the last session, that every comment I make to you is a put-down. [sisters laugh]

TIM: And I don't think it's a joke. One thing I need from you is to tell me what you are thinking and feeling about me.

LEVINE: You're wanting them to be direct?

TIM: To be direct with me. I can deal a lot better with that.

FRAMO: Are you both agreeable to that? If there's something about Tim you don't like you will tell him?

TIM: I'd like to know whether this gossip is going on because I feel it. You know, I don't know where it's coming from.

LEVINE: Is Tim accurate? Can we get some reality testing here?

KATIE: Well, Lynn and I, we talk about everybody.

LYNN: Well, you know what I think it is most of all is that Katie and I have the same sense of humor. We really do.

FRAMO: What kind of sense of humor?

DAD: The same sense.

LYNN: The sarcastic sense. The way we deal with things. We don't talk about Tim like, "What a brat. He's such a big jerk." It's not that way at all.

KATIE: I'll tell you one thing that came up about you between us this summer. You want to hear it?

TIM: Yes.

KATIE: When you called this summer did you ever say, "Let me talk to Lynn while I have you on the phone"? Did you ever take a personal interest that she was visiting? Did you ever ask about all these crises in our family this summer? Have you asked about them?

TIM: Yes, on the phone.

KATIE: You want us to be personal and talk to you, and you're not doing the same thing. You want us to treat you differently, and yet you're not acting any differently.

(Framo: As the siblings squabble over who is neglecting whom, and who is being most deprived, long-buried feelings are being revealed.)

(Levine: I am also struck by the openness and directness in their communication. I think this is progress.)

TIM: I think I am. I think I made a heck of a lot of effort to get this thing going, and it's not just because of my professional intent. I did a lot of work, and I don't think that you realize how much work it took to put this thing together. It's like arranging for a national conference. I sent letters out to you all; I don't know whether you got them; I don't get any feedback. I have to keep calling; I have to keep it going. I'm calling a lot, and it's not only around this family meeting, but I sometimes call to ask how things are going.

(Framo: Tim feels unappreciated for all his efforts to organize the family meetings. He not only wanted something for himself from the sessions, but, from his perspective, he was giving his family a gift. I wondered whether the family members had the unexpressed belief that one of Tim's motives in arranging the meetings was to advance himself professionally.)

LEVINE: Thomas has been trying to say something. [general laughter]

THOMAS: Next time, I want to see Tim in April, and I want to see him a lot. I want to see Katie. And I call Dad once a month, and he gets after me. Lynn doesn't call me, but I call her. I wish she would call me.

LEVINE: So you are also feeling that you want somebody else to call you besides Dad.

THOMAS: Yes. Lynn doesn't call me; I call her. I wish she would call me. Her and I are far apart. I call Lynn, but Lynn doesn't call me.

FRAMO: Lynn doesn't call you? Listen folks, Thomas has taken his position here. The sense I'm getting from this is that it shifts around from one to the other. Ann felt at one point that she was not getting enough closeness with the family. Katie was saying it, Tim was saying it, Lynn is saying it, Thomas is saying it; you're all saying it. You're not getting enough from each other. What's going on? What's behind all of that? Paul, you're the head of the household. Your kids are saying they all want more from each other, and they want more from you. Are they being oversensitive?

DAD: Obviously. Oversensitive to certain things. The second thing is that, when they are separated so far apart, they obviously aren't going to see each other as much as they would like. Another is the fact of dollars.

FRAMO: Yes, it's expensive to visit each other.

DAD: When you incur $250 per month in long distance calls that's no small amount. Therefore we can't call as often as we would like, and we have to measure our calls.

FRAMO: I can see that all those are realistic factors. But I have a sense there's something else, and I'm not too sure what it is. I'm wondering whether what's happening here is a reverberation of the loss of Mom.

TIM: It's a part, but I have an idea it's more than that.

KATIE: Tim, your family is doing this partly because you set it up, but I'm doing it for you. So if you want to talk about personal relationships [tearfully] I'm doing it for you.

TIM: I appreciate that.

KATIE: [tearfully] And my family is coming here for you. We didn't come to your home this year; we came here and this is our only vacation. You're asking us to be personal and close to you. We're doing it. We're trying.

(Levine: Again, we hear the shared longing for appreciation.)

TIM: I know, I know.

FRAMO: Why is there so much hunger here? I call it a kind of hunger. I guess I'm looking for some kind of common denominator that helps explain what's going on, and the only thing I could come up with is the loss of Mom—what it has done to this family. Tim, do you have a different hypothesis?

TIM: If I remember the family history, it's a series of crises.

FRAMO: That's true.

TIM: One after another.

FRAMO: It took its toll?

TIM: I survived by being busy. I can remember that I just stayed away from home, that was the only way I could make it. Now, I need people to be more direct with me to help me get out of it, so I can be more present with them.

FRAMO: What were you isolating yourself from?

TIM: I was always wondering what's going to happen next. If it wasn't some medical crisis it was some social crisis, like we talked about last session. You know, Thomas, when you had your flare-ups, you would become angry. I know it's hard for you to help that, Thomas, but it could happen any time.

FRAMO: You mentioned arguments between Mom and Dad. Were they unsettling to you?

TIM: Well, it could be like anything, a whole assortment of crises, year after year after year. It just kept going, anytime, anything could happen, and I'm just tired of trying to hold it together.

(Framo: I took the cue from Tim that he'd rather not, at this time, discuss the marital relationship of his parents.)

FRAMO: Was it your responsibility to hold this family together?

TIM: I think I checked out doing that a long time ago. The way I made it, I just stayed away from home. Being the oldest, I was the first one to leave home, so I had other connections. But I think I've learned to survive by basically shutting myself out. I think I don't trust that when you really sit down with something, that something bad isn't going to happen. I know I've stuck myself into this corner, but I need you all to be more direct with me because I think that people are gossiping about me and putting me down. I feel that way a lot. It's not only with this family, sometimes it's with the work group; I feel really apart from them, too. So I'm working on this with other groups.

(Framo: Some of Tim's statements had a paranoid tinge, which I did not think was pathological in nature. Indeed, the women in his family did talk about him, although more benignly than he thought. Because I was uncertain about the deeper meaning behind his feelings, I turned to someone else.)

FRAMO: Ann, what are your thoughts about what he is saying?

ANN: Well, not so much about what he's saying. There are two questions I've been thinking about all this time. One is that, as I was telling Dad, I think we all know there is something specific in each one of us that needs to be changed. For me, I had to make a mental decision, and I had to say to myself that this area needs to be corrected in my life. For instance, when I was small, and I agree with Tim, because of all the stress, everything was locked up.

FRAMO: Shut down?

ANN: Yes. Just terribly. After I was married I realized that I couldn't do that anymore. It was hurting me, it was hurting those I cared about very much, because I was not acting in accordance with the way I was feeling. I was so confused about the way you were supposed to act. The way you act at home would not come out the right way, and then you are in trouble. If I didn't act at all that was the most comfortable position. So as I grew older I realized what I was doing. I had to come to grips with what I was doing and make a change. I don't know whether anyone else has gone through that same feeling. I don't know if it was a crisis or not. I knew that something had to get changed or whatever. I was not able to pinpoint the reasoning.

FRAMO: What did the last family meeting do for you?

ANN: Um, I think the change started before then. But last year's session made me realize what I was doing. You know, it was part of me to change. And also, our last session made me realize that all of us are in the same boat, more of a self-examination.

FRAMO: You're all struggling.

ANN: Uh huh. We were always trained to think intellectually, but when it came to emotions and reaching out and being able to communicate on that level it was always negative. So when the emotions come out now we all close up. There's no way of communicating.

FRAMO: Except when we get into this kind of situation the emotions come out.

ANN: That's right; and it's so difficult, and at the same time it's so touchy. When they come out they come a little bit, and when they go too far everybody pulls in.

LEVINE: You seem to indicate this is because of the loss of Mom, Jim. I have a little different thought: it's associated with the meaning of Mom, and not necessarily only with her loss. There seems to be a good guy–bad guy split in the family: Dad was idolized and Mom was seen as the bad one. Mom was the one who lost her temper, she was unpredictable, she seemed to be in and out of crisis; and Dad was looked up to as sort of a stabilizer. So intense emotions got associated with a bad, out of control Mom. It is scary for people to have strong feelings; they worry, "When I lose my temper am I losing it like Mom?"

(*Levine: Through much of the session I felt like an outsider to Jim's relationship with the family because I was not present in the first family-of-origin consultation. I wanted to make an impact, and my overly wordy interpretation reflected my competitive struggle with Jim. During our work as cotherapists, we have each felt competitive on occasion. I think competitive and envious feelings are normal parts of family life, and are to be expected in the cotherapy team. I also believe that my struggle to feel important in this family was an instance of projective identification, in that competition, envy, and need for admiration are core conflicts in this family.*)

FRAMO: So then, it's safer to be like Dad, and you stay with the thoughts instead of the feelings.

LEVINE: Yes. It's a heck of a lot safer like that. To be like Mom is to express strong feelings, some of which are unpredictable.

(Levine: I was so glad that Jim simplified my words.)
(Framo: Here is an instance of cotherapists having a dialogue about the family in the presence of the family. Different interpretations can be expressed by the cotherapists, which can often give rise to new insights.)

DAD: Ann, you had a pretty realistic evaluation of Mom when we were coming out here.

ANN: I was telling Dad that I identified with Mom a lot, but I don't know why.

FRAMO: Who is most like her?

ANN: I don't know.

LEVINE: Who looks most like Mom, Paul?

DAD: Katie is beginning to have her nose. If you had my nose you couldn't see your eyes.

FRAMO: Go on, Ann.

ANN: I realize it now, but not while growing up, that when Mom would go through a crisis I knew it. I knew it even before she would, or before she showed it. And there would be times—I don't know whether anybody else had it either—when we would talk without words. I've never done it with anybody else except my husband. Not even words being exchanged. How deep.

FRAMO: It's like you were in communication with each other.

ANN: Yes. As I was growing up and realizing things that were going on inside of me . . . It wasn't a feeling that I was becoming like Mom, but I could feel the tendency of it. I don't think she was able to stop it. And, like I said before, I made a mental decision as to what was going on.

FRAMO: Do you mind if I ask you something? In the last session you mentioned that you wanted to kill yourself.

ANN: Right.

FRAMO: By stopping to take your insulin. Was that after Mom died, or was that before?

ANN: Before.

FRAMO: Do you have some sense as to why you wanted to die?

ANN: Well, it was because of all the confusion. I was not able to be in touch with what was going on inside because of everything else that was going on. It was after Mom died, you know, and me growing up and seeing myself the way that I was growing up and what Mom was doing.

FRAMO: So you describe making a decision that was a real turning point.

ANN: It was, it was. It was a struggle to do it.

FRAMO: Is that when you moved to the other religion?

ANN: I think I became more aware of it in my new church. People in that church were very concerned about what was going on physically and spiritually—how you're doing in your relationship with people and with God. At that point, I came to the realization that something had to happen. I was looking at myself and knowing where I had come from, all of a sudden seeing myself and to where my mom was going, too. I was seeing the parallel between us. It was a difficult decision because I felt pulled in her direction, and I was saying no. I was realizing where I could have gone.

(Framo: Ann's fusion with Mom must have been so frightening that she knew she had to establish a separate sense of self. I am reminded of Greenson's [1954] classic paper, "The Struggle Against Identification.")

FRAMO: I'm wondering, when your mother died, whether you thought you needed to die, too.

ANN: No, no. It was before that.

FRAMO: Okay.

DAD: I think I was referring to the evaluation of instead of a negative feeling. Some positive strokes came through for you since that time, in respect to mother.

FRAMO: I don't know what you mean, Paul.

DAD: She was evaluating mother in a rather negative way. Elizabeth did things in a positive way rather than the negative way, which largely came through in the last session.

FRAMO: I heard both. Mom could be real caring, be a real mom and do things like a mom is really supposed to do.

(Levine: It seemed that each family member had an agenda for this session. Dad's was to rebalance the impression that Elizabeth was a bad mother. Jim is trying to help Dad hold both images of his wife and to tolerate the natural ambivalence toward her.)

DAD: I think Ann's perception of the situation is . . .

ANN: It is not like I'm doing that to shut it out; but it's like I was telling
        Dad, when I get in an argument with my husband he may bring
        it up, and I'll say a week later, "I don't remember doing that." It's
        not because I'm trying to block it out, but because it's not that
        important. The things that are good and lasting are the things I
        hang on to, and that's the same thing with Mom—when she died.
        When you're young you don't relate in those kinds of words, so
        that when growing up I had to basically evaluate my childhood
        to see how it all fit together. And then, in that instance, I remem-
        ber the good things and not the bad.

        *(Framo: Although it still was not clear what Ann's decision was, her an-
        guish over trying to reconcile the two sides of Mom was clear. She expends great
        effort to block out negative feelings about Mom. When Dad focuses on the
        positive aspects of Mom, Ann fragments somewhat and pulls back.)*
        *(Levine: I wish we had explored Ann's past suicidal thoughts. In the initial
        family-of-origin consultation, Jim worked on Ann's struggle against identifica-
        tion with her mother. I think this theme needs more intensive work.)*

FRAMO: You know, one of the things I wanted to comment on is that
        when I ask someone to speak I ask them directly. But I want you
        to know that you can interrupt each other, and you don't have to
        talk in turn. It's alright for you guys to talk to each other—this
        isn't a classroom.

THOMAS: I have something to say. I care about my brother a lot.

FRAMO: I figured that. You've been rehearsing some of the things you
        wanted to say today?

THOMAS: Yes. I just care about my brother.

TIM: Thomas, you said last night that you wanted me and Katie to call
        you more.

FRAMO: Katie has not had the opportunity to express herself.

KATIE: Thomas, I'm going to call you. I'm going to call you more.

DAD: Yes, I think it should be said that, of all the members of the fam-
        ily, Katie and Thomas get along the best.

KATIE: Adults in our family are not really affectionate. Lynn was talking
        about that, too. You tend to feel things on the surface level rather
        than emotionally, because it's easier that way. Except with my
        own family—my husband and daughter are really important to
        me. [tearfully]

FRAMO: Sure.

LEVINE: What do you think makes it so hard in this family to express emotions?

KATIE: With me, it's not really hard with my sisters. I don't feel that it is. It used to be less hard with Ann, but Ann has become more difficult.

ANN: Can I tell why?

KATIE: Not yet.

ANN: I think this was brought up in the last session . . . The distance that has come about, and it was not due to a change of religion. It's a step beyond where everyone else is. That's where the barrier is, especially between you and me. When you said I found a new family when I stopped going to the Lutheran church it was a misconception. I put a new barrier up because what you perceived was totally untrue. You made an assumption and went from there. I didn't want to be around because I think it was just the opposite. Realizing how important God is, my family becomes even more important!

LEVINE: So you have not replaced this family.

ANN: [emphatically] No!

(*Framo: Following Ann's emphatic statement that she is still very much in this family, Katie returns to a matter which has been bothering her.*)

KATIE: . . . it was brought up in the last session. Tim, I don't feel in competition with you. I just feel that you don't want to be around, and I thought it was because you didn't like us. You were gone and I had relationships with Ann and Lynn, and I never had it with you. All of a sudden you want intimacies that we sisters have had, and it's difficult. First of all, you're a male, and secondly you weren't there. It's difficult.

TIM: I know it's difficult. I'm trying to do something about it. I don't have many friends—male or female. I've felt very isolated.

LYNN: I think I'm hearing you say some things for the first time. When Dad was dean of the university, he seemed to have it all together. You know, he had all the friends and we went to all those parties together. [turning to Dad] But when you retired you felt all alone. I never felt Dad was ever all alone. I felt almost like being his mother, because when we're on the phone I worry so much about him because I want him to be happy. [speaking through tears]

DAD: You made me happy when you bought me those golf clubs.

LYNN: I worry about him because I see him as a human being because
          he's hurt. [looking to Tim] And now, for the first time, Tim, I'm
          seeing you as a human being. But I think that I'm different from
          everybody else here because I don't deal with things on the intel-
          lectual level. At school I'm very emotional, a "touchy-feely" per-
          son, and the only person I get that from is Ann. I can cry one
          minute, and I'm of extremes. I'm not a calm intellectual. So now
          I'm seeing you as a human being. [pointing to Tim] I'm not as
          intellectual. I'm not that person who reads a hundred books a
          summer and sits there and talks about his practice.

FRAMO: So you're hearing a different Tim? About his neediness?

LYNN: Right.

KATIE: We're all trying to get closer. [addressing Tim] We're all trying, in
          our own way, little by little I think—like us coming here. Our
          coming here was hard to organize. Like Mother said, "If anybody
          knew how hard it was to have all this company . . . " Maybe you're
          seeing what it's like; it is difficult.

TIM: And I appreciate your coming here.

FRAMO: I'd like to ask a question. What has happened in this last year
          since I saw you all? Have there been any changes? What has
          changed? What has not changed?

*(Framo: I was not tracking well here, because in the last few minutes some
changes in the family had been clearly demonstrated. There was a breakthrough
when Lynn said to Tim, "I'm seeing you as a human being now." And Katie,
perhaps disarmed by Tim's self-disclosures, was more open to closing the distance between them. Family-of-origin sessions create the context for family
members to develop different, more real, and compassionate views of each other.)*

*(Levine: Despite Jim's more factual questions, the family continues to talk
openly, taking emotional risks with one another.*

THOMAS: I call Tim and Katie a lot, and I appreciate Tim, and he asks me
          how I'm doing.

FRAMO: Okay.

THOMAS: And I talk to him.

FRAMO: Has there been less or more contact with each other, or the same
          contact?

LYNN: About the same.

ANN: [tearfully] I think that has a lot to do with perception. I have
          made a lot of effort, and it takes time; so I say to myself I need to

concentrate on what I think is really important . . . [Ann struggles to speak but, because of her tears, she cannot and gestures with her hands]

FRAMO: Go ahead, Ann. What are you trying to say?

ANN: I'm trying . . . Because of Lynn being in school, I thought that it was important to contact her. I thought she needed help. I didn't get the response back. If you are trying to make a change and nobody says that you're doing something right or doing something wrong you stop. If it doesn't make a difference, why do it?

LYNN: [looking at Ann] And then I sent you a response.

ANN: But after how many tries?

LYNN: I do wrap myself up in so many things, and I do forget; and I'm so busy at school and moving to another state and all that kind of stuff that I do forget.

ANN: Right, right.

FRAMO: One of the things you've been trying to say is that people have been making the effort, but there haven't been many results.

LEVINE: Ann's saying she's made a conscious effort.

ANN: If you're doing something you hope people would notice it.

LEVINE: You need a little more acknowledgment from people that you've been really trying to turn things around?

ANN: Not so much the acknowledgment, but . . .

LEVINE: Feedback?

ANN: Yes, feedback. Not only for me, but for everybody. I wanted to give her that extra special lift. Lynn was motherless. When I was going to college I didn't get it either.

(Framo: Apparently, the void of the loss of Mom impelled the females to mother each other at times. Presumably, Tim was perceived as being able to take care of himself.)

FRAMO: Yes, yes.

ANN: Regardless of whether she responds or not, I'm going to keep on doing it. I did it for a while, but I don't get any feedback.

FRAMO: It's hard to be a mother when you don't get feedback.

ANN: It's hard being a father without any feedback, too.

FRAMO: That's true. Paul, Tim mentioned that you started getting interested in your own family as a result of our last meeting.

While Dad claimed he had little or no memory of the trip that he, Thomas, and Tim took following the first consultation, Tim elaborated on what happened on that trip across the country. He said they talked to members of Mom's family, and even visited the graves of her relatives. Further, they spent some time with Dad's siblings. Tim was motivated to learn more about the family relationships in both parents' families. He had taped the conversations, and offered the tape to anyone who wanted to listen to it. Although Tim said Dad learned some things about his parents from his older sister, it became apparent that Dad was, at this point, reluctant to discuss his own experiences in his family of origin. Ann said, at one point, she did not even know the names of her dad's parents.

There was some discussion about Dad and his second wife, with the adult children generally feeling positive about their stepmother, Linda. They were grateful that Dad had someone in his life.

Toward the end of the session, we asked whether those who were married had noticed any changes in their relationship with their spouse over the past year. Tim said that as a result of this work with his family of origin he was trying hard to improve his relationship with his wife and kids, particularly in the area of his not working so hard and making himself more emotionally available.

The first two hours of the follow-up consultation concluded with the discussion of relationship with spouses, leading to the second two hours where two of the spouses were included: Tim's and Katie's.

Chapter 11

THE SECOND FOLLOW-UP FAMILY MEETING
Becoming a More Connected Family

JAMES L. FRAMO, PhD
FELISE B. LEVINE, PhD

When family-of-origin sessions are divided into two segments the break in between allows the family members to reflect on and be more prepared to deal with deeper issues in the family—what one client called "the real stuff." Generally speaking, family members become more open and personal after the break. This second follow-up meeting took place several hours after the first follow-up meeting.

Although we believed that including spouses in the second segment of the follow-up session would lead to observations from those not a part of the immediate family, in truth only one of the spouses (Tim's wife, Annie) was able to contribute her views. Katie's husband, Steve, had not been a part of the previous process, and did not seem to have that much investment in his wife's family. It probably never occurred to him that if Katie came more to terms with her family-of-origin conflicts, he would be the beneficiary. On the other hand, Annie had a closer relationship with Tim's sisters than Tim did. She also shared similar feelings about Tim's distancing, so she had a large stake in the outcome of these consultations. It was not fully clear why Ann's husband, Mark, was not present in the session.

FRAMO: I suppose all of you saw the tapes of previous sessions.

STEVE: I've seen only a part of it, not the whole thing.

FRAMO: You haven't either, Annie?

ANNIE: [shakes her head no]

FRAMO: Oh. I thought you guys would have spent hours studying it.

LEVINE: Steve, what did you hear about that session?

STEVE: From what you [Katie] told me, there was a lot of emotion. They came down really hard on Paul, more than other people. That bothered Katie a lot.

LEVINE: Any other impressions that you had?

STEVE: Well, I'm not too sure what the intent of all this is. So far, what I'm able to see, I'm not sure what kind of impact it has had on the first group which had the session previously.

(Levine: It is clear that Steve is skeptical of the value of these meetings.)

FRAMO: Could you see yourself doing that with your own family: everybody sitting around telling the truth?

STEVE: I could picture that, but I doubt if that would ever happen.

(Levine: Translation: "No way!")

LEVINE: Annie, what impression did Tim give you?

ANNIE: Well, it made me want to do it with my own family. I would really like to do it. I have been interested in something like this for many years, but didn't really know what it would be like, so it was fun to see an example and made me feel less fearful, I think, of doing it with my family. I talked with my brothers and sisters about doing this.

FRAMO: Are your parents still alive?

ANNIE: Yes they are, but I haven't spoken to them about it. I think it would be harder for them, and I admire Tim's family a lot for having the courage to do this. I was amazed that they agreed to do it, especially in front of all those people.

LEVINE: They were very courageous.

(Levine: I was pleased that Annie acknowledged the family's courage. Sometimes spouses are threatened by their partners' attempts to strengthen family-of-origin relationships.)

FRAMO: We don't have any audience this time.

(Framo: The follow-up consultations were videotaped, but unlike the initial consultation, this time there was no audience observing the sessions.)

ANNIE: Except on the tape.

FRAMO: That's true. But after a while you usually forget the tape is on. So, you would like to have a session with your family?

ANNIE: Yes.

FRAMO: After the session, we'll give you our card. [there is general laughter and chuckles throughout the entire group]

LEVINE: Nobody gets off the hook easily.

(Levine: Humor and playfulness are important parts of our work.)

FRAMO: Steve, how did you feel about coming here today?

STEVE: Oh, I wish I had a little more time to spend. We're so rushed.

FRAMO: You have to get back right away?

STEVE: Uh huh.

FRAMO: Are you going to spend a few days in sunny Florida?

STEVE: Well, I wish we could. But all of a sudden we have work to do back in Phoenix, so I have to be there on Monday.

FRAMO: So this was kind of an imposition on you?

STEVE: Well, this summer has been hard on us. We've been trying to sell . . . Everything culminated this summer, but I wouldn't really call this an imposition. But just right now, I'm tired and I don't have all the energy that I would like.

FRAMO: It could have been better timed?

STEVE: Uh huh.

FRAMO: Annie, how about you? How did you feel about coming here?

ANNIE: I was looking forward to it.

FRAMO: Was that because of Tim?

ANNIE: Well, I suppose a little bit, because I know this is something that is important to Tim. But it's also because of my family, and my family has enjoyed sitting around and talking about it. So this is an opportunity—I like going to therapists [general laughter], although I'm not allowed to because of money.

(Levine: Sounds like Annie thinks that she and Tim should be in therapy.)

FRAMO: Don't you have medical insurance or something that covers therapy?

ANNIE: Oh yes.

TIM: Yes, part of it is . . .

ANNIE: But you have to have a problem.

FRAMO: Well, create one . . . How often do you guys get together as a family? Does it happen on holidays, or any days like that?

DAD: Weddings, funerals.

TIM: Ann's wedding.

FRAMO: How long ago was that?

ANN: Three years ago from last summer.

FRAMO: Okay. The rest of you guys had some time to do some thinking the last two hours; did you go out to lunch?

LYNN: I was freezing inside, climbing under the covers.

TIM: Ann, Annie, and I talked.

THOMAS: My dad and I talked for a while.

FRAMO: You did; what did you talk about?

THOMAS: I forgot. You tell them, Dad.

DAD: He was saying that since we spoke this morning he'd speak this afternoon.

FRAMO: [To Thomas] You spoke a lot more than you did last year.

DAD: I guess that's right.

FRAMO: Thomas, I'm glad that you participated more.

DAD: Yes. And he's a little concerned because he lost his pants, and he has a suit with a coat and a vest.

LEVINE: You have only part of a suit with you?

THOMAS: Uh huh.

LEVINE: Well, you look just fine.

THOMAS: Thank you.

LEVINE: So, you have a lot more to say this afternoon?

THOMAS: Yes.

FRAMO: One of the impressions I got this morning . . . [turning to Tim] I was picking up some of the stress you've been under. Apparently, there are a whole lot of things going on for you: You work in private practice, trying to organize this meeting, and you have a new baby. What else has been impinging on you?

TIM: Well, we may move to another state. Back to the Northwest. We were just talking about that over lunch. We've been thinking about that for a couple of years.

FRAMO: Why do you want to move? To be closer to your family?

TIM: Yes. To be closer to an area where we think most of us are going to be. We also like the Northwest better—more water, more green.

FRAMO: Tim, I noticed this morning that you were expressing your needs more than you did in the first family meeting.

TIM: Yes. I'm more concerned about that. I've been operating in such a professional way such a long time that I think I've neglected other areas of my life. I think I'm approaching midlife—thirty-seven is kind of a beginning point for that. I think I need to be thinking about things that I didn't think about before. I don't think about a lot when I'm under stress.

FRAMO: I think you're a little young for a midlife crisis.

TIM: Well, I don't know.

ANNIE: Some people think it comes earlier.

FRAMO: Some people earlier? Have you noticed Tim's stress?

ANNIE: Well, yes. I think that's part of the reason he has been sick. He's had this sinus infection for the last couple of months, and that's unusual.

FRAMO: He said he was worried about a brain tumor.

(Framo: Dad had had a brain tumor, and Tim's identification with his father may have contributed to this preoccupation. I could recall, after my father's death from a heart attack, developing a temporary numbness in my left arm.)

ANNIE: He's had a lot of headaches. Yes, and maybe I think it's stress.

DAD: You should ask him how many hours a day he works, and what jobs he has.

(Framo: Apparently, even Dad was aware of Tim's grueling, workaholic schedule. Tim, perhaps, best exemplified the family theme of working hard and always being busy.)

FRAMO: [to Tim] How many hours a day do you work, and how many jobs do you have?

TIM: I have worked more in the last few weeks, and I have a consultant's job. I am also an assistant at the church for the pastor—deaths, funerals, weddings. I see about thirty-five people a week.

FRAMO: A lot of hours. And teach, too?

TIM: No. But I do a number of things that might be related to teaching: workshops, seminars, and consultation.

FRAMO: Tim, when you were getting this family together for this meeting, did you find that some members of the family were resentful having to come here? Katie, for instance, said "I'm doing this for you."

TIM: Not so much resentful. There wasn't the resounding enthusiasm of coming here where people were saying, "Oh, boy. I'm glad we're having this. I just can't wait to be here." I appreciate that everybody came. There hasn't been outstanding enthusiasm. It's more like, "We're glad to do this for you, and it may be of value." I've been the one who clearly had the emotional drive to do this.

LEVINE: Lynn felt a little discouraged because there weren't as many changes as she had thought from the last session until now.

FRAMO: Is that true, Lynn?

LYNN: I think I was more excited last summer. Maybe the older I get the more distant I get. I think I was a lot more talkative, and when I watched the tapes of the previous session I couldn't believe the things I said. I didn't believe that I was that open. I think that the older I get I don't trust people as much as I used to, or it's hard for me to open up.

ANNIE: I'm curious to know whether other people felt they benefited? I really have. That's the reason I'm excited—because I've seen a lot of difference in Tim, and our relationship, and our family life. It was a real positive experience, and I wonder whether other people have had the same experience.

FRAMO: [to Annie] Why don't you share that with the family. What changes?

ANNIE: When I look at the tape a little bit, I thought Tim is like a different person than he was then. It's hard for me to think what he used to be like. Changes happen; changes take place gradually, and it's hard for me to know what he used to be like. When I looked at the tape it brought back some memories of how he used to be less open, less warm, and less involved with our family. I've experienced where he has become more involved with the children, with me, and no doubt with other people.

FRAMO: As I recall, Tim reported that you have said he wasn't relating intimately enough.

ANNIE: That's always been a problem with him. That's something he's working on. But I have seen changes.

FRAMO: In his relationship with you. You don't think this has taken place yet with his sisters, brother, and with his dad?

ANNIE: I don't know whether that has improved. I would like it more in our relationship, and also I think other people would like it more.

(*Levine: Annie is closer to Tim's sisters than Tim. She identifies with their feelings about Tim's emotional remoteness.*)

FRAMO: Well, the sense that I got from this morning is that, instead of Tim just being thought of as being up on a pedestal and playing football and writing books and getting degrees, he expressed his needs about wanting more closeness with the family and the family responded by saying that they now realize he is more human.

ANNIE: Well, I think that's part of it: being willing to admit more vulnerability.

FRAMO: Is it perhaps true that Tim is the one person in the family that has changed the most?

TIM: I know there are certain things I've been working on, certain things I'm conscious of. I would think that everyone here is working on some personal agenda. We've talked about changes in terms of how much we have contacted each other. But I think there is another thing going on. I'm working on my own personal stuff, my agenda, and I think that everybody's doing that here. I've been curious as to what you've all been working on.

(*Framo: Tim's statement that his personal agenda for the family meetings was primary did not, in my judgment, exclude his interest in improvement in the relationships among all his family members.*)

FRAMO: But is it possible that the relationships among the members of the family did not change that much, but some internal stuff in each individual has changed? Let's hear about that. Lynn, earlier today you were suggesting that you're not so much the baby in the family, but you are growing up to an adult, and becoming more independent.

LYNN: Yes. This is the transition. Instead of being thought of as a teenager, I want to be thought of as an adult. That's what is difficult for me now, because all the kids are married except me. Everybody has a spouse but me. They have their own families that they can identify with. It is difficult for me during this transition.

FRAMO: Because you are undergoing certain developmental changes yourself?

LYNN: Right. And they're so much older than I am, so that it's some-
          times hard for them to relate to me. It was so long ago that they
          went through the transition of being dependent on your parents
          and then being independent. I have no place to go like home.
          Therefore, I don't have a place that I can call my very, very own.

FRAMO: But since last year, you seem to look at yourself differently.

LYNN: Yes, older.

LEVINE: Lynn, are people responding to you as an older person?

LYNN: Yes. Sometimes it bothers me, because I still am a child. I still
          want to be an adult, definitely. Yet I still want to be a child. But
          I'm the adult, definitely, and that doesn't mean I'm not a physi-
          cal person. I've always been a physical person. People tease me
          about this because I like hugs, you know. But that's the way I am:
          I'm still touchy.

LEVINE: Who gives the juiciest hug in this family?

THOMAS: I do.

LYNN: Tim, for the first time, gave me the best hug.

FRAMO: Ann, what's happened to you since last time we met? You said
          you were making certain efforts to contact people.

ANN: Uh huh.

FRAMO: What, in turn, took place within you?

ANN: That I always was the person who was trying to reach out, but
          now I'm realizing more that everybody else is in the same posi-
          tion, too, but they just don't say it. I realized the last time that
          Tim also was a human being. And I could relate to him. We are
          more similar than I thought.

FRAMO: Were you surprised that he felt emotional pain?

ANN: No, not so much about that, but that we felt the same things.

FRAMO: Does that close any distance between the two of you?

ANN: Yes, I think so.

FRAMO: What changes have you seen in your dad?

ANN: Have I seen any? No.

FRAMO: He's the same as he ever was?

ANN: Well, when we came down here he was talking about the things
          that were going to happen in this meeting. That's the first time
          that has ever happened.

FRAMO: So that's a change?

ANN: [nods yes]

LEVINE: Has anybody else in the family experienced Dad in a different way in the course of this past year? Tim, how about you?

TIM: On our trip last August, to visit Dad's family of origin, we talked a lot.

LEVINE: Was it on a different level?

TIM: Yes. We talked about ourselves, and about our families—his family and Mom's family. Things that I would normally censor, I'm less concerned about censoring. I don't have the kind of censoring filter that I used to have.

FRAMO: Tim, can you bring up a controversial issue, like money, without your father getting angry and walking out of the room or keeling over?

TIM: Yes. I don't think, now, that there is any taboo topic that I can't talk to Dad about. I feel more spontaneous.

(Framo: In a half-humorous way, I was dealing here with the near universal apprehension that men have about confronting or raising certain issues with their father.)

LEVINE: Paul, do you sense a new level of honesty between you and Tim, that he's being more open and less careful?

DAD: Less careful? I never sensed any necessity for the change. At the last family meeting I became aware of feelings that I was not aware of before.

FRAMO: You weren't aware that he had some trepidation of bringing up certain topics with you?

DAD: I wasn't aware of it at that time. In fact, I don't think it existed.

FRAMO: Could you picture yourself bringing up certain topics with your own dad? It's scary.

DAD: My relating with my father was substantially different from that which I have with my family. He came from the old school, and he didn't raise such questions.

FRAMO: And *you* didn't raise such questions.

(Framo: It is interesting that while Tim feels there are no longer any barriers between him and his father—that he can talk about anything with him— Dad is unable to acknowledge this change in Tim's attitude toward him. Yet, at the same time, he does say that at the previous family meeting he became aware of feelings that he was not aware of before. I erred in not asking him what feelings he became aware of.)

LEVINE: And now, Tim, you've taken a step beyond where your father and his father were. Change is taking place slowly across the genera- tions.

TIM: One thing I have struggled to say is, "Dad, I love you." I can remember last summer when we were traveling I would say, "We love you," in some general way. I think it is hard to say those words, and I think, therefore, it's so hard to say it to Annie.

DAD: Verbalization like that is nice, but that is not the substance for me. The substance is the way you relate, the way you handle cer- tain things. Perhaps my reactions are from the family I came from. I take you for what you are. You are my kids, and I love every one of you, regardless of what you do. It's nice that people relate to me, not saying this or that, but it's more in their actions rather than in the words which they speak.

FRAMO: I think I know what you mean because there are certain families who say to each other all the time that they love each other, but they don't *behave* lovingly toward one another.

There then ensued a discussion as to how Tim was perceived by the rest of the family. Ann indicated that when she was growing up Tim seemed more like an uncle than a brother. Lynn, commenting on the 17-year age difference between her and Tim, said that earlier in her life she perceived Tim as a kind of father. However, she said that now that she can talk about adult things with Tim (e.g., career choices) he is more real to her. Annie stated that she has always had a closer relationship with Tim's sis- ters than he did. This last observation again gave Tim the feeling that he was the odd man out in this family.

FRAMO: In the previous meeting, I got the impression that it was better to be a boy in this family than a girl. And now the opposite seems to be coming out because Tim is saying how difficult it was to be a male in this family with all these sisters.

ANN: Dad feels the same way.

DAD: For reasons beyond description.

(Framo: I should have asked Dad to elaborate on this statement.)

TIM: Dad was in a similar boat as I am in this family. There were four males and four females, right? The males are sort of out of it. Dad is the darling of his sisters.

FRAMO: And he didn't relate as closely to his brothers?

TIM: No.

(Framo: Many parents in family-of-origin sessions spontaneously talk about their own original families in order to explain their attitudes and behaviors in this family. For those parents who do not volunteer this information I routinely ask them to talk about their own family background. Revelation of the parents' family histories helps make the parents more understandable to their adult children.)

DAD: Well, not because we didn't want to, but because circumstances didn't even suggest that. My youngest brother was so much younger, and I went away to school at fourteen. I wasn't around in the early years, so I never got acquainted with him.

FRAMO: Wow! You were so young to leave home for school.

DAD: I went away as a freshman in high school, virtually went out of the home so that my oldest brother . . . I didn't know him very well either, because he was much older. I had another brother, and he and I peddled papers together. He is possibly the one I know the best.

FRAMO: He was closest in age?

DAD: Yes.

FRAMO: Are all your brothers and sisters still alive?

DAD: Yes.

LEVINE: Tim, do you know your uncles and aunts?

TIM: Yes.

DAD: Have all of you met my oldest brother?

TIM: Yes.

FRAMO: Are they all scattered around the country?

DAD: Yes, they are.

FRAMO: Do you try to keep in touch with them?

DAD: Yes.

FRAMO: Are you the one member of the family they communicate through?

DAD: No. They really all communicate with one another, except possibly my oldest brother.

FRAMO: What happened to him?

DAD: Well, he's a more independent person. He's the oldest in the family, so he wanted to chart his own way through life. But there's nothing evil about him. He's different.

FRAMO: Does he ever come to family gatherings?

DAD: Well, he may have, but with reluctance.

LEVINE: Was he the black sheep of the family?

DAD: No, he wasn't.

LEVINE: What do you mean that he's "different"?

DAD: Well, he was more independent than the rest of us. He also went away to school at fourteen years. He wasn't even home for the summer because he couldn't be gainfully employed. So we didn't even get to see him all that much.

(Framo: Over the years I have heard many times of the lasting, painful effects of being sent away from the family to a school at an early age. While some youngsters are sturdy and resourceful enough to survive the experience, others carry the scars of that deep rejection for a lifetime. For some, that experience is as much of a defining event as the effect of the breakup of a family through divorce. I am speculating here as to why Dad's older brother is cut off from his family; other factors may be involved.)

FRAMO: What does he do now?

DAD: He's retired.

FRAMO: Do you ever call him?

DAD: Yes. I called him on his birthday, and visited him last summer.

FRAMO: Now I see why you spend two hundred and fifty dollars per month on telephone bills.

(Framo: I should not have diverted the discussion away from Dad's family with this quip. It would have been more productive to get more information about his family. For example, what were his parents like? What were the family themes, stories, what was the emotional atmosphere, etc.?)
(Levine: I don't agree. I think Jim was intuitively tracking that Dad had said, "Enough for now.")

DAD: Not because of me. [general laughter throughout the entire group]

FRAMO: I wanted to ask Katie a question. Katie, have you seen any changes in your dad?

KATIE: Well, yes. What I was thinking of was we know some of the things that happened, but we in this family have forgotten some of the positive things that happened. When we got together this past year we bought Dad some golf clubs for Father's Day.

DAD: And I really appreciated that.

FRAMO: Did you all contribute?

KATIE: Yes. We all decided that it was important.

DAD: And Katie was the leader.

FRAMO: So you didn't get him a Mercedes?

KATIE: Well, nearly.

THOMAS: I helped out. I paid for it.

FRAMO: Good for you, Thomas.

KATIE: But we put together a card, a really cute card.

DAD: Marvelous.

KATIE: [begins to cry]

FRAMO: Katie, why should that bring tears to your eyes: giving a gift to Dad?

KATIE: I'm just tired. I was thinking of Dad. The college dedicated a portrait of him when we were there last summer. Up until last summer they never expressed appreciation for all the work he did. We thought it was an injustice, and we got together and talked about writing a letter to the college. It was really important for us, as a group, to do this.

FRAMO: Dad was treated unfairly?

KATIE: Yes.

TIM: Yes.

KATIE: Someone took over his position. So we decided that Tim should write the letter because he was the best one with words, and we all signed our names, and that was something that we all got together on. And another thing I was thinking of is Lynn's job situation. She needed contacts to get a job, so we helped her. And another thing, when Stacy [Tim's daughter] was ill, Tim called every one of us, out of panic, just to talk. We called back every time.

(Framo: This statement of Katie's was the clearest example of change in the direction of more family cohesiveness.)

FRAMO: So you're saying that the family has really pulled together since the initial meeting?

KATIE: I think things really happened. The other thing I wanted to say was that part of our relationship is remembering simple manners. When you're with someone you say, "Tell us about yourself. Tell us something you have done." We don't do that; I don't know if it's being neglectful. It's just simple communication skills and manners. I really don't know why it doesn't happen. I suppose it's busyness again. I do feel a lot has happened. Over Christmas,

Dad and Linda talked about more personal things, and they bought us a very special Christmas tree cover that we wanted for several years . . . Tim and Annie asked us to be godparents to their child. So we can talk about all the problems, but there are so many good things that happened. It shows there is communication. Ann has written more this year than in the last four or five years. I think things are happening.

FRAMO: So why do you think this morning there was an emphasis on what *didn't* happen?

KATIE: Well, I'm concerned about Lynn. She still needs attention. She's without a mate. If you have a spouse your attention and affection come from that source.

FRAMO: Are you saying that it is difficult for this family to deal with positive things? Is it easier to deal with the negative?

(Framo: I took a leap, here, by jumping to the family theme of self-abnegation—that life is to be endured, sometimes suffered, not enjoyed. I wondered whether, for this family, enjoyment is too closely associated with guilt.)
(Levine: I agree.)

KATIE: Yes. Yes.

FRAMO: That you don't deserve it or something?

KATIE: We want to dwell on the negative.

TIM: That's probably true.

KATIE: I think I do that with myself as a person. In my life, I tend to do that, too. And that's all of us.

ANN: That's sort of an error in the family, and that's one of the things I saw in my life. I saw how it was affecting the people around me, and I made a mental decision to try to change that.

FRAMO: To stress the positive?

ANN: Uh huh, rather than the negative.

LYNN: It's hard to be happy because, as Tim says, you wonder what's going to happen next. Is it okay to be happy and just to be carefree? Instead we marry, we have bills to pay, we don't have any money, and we can't do this or that. It's really hard to have a good time and not worry.

TIM: I've noticed that when things are going along well for a while you just can't trust it.

LEVINE: Is it all right in this family to appreciate the good things?

KATIE: No. It's hard to accept compliments, too.

DAD: With respect to the golf clubs, what I appreciate most was not the golf clubs but the effort that was put into the card. That's not saying I won't enjoy the clubs.

ANN: When something is given to you, it's difficult to say the right words. It's difficult to receive compliments.

KATIE: Lynn and I said this summer, we don't want to owe anything to anyone. It would be hard for us to accept anything from anybody. We always want to be on the giving side.

LEVINE: Right.

FRAMO: I've got a brother like that. He can't accept. He can only give.

(Framo: I self-disclose here about my own family, but the comment does not make much of an impression. Therapist self-disclosures, appropriately timed and relevant, however, can be very therapeutic.)

LEVINE: Earlier, Katie, when you were describing Dad and Linda's gift, you became tearful as you acknowledged your appreciation.

KATIE: Yes. That's true. But sometimes it's hard to accept.

TIM: I was recently enjoying myself for a day or two, and I felt guilty about it.

LEVINE: Felt guilty about it?

TIM: Yes. I felt unnatural about it. It's hard to accept gifts from members of the family, or from anyone.

FRAMO: Tim, can you imagine spending a day doing nothing?

TIM: No. I don't think I've ever done that.

FRAMO: Sitting down and reading a good novel, or watching television?

ANN: I don't think any of us can do that.

TIM: At home growing up there was no way we could think of doing that. We got a lot of practice working and being busy, and that was just continued.

(Levine: I felt that Jim had diverted the discussion and I wanted to get back to the issue of appreciation and taking gifts.)

LEVINE: I'm still interested in the feelings about the giving and receiving of gifts. There was a lot of gift giving this year, with all of you kids trying to right the wrong, like at your dad's college. And the way you pulled together to do what you did was a gift of sorts. The golf clubs and the Christmas tree cover were special gifts. Lynn, your coming to Katie's place to stay, and Ann, your reaching out and writing letters . . . There seems to be more giving, and I wonder why the taking seems to be so hard. Could it be that receiving a gift makes you feel too vulnerable and hungry for it? If you get the taste of receiving you become aware of the hurt of not having had it; so instead you say, "I don't need anything. I'd rather give than receive."

(Levine: I believe that the need to always be the giver is a defense against dependency longings and vulnerability.)

TIM: It's hard for Annie to give me gifts because I haven't had practice to know what I need in my life.

ANNIE: That's what I would like to see change in our life: where you, Tim, would actually want something. There's never anything special that I can give him or do for him. You know, we've had marriage retreats where one of the things we do is make a list of loving things that you could do for your spouse. Tim can't even make a list of things that I could do for him. He can't think of four or five things except such things as doing his laundry [group laughs] and that's not the kind of thing I have in mind. I would love to have things that I could do for him or I could tell him he's special, but that is a vulnerability. Tim, you cannot admit that you have any needs, or what you really like.

LEVINE: Is that a struggle with you and Katie, Steve? Does she take gifts from you?

STEVE: Oh, yes. But they're so few and far between. [group laughter]

LEVINE: You shouldn't spoil her too much.

STEVE: That's right.

FRAMO: That's interesting. People usually claim that their spouses are too demanding, but you're saying that you wish they would demand more.

ANNIE: I'm also thankful that he's not too demanding. He doesn't complain about a lot of things that other men would complain about. He's so laid back about it; but on the other hand, so laid back that there's nothing that I can really do to please him.

FRAMO: Does he give you lists of things that he would like for Christmas?

ANNIE: No.

FRAMO: So, you really have to guess.

ANNIE: Yes. I guess so. It might be that he really doesn't want anything, because he has conditioned himself to the extent that he doesn't really know what he would like. He's not really free to say, but he really doesn't buy himself anything. He doesn't want to have pleasure, to have fun.

FRAMO: Does that sound familiar to any of you? Having difficulty having fun? Can you have fun, Ann?

ANN: When I'm working, or when I'm on vacation, I can't relax. I can't relax at all. When I'm home I work until I go to bed.

FRAMO: Did you ever play hooky from your work?

(Framo: In a playful way I was working here on trying to reduce the force of a punitive superego that permeated the family.)

ANN: That would be terrible; I could never do that.

LEVINE: Is your husband, Mark, like that?

ANN: No. He yells at me because I'm unable to sit down.

LEVINE: So, he encourages you to relax sometimes?

TIM: That sounds like home, growing up.

ANN: It hasn't worked. I've tried, but it's uncomfortable for me to relax. I have this thing in my mind that I should be doing instead of relaxing.

FRAMO: Steve, is Katie like that? That she can't relax, but has to work hard?

STEVE: I think so. She's very dedicated to her teaching profession, and in just about everything else she does. She does it very thoroughly.

FRAMO: What do you guys do for fun?

STEVE: Well, that's what we were saying just a few minutes ago. Fun, well it seems we are always *almost* there. We never quite get there, something else seems to come up.

FRAMO: Katie, did you know he felt that way? That it's so hard for you to have fun?

KATIE: I told this to Tim over the phone before our coming.

TIM: You said that this family thinks too much and doesn't play enough.

FRAMO: Lynn, can you play?

LYNN: Not at all. I think I can when I'm with Ann.

FRAMO: Really?

LYNN: When I'm with Ann, I can really concentrate on having a good time; but I really worry a lot. I think that tomorrow I have this to do, and my friends at school. And my boyfriend, in particular, gets on me a lot saying, "Why don't you just calm down. Sit down and just rest."

FRAMO: Could you imagine yourself the night before a final examination going to the movies?

ANN: My gosh! My gosh!

(Framo: I knew this idea would sound strange or foreign to the family, but I wanted to lend them my own less serious approach to life and my fun side. In more technical terms, I was introducing variance into the system.)

LYNN: I worry about the final examination the week before.

FRAMO: I have done that. I figured that I studied enough and that I know as much as I'm ever going to know, so I go to the movies the night before finals.

LYNN: I think that we want to make everything perfect; we strive for perfection. It's never good enough. We're never satisfied with the job and, "It's done, so let's go and have fun." Maybe there is something more we can do. We're never satisfied with what we do or pleasing people. There's always more that we can do in the world. I think that's my problem.

FRAMO: Would you all like to get off of this treadmill?

TIM: I know I need to get off of it, otherwise it's going to spell disaster.

THOMAS: It's hard for me to have fun. I don't know why, it just is.

LEVINE: It is?

FRAMO: What *do* you do for fun, Thomas?

THOMAS: I like to watch baseball.

FRAMO: Did you ever play baseball?

THOMAS: No. I like to watch. I don't play baseball. I just watch it.

FRAMO: Uh huh. Do you play any sports, Thomas?

THOMAS: I used to; I don't anymore.

FRAMO: It might be a good idea to do so. Get active.

THOMAS: I doubt it. I just like baseball for right now. It's hard for me to have fun.

DAD: His stepbrother took him out bowling this Christmas, and he bowled a game of two twenty-one.

FRAMO: You did! Good heavens. I bowl ninety.

DAD: Two twenty-one. He's a very respectable bowler.

LEVINE: You bowl, Thomas?

THOMAS: A little bit.

LEVINE: So you even downplay your accomplishments?

THOMAS: Right.

LEVINE: Ann, if your husband, Mark, were here would he say it would be hard for you to take gifts, in light of what Annie was saying about Tim?

(Levine: I was using the Milan technique of circular questioning.)

ANN: Uh huh. Probably not as bad as Tim, because I'm able to say the things I want. It's hard to take things, but I can take compliments.

FRAMO: Dad, can you have fun?

DAD: Possibly. I've learned it over the years.

LEVINE: You're working at it?

DAD: Well, yes. I came back from our family reunion in June, and Linda and I had been there for seven days, and we had fun.

FRAMO: But what do you personally enjoy?

DAD: Well, anything in sports. Golf.

TIM: Most of your relaxing has taken place since your retirement. When you were working, you worked hard.

DAD: I think the family has oriented to a little different format or formula than the average family because when you work you work, and when you go on vacation you really go on vacation. Other families say, "Well, let's have some fun in the course of that work week." But with our family there's not much of that.

FRAMO: There's a very powerful work ethic in this family.

DAD: That's right.

(Framo: I should have asked Dad how he felt about his children's inability to enjoy themselves.)

FRAMO: Tim, I want to go back to a statement that you made a few moments ago: "Unless I get off of this treadmill it's going to be disastrous." What did you mean?

TIM: I think I work myself to death. I think I'm like Mom in that sense. I think I'll miss things that I'll later regret. I worry that I could miss important opportunities with my kids. I think Annie and I need to keep on working on our relationship so that I don't get on this work thing. We need to keep in touch in that way. I think I'll be disappointed in myself if the years go on and I keep this work thing up at the pace that it's been. I don't think I'll be satisfied with the choices that I made.

LEVINE: You don't want to look back at your life with regrets?

TIM: Yes. Nobody has ever died regretting that they didn't work enough.

FRAMO: They usually die regretting that they worked too much.

TIM: Yes. Yes. I don't want to have that regret. Yet I don't want to be that person who is reviewing his life saying, "I didn't work hard enough." I want to have fun.

FRAMO: The whole idea here is balance, and you have to balance fun and enjoyment with work because all work and no play makes Jack a dull boy—to coin a phrase. [general laughter]

LEVINE: Annie, you're making all of these wonderful faces.

(Levine: Sometimes nonverbal comments speak louder than words.)

ANNIE: I wonder if Tim works so hard because of the income.

TIM: We grew up in a family that really didn't have a lot of money. I think we were really deprived of things that families with money have. We grew up in a very conservative family when it comes to money, and I think all of us are money hungry. I know, for me, I want to develop a big bank account, not necessarily to live high off the hog, but I want to have resources there so that I can use it. Sometimes I think I have been leaning over into that direction too much.

FRAMO: Felise and I are seeing a very wealthy family right now, and they're fighting over money all the time, too. They never have enough.

LEVINE: And they bicker over hundreds of thousands of dollars.

FRAMO: That's right. So no matter how much money you've got, money represents a lot of different things besides it inherent value.

TIM: It's a big problem among us—money. Who's going to pay for what? How much money can we afford to spend at what restaurant? And we're not casual about it at all. I want to make more than what my dad did, because I think he suffered because of that to the point where instead of parents giving you things it's the other way around. Dad doesn't have money to dole out to us. I want to be in a better position than my dad is with money, and with financial security. Right now, for every hour I don't see a patient I lose money. I'm trying to work this one out. I'm trying to see what I can do about it. Sometimes I'm perceived here as the rich, rich brother by other family members, and I don't think that's the case. I feel it's too dangerous to talk about money, and I'm feeling it now.

FRAMO: Is money a taboo subject in this family?

DAD: No; I don't think it is.

FRAMO: Tim, are you alluding to something we talked about this morning: about the way your dad and his wife are handling their finances?

TIM: It spills over onto all of us. We talk over the phone about it, about how Dad is doing with money, and we're concerned about his impoverished condition. He talks about it. I wanted him to come to David's baptism in September, but he can't come because he doesn't have enough money to pay for the plane fare. So what do I do? Do I write out a check to him so he can come?

FRAMO: Why not?

TIM: Because I can't keep on writing out checks. But he said on the phone, "I don't want to accept favors from anybody. I don't want you to write out a check for me." But Annie and I continue to write the checks.

DAD: And you have. You are paying for all the hotel rooms now.

LEVINE: Does money pull you all apart? Do you feel separate because your financial situations are different? Is there resentment over that?

(Levine: Because Dad's wife, Linda, was not present, I was hesitant to pursue their feelings about Dad and Linda's financial arrangement. Yet it was clear that the Weber kids resented their arrangement, and felt that their father was getting the short end of the stick.)

TIM: When Katie and I are on the phone there are references to all the money we have. [group laughter] [Tim turning to family] Don't you know that?

KATIE: Have we ever asked you for money? I don't know what the issue is, I really don't know.

TIM: Oh no, no, no . . .

FRAMO: Do you see him as rich, Katie?

TIM: I think she does.

KATIE: Let me tell you what I see Tim as, this is what bothers me. He acts like the cheapest person in the world. He will go down to the happy hour because it's free food, and he will take everybody down there saying it's free food. We make hotel reservations two or three times to get the cheapest rate.

TIM: No, we changed it twice from the Marriott to the Red Lion.

KATIE: Oh no. We looked through the Disneyland directory, and looked at various prices.

TIM: I am conservative, yes; and I will always be that way.

KATIE: Or he'll say, "Let's take the food to Disneyland, and we can hide it." And Annie says, "Well, the rule is we can hide it in the bag." Here is this person who, at the one end has money, and that's where the digs come in. He plays the game with us, and it bothers me.

TIM: It's not a game. I am financially conservative. If I go to happy hour to eat food free, I'll go to happy hour and eat food free.

FRAMO: But as I recall, last year when this subject came up Dad was seen as the stingy one. You all stayed in Motel Six. Do you remember that?

TIM: Yeah, yeah. That was true.

FRAMO: Are you, then, just a carbon copy of Dad?

TIM: I don't think I'm *that* stingy. I think I've loosened up. [general laughter in the background, especially from Paul] I think I've loosened up in terms of spending money.

KATIE: You felt that in order to get everybody down here you offered to pay. It was a real struggle even for you to offer that.

TIM: But I wondered if I should pay for everything. Do I pay for the hotel? Do I pay for food? Do I pay for tickets to Disneyland? Do I play Santa Claus? Where do I cut boundaries? I think that's an important question. I paid for this because I wanted this family gathering to happen.

KATIE: But it's such a struggle with you to enjoy your money.

TIM: Katie, I'm doing it! I'm doing it! Okay?! Right now! This is something that pisses me off! It looks like you're coming down on me for being concerned about money, that I'm one of the worst penny-pinching people in the world. You give me these digs on the phone.

KATIE: I'm telling you why. The reason it came up is because you play both sides. You've got the money, you play the penny-pincher.

TIM: And I always will.

KATIE: It embarrasses me to be with you sometimes.

ANNIE: I can understand, Katie. What Katie is saying is true. What they are saying is true, Tim. You are working hard to change it.

FRAMO: What's the two sides that you see, Annie?

ANNIE: That he's a penny-pincher, and at the same time he's very generous. Well, he's trying to be more generous. He's trying not to be a
penny-pincher. He's trying to be different from his parents. They
didn't have as much money, so I guess he's trying to spend more
money. Your mom was like that. She was always very generous,
and of good will, like going to those places where you could
have as much as you wanted to eat. You still like to go to those
places where you can have all you want.

FRAMO: So, Annie, you want to see him loosen up a little bit more?

ANNIE: Yes. And he can allow us to spend money, but I'm not too sure he
can feel good about it.

TIM: It's really a struggle for me. I want to work at both ends, you
know.

KATIE: My daughter spilled French fries on the chair at the restaurant
yesterday. All of a sudden I was nervous. This is a ritzy hotel, and
Tim started taking a fork and eating the food up from the seat.
[laughing considerably] It embarrassed me.

LEVINE: But he's working on it. It's a conflict for him.

KATIE: I'm a teaser. But you seem angry at me, Tim, and I don't know
why.

FRAMO: You're angry at him, too. Don't you hear that?

KATIE: I am? [everybody nods "Yes, you are"]

LEVINE: Sure you are.

FRAMO: Sure you are.

TIM: Often, when I look at you, you have that dour face toward me.
You don't smile. You look mean. I've noticed that it's not an angry face, but it's . . .

FRAMO: Disapproving?

TIM: Yes, that's it.

FRAMO: You guys got stuff to work out, you two. Don't you?

KATIE: I guess.

*(Framo: The old conflicts between Tim and Katie flare up again during
these exchanges. I speculated to myself about the possible bases for their ongoing
feud. Katie's envious and resentful feelings over Tim's privileged position in the
family have never left her. Katie is quite out of touch with her anger, and cannot
own such feelings inside her. The closest she can come to acknowledging any
hostile feelings is to call her sarcastic remarks "my sense of humor.")*

I considered further that Katie and Tim were dealing with parental trans-
ference distortions to each other—that is, neither was able to fit the role of
parent to the other after Mom was gone.

In addition, could it be that their conflicts with each other were a replay of
their parents' marital struggles? Avoidance of discussion of the parents' mar-
riage is common in family-of-origin sessions. The therapist is usually given the
message, spoken or unspoken, not to bring up this topic. I had come to realize
how little we knew about the marriage of Tim and Katie's parents. For instance,
there was no information on how Dad handled his wife's emotional outbursts.

Finally, Tim had earlier stated that he thought Katie was taking out on
him the anger she could not express toward Dad. I wondered: Did Katie per-
ceive Tim as a potential giver of the love and admiration she could not get from
Dad? Unfortunately, we were approaching the end of the session, and there was
not enough time to pursue any of these hypotheses.)

(Levine: I also think that this discussion diverted from the more difficult
subject about their father's financial arrangement with his second wife.)

LEVINE: There is a lot of misunderstanding between the two of you. So
much so that you're barely finished with a sentence when the
other person is already in the process of defending themself. When
you watch the tape you'll see that. I'm not too sure you understand each other's position.

FRAMO: Do you, Katie, feel his digs, too?

KATIE: No, no. I'm afraid to talk to him now, to tell you the truth.

FRAMO: Why?

KATIE: It will be misinterpreted.

FRAMO: What is it you feel will be misinterpreted? Will he ascribe to you
a negative emotion that you don't have?

(Levine: I think Katie was feeling ganged up on when all of us, including
Jim and I, called her on her anger.)

TIM: I think this is helping me to talk to you about it. [Katie begins to
cry]

FRAMO: You see, I think your sister is trying to tell you she has good will
toward you, and she's annoyed at some of the things you do.

TIM: Yes.

FRAMO: You embarrass her with what she perceives to be your penny-
pinching. There may be some other issues here that aren't clear.
Is there anything else involved between the two of you? What
was it like when they were kids, Paul?

(Levine: Sometimes when two family members are in a stalemate it is helpful to triangle another person as a commentator.)

DAD: I don't remember.

FRAMO: Did they fight like brothers and sisters do?

DAD: Not that I can recall on reflection. Last year, Katie brought up that she was being discriminated against, because invariably Tim was given the better of the deals since Tim was permitted to go out to play football and other things.

FRAMO: And she had to work at home.

DAD: Right. In the light of today's definitions that no doubt is true. That was a mistake.

(Framo: This acknowledgment by Dad was noteworthy.)

FRAMO: But she must have felt jealous that he was getting all the fun and she was getting all the work.

LEVINE: Was that part of the struggle?

DAD: You asked me whether they got along well as kids, and I remember reflecting on this one. Generally speaking, they got along very well. That's my naiveté in respect to the entire relationship.

FRAMO: Tim, do you remember her saying that last year? That she had to work while you were out playing football and having fun?

TIM: Yes I do.

FRAMO: So, she is bound to have some resentment.

TIM: That's true. But Katie has overestimated the amount of attention that I got from Mom and Dad. Often, I played football, basketball, baseball games and my parents weren't around at all. I didn't get as much from my parents as Katie thinks I got.

LEVINE: Annie, what do you think is the reason for this tension between Tim and Katie? Do you have any sense about it?

ANNIE: Well, I don't know about that, but I have some of the same feelings that Katie has, so I can identify with Katie. I sense some of the same things. The relationship between Tim and Katie . . . I can understand why she would feel some resentment for having to go through some of the childhood that she did as Tim learned to be independent and went off do to his own thing. He probably doesn't think it was all that great, but it was probably better than Katie's experience—having to have a lot of responsibilities and not being able to have fun. Tim at least had fun. He felt neglected in the sense that his mom and dad weren't there, but he was still having fun with his friends. He was doing the things he wanted to do, and he got a lot of strokes.

FRAMO: You think that Katie is resentful because Tim advanced farther educationally?

ANNIE: I doubt it.

FRAMO: You don't think that is part of the picture?

ANNIE: I don't think so. I wouldn't think so, but I wouldn't know.

FRAMO: Or that he's less interested in what she has done with her life?

ANNIE: That could be.

KATIE: I worked through a lot of this since our first family meeting. You know it was my perception of Tim, and Tim's perception of me. I thought it was worked out then because I thought he didn't like me.

FRAMO: Because he didn't like you?

KATIE: Yes. But after our first family session I realized that he coped by abandoning the family. It doesn't bother me anymore. [tearfully] I don't have resentments. Educationally, that doesn't bother me either.

LEVINE: What do you think the tension is between the two of you, then? What are your ideas about that?

KATIE: I didn't think it was that bad until it was just now brought up.

TIM: I think it's better; I think it's better. But I still think there is some difficulty connecting. I guess I'd like to break through this. What I fear is that there are certain things you feel about me, but you don't say to me directly. You talk to Steve about me, you talk to Lynn about me. If there is anything you want to say to me say it to me directly.

KATIE: Well, they can speak, but I don't think there's anything that I haven't told you that I have told them. You know, it seems that you are much more upset with me this year than you were before. You know I have this sense of humor, but I really don't know what to say to you. I don't know how to approach you.

(Framo: I should have mentioned that sarcasm, under the guise of humor, can be quite hostile.)

TIM: But I have a sense of humor, too. I think I can appreciate humor, too. I think we can work through this. I just need to know that you can be direct with me when you have something to say.

LEVINE: Katie, I have a hunch that you're struggling with Tim about whether he likes you. If you say something Tim doesn't like, is that going to mean he doesn't like you anymore?

KATIE: It kind of came through on the tape. He said that whenever I talked to him I talked to him with sarcasm. That's how I talk. That's how I relate intimately with people, because I don't do it to people I don't like.

(Levine: Sarcasm is often a defense against intimacy.)

TIM: I think the reason I'm more direct this year about my feelings is that I wanted to be sure that things were out before this meeting was over. One of you made the comment after looking at the tape from the first session that I wasn't myself, I wasn't real, I was pretending. I think I'm making a strong effort to be direct about what's going on.

KATIE: I was wondering whether you may have some jealousy because Lynn and I got closer to each other this summer.

TIM: Yes, I probably do, because Lynn doesn't come to our house, but spends three months with you. I'll just have to get beyond that. I *am* jealous.

Lynn said she had been very upset that she couldn't afford to visit Tim. Dad defended Lynn to Tim, saying she really wanted to visit Tim. When I commented on one theme of the family—that there was a struggle over who got more—Dad said that the format of these family meetings promoted oversensitivity toward each other. Dad was implying that sessions like this, where the family members react to each other, were creating problems that weren't there.

FRAMO: I have an alternative hypothesis. Namely, this family has tended to be more intellectual, and dealing with a hard session like this brings out a lot of the deeper emotions. It does stimulate a lot of feelings, a lot of oversensitivity. But because you all lived at the intellectual level doesn't mean that the emotional level wasn't there. It was always there, but was never looked at. The point is, when you guys look at these tapes following this meeting, you will see how it's put together. These sessions start a process, and we only open the door. We start the ball rolling. Now it's up to you guys how to deal with all these matters.

LEVINE: I agree. It's clear that these sessions brought feelings and issues into the open that were discounted.

DAD: I agree with you. I would have no problem agreeing with that. But there is oversensitivity and overreading of the situation.

FRAMO: But the other point we're trying to make is: Let's assume for a moment that Katie has some resentments toward Tim, and let's assume for a moment that they have never talked about it. The resentments would come out in another form such as not visiting him for four years. I firmly believe it's better to be very direct. That's more open and more clear, rather than expressing resentments obliquely or indirectly.

DAD: I would agree. So there's very positive things going on here. But like everything that's positive, there's something that can always be overdone. You can make people so sensitive that they get to be oversensitive.

FRAMO: That's true.

DAD: And therefore suspicious.

FRAMO: I think that's true.

(Framo: This colloquy between Dad and me, where we each concede the other's point of view, showed me how far we had come in our relationship. He could admit having been moved by the family meetings, and that some of his perceptions had changed. I could acknowledge that therapists do sometimes overread into situations. In the previous session Dad had expressed wariness about the therapy process, as seen in the metaphor of his accepting mints from me. His doubtfulness was still present at the end of this session.)

FRAMO: Well, you know, we have about fifteen minutes left. What would you guys like to do in the future with each other? How would you like the family relationships to be?

(Levine: We usually try to end family-of-origin consultations on a positive note by asking members to tell what they like and admire about each other, but unfortunately there was not sufficient time in which to do this.)

TIM: I have one concern, and I had this concern following our initial meeting. There seemed to be kind of a peak of emotions and then a letdown. But I think there have been changes. I think the changes have been ongoing, and I think it's impossible to keep up the momentum. What I'd like to do in a slow way is make connections. One thing I need to do is remember important dates like birthdays. It's very hard for me because I get caught up in so much stuff during the year. But I need Annie's help for me to do this, and then connect with you all on your birthdays.

(Levine: Tim's description of his letdown following the original family-of-origin sessions is not unusual. Clients often experience a huge emotional release after the session is over, but then, as the system settles down and reverts to the familiar patterns of interaction, disappointment follows. Although the actual consultations are an intensive, brief therapy experience, lasting changes in family-of-origin functioning is an ongoing process that is accomplished by the family over time. These consultations "kick-start" the process.)

FRAMO: Is it just a question of being in touch with each other by telephone or on birthdays?

TIM: Well, it's being more emotionally close when we do get in touch. I need help in doing that. I need to cut through the surface of "How am I doing?" or "How are you doing?" We talk about our work and what we are doing, and I think it would be nice if we could get beyond that.

LEVINE: So you want to communicate, "How are you *really* doing?"

TIM: It's the quality of contact, not just the amount. I also want people to tell me directly if anything's going on with them about me.

ANN: And another important thing is if you have any questions about something which has been said to you, always ask, "Is this the way you are thinking?" Go on and address it right then, instead of jumping to assumptions.

FRAMO: Ann, what would you like for yourself from your family?

ANN: More recognition and more positive strokes.

LEVINE: More reaching out?

ANN: I think everybody wants to see change, to make an effort to keep going in the right direction. I also think that not talking about important things would be going in the wrong direction. Things will come up, and it's going to be important that we talk about them.

FRAMO: So what you're saying is that there are no taboo subjects anymore.

ANN: Right. And not to make this family meeting a game, something we're doing for Tim. To realize that this meeting isn't just for Tim, but for everybody else.

LEVINE: That's a good point; it's not just for Tim, but it's for the whole family.

FRAMO: Yes. I never conceived of these sessions as just for Tim. Not at all. But just for me. [everybody laughs] Paul, what would you like for your family?

DAD: I'd like to have them continue the way they are. Misunderstandings that take place can be taken care of by conversations at some time. I'd like there to be family reunions where we're trying to get the kids together. Whether that's ever possible I really don't know. I would like it if each summer they'd come to our place, as many as possible, and that we'd have a good time together.

LEVINE: Is there anything you would like changed in relationship to the children, you and Linda? You might speak for her if she were here.

DAD: I don't know if I could say what she would really want changed. I suppose if they come to visit us more often, that our two families become merged, more than they are right now.

TIM: Which two families?

DAD: Her family and our family.

TIM: I don't know how realistically possible that is. I have an interest in seeing her family when I can, but I don't have a lot of interest in pushing together for a reunion. It's because I think it's really too much, because all of us are adults and really never spent much time together.

FRAMO: You wouldn't feel the need for a reunion?

LEVINE: [looking at Paul] You're not talking about a reunion; it's more like a union, connecting these families for the first time.

TIM: Well, maybe I really don't see a real need to push for it myself.

FRAMO: Do the rest of you share this?

LYNN: I know Linda's kids, and I'm probably the closest to them, especially to Debi. I consider them to be relatives, because I know them, because we lived together for two years, and Debi and I were sisters. It would be neat, I think, if Katie could meet them. I think it's terrible that they haven't met yet.

TIM: Katie, would you want to?

KATIE: Sure I want to. I'd like to get to know Linda better, but I feel she and Dad come down often, so I feel I know Linda real well. You have to prioritize things in life, and with all the stresses we've had it has not been a priority in our life to meet her children.

FRAMO: Ann, would you want to?

ANN: I don't know whether it's a top priority. I think it would be good to get together. I think, with this family, it's important that we don't spread ourselves too thin. This is a problem with our family in general. We should concentrate on what we're doing here, and not spread ourselves too thin, but it happens. Yes, I would be willing to try it.

TIM: I would go to a reunion, but I don't have energy to spare.

LEVINE: Apparently, it's important to Linda and your dad. They have said
           it would be a blessing if they could see all their children in one
           place. I can see your point: that you're not eager to get new broth-
           ers and sisters. You're still dealing with your first family. But ap-
           parently this is important to your father and Linda, and I hope it
           could happen for them. That would be a gift for your parents.
           What happens after that will be up to you all.

FRAMO: Katie, I didn't give you an opportunity to say what you would
           like from this family from now on.

KATIE: Well, I guess, with everyone except Tim, to continue the way it is.
           I feel comfortable with Dad and Lynn. I guess with Ann, to keep
           in touch more.

FRAMO: What would you like from Tim?

KATIE: Well . . . [she smiles and looks toward Tim]

FRAMO: That you continue to work out stuff with each other?

LEVINE: Do you ever give each other a hug?

TIM: Yes.

KATIE: Yes. [begins to cry]

LEVINE: I'm just checking.

FRAMO: Let's ask Thomas. What would you like from this family from
           now on, Thomas?

THOMAS: To get along.

FRAMO: Get along, Thomas?

THOMAS: Yes.

LEVINE: Steve and Annie, how about you in your relationship with your
           in-laws? Would you like anything different?

STEVE: I would like to develop relationships more than they are. We
           don't get to see Ann and Mark much, and Tim and Annie. Paul
           and Linda have been coming down the past couple of springs. So
           I want those things to continue, and I will make some efforts to
           come closer to the family. We don't want to lose our contact with
           Lynn, even though she is in the Midwest.

FRAMO: Let's give Annie a chance.

ANNIE: I'd like to see people more often. It's always been a point with us
           to have family and friends visit. I think we've been trying to find
           a place to live that would get the most people to come.

TIM: It's important to both of us that you visit us. And I don't know if
           you know how important this is to us.

LEVINE: Ann, if Mark were here, what do you think he would say he would like changed?

ANN: He doesn't know any of my brothers and sisters, except Lynn. I think that's very important, because he wants to be a part of the family very much.

LEVINE: So he'd like to be more a part of the family, and get to know people better?

ANN: Yes.

LEVINE: Is it difficult for him to take initiative, like calling Tim up to chat, saying, "Hey, I don't know you; you're my wife's brother. Who are you?"

ANN: Not really. If the opportunity were there he would do it, but it's hard for him to take that kind of initiative.

LEVINE: Before we end, I would like to say a few things about my impressions about this family. Although I wasn't present at the first meeting, I did watch the videotape. Last year, the family talked about Mom's death, and the good and the bad parts of growing up with Mom. You also talked about your struggles with Dad, and how you could emotionally touch Dad, and how Dad could touch you so that you might have more closeness. You dealt with your relationships as brothers and sisters, and there are a lot of feelings about stepfamily relationships. But the themes keep developing, and I would hope this process will continue. I think one of the things that is important about this kind of work is that when raising your own children you will begin to notice the struggles you have with them, and the ties to this family. That's when you take the next step—from what happens with you all to what happens with the next generation and your extended family.

FRAMO: When your kids grow up they'll get to see what the last family was like, what heritage you are passing down, because the growth just continues. For example, your dad has gone beyond what his father gave, and as parents you will go beyond what was given to you . . . Okay, folks, I think it's been great to be with you all again. If we can be of any further service to any of you let us know.

DAD: Let me say, again, our thanks to both of you. You've been very, very kind, introspective, on target, very helpful, very kind.

FRAMO: Okay, folks. It was good to see you all again. [everyone shakes hands with Framo and Levine]

(Levine: By the end of these sessions, I had grown fond of this family. I also respected their willingness to discuss the hard issues that had remained underground for so many years. I also noticed how the family had changed since their initial consultation. First, Paul spoke more directly and seemed more aware of his children's feelings. Tim and Katie were continuing to flush out their differences in a more honest and open manner. Ann had moved from feeling like an outsider to a more insider position; and Lynn, although she was less open in these sessions, was beginning to make her statement as an adult in this family. Although Thomas had not changed, his siblings seemed more responsive to his desire for more contact. In terms of our cotherapy work, I always learn more about therapy when I work with Jim. He is very down to earth, a good antidote to my hyperintellectual tendencies.)

(Framo: At the end, here, I became aware of how much I had come to care for this family. Each person in the family had come to mean something to me; they were real people, not just clients. I knew I would remember them. I knew I would, through Tim, find out what happened to all of them in later years. Felise and I are a smoothly functioning cotherapy team. I always appreciate her presence in sessions because she notices things I do not see, and she has a way of couching uncomfortable interventions in a palatable way. When we see things differently we discuss these differences in front of the family, presenting a model for the handling of differences.)

Chapter 12

RESPONSES TO THE FOLLOW-UP FAMILY CONSULTATION

TIMOTHY T. WEBER, PhD

This follow-up family meeting, one year later, was less surprising and dramatic than the first family consultation. We were more familiar with the "procedure," with Jim's style and temperament, with our own family dance around our emotional life. I felt consoled with Felise's presence as she buttressed the "holding environment" for the family, especially bringing a female sensitivity to the emotional "hunger" of the family, attending to the continuing impact of the "loss" of mother, and more directly supporting my sisters. The balance of the consultants' genders as well as their own personal styles added richness to the conversation, although it seemed Jim was more in charge because Felise had not participated in the first family consultation.

The inclusion of Katie's husband, Steve, and my wife, Annie, for the second half of the day lessened some of the intensity of the morning session. Having my wife present did add to my sense of increasing accountability; it would be difficult for me to make promises about my own life and not keep them because she would be following me. It didn't take long. Right after the meeting, she had direct feedback for me: "You're writing off what Katie says." Annie also felt relieved as she heard how other family members experienced me, especially the "problems they have with me." She felt at least partially exonerated, exclaiming, "I'm not crazy."

In spite of the greater support and familiarity in this meeting, I also felt more fragile. The first family conversation felt shocking, revealing, and dramatic. Now we were at a point where we could deepen and intimately explore the issues identified in the first consultation. I felt less certain, more exposed, more challenged toward authenticity. I could hide less behind the drama and the novel, the initial "getting to know you" of a family having this kind of encounter for the first time. Ongoing conversations feel more threatening and, at the same time, afforded greater potential for change and honesty.

Shortly after this consultation, Katie phoned me one night reporting her experience that the family meeting was "good, but it seems, Tim, like you've got a lot of problems." Immediately I felt the cost of having risked in the family meeting. I tried to respond less defensively and more openly about the problems that I struggled with and challenges I faced—more real, less controlled, less reactive, more affectionate. I had to bridle myself from pushing back into a competitive match over who, really, had the most problems!

Although Jim and Felise did inquire about changes in the family, I also felt under examination in the follow-up family consultation with my own internal test questions: "Did the first consultation make any difference?" "Has all of this been a disappointment and failure for the family?" "Did I, did any of us, really make any substantial changes, or was the first session all hype and no action?" On a larger scale, "Does psychotherapy, at least in this form or in any form, really help healing between people?" On a smaller scale, "Would the consultants be pleased or disappointed in how our family responded to the family intervention last year?" "Did we pass the test?" The most important question: "Were we evolving as a family toward more honesty and love, a feeling of greater confidence and less weariness in life, or were we stuck, mired in impossibility in spite of a high-powered family encounter with consultants?" I had a deep investment in wanting to hear stories of hope and possibility. I wanted to believe that something better was evolving.

The family interactions during the past year appeared to embody new stories of connection, compassion, deeper honesty and directness. Thomas, my father, and I took an extensive tour to my father's family of origin in the Midwest, visiting his siblings and inquiring about memories of family relationships, emotional struggles, and secrets, as well as fond recollections. All of us in the family seemed to be taking increased initiative in contacting each other with conversations that felt more real and authentic and courageous at times. Annie, my wife, had been telling me that she noticed some differences in my parenting. She saw me embracing the father role with more gusto and care, especially with David, our youngest child. She felt more confident in my ability to be a father. And yet I wondered if my personal enthusiasm was shared by others. How did others in the family experience themselves and family members changing, if at all?

I was anxious when Jim asked the question several times, "What has changed in the family since our last meeting?" My worry grew when family members appeared to have a slow, cool response. Although I had perhaps hoped for a few "born again" testimonials about how this family consultation had been riveting and life changing like some hyped movie review, I was willing to settle for some tepid reports of change and satisfaction. I didn't want to hear what Ann said as she responded, "The effort has been there, but not the results." I wanted to leap and defend our work, but did not, restraining myself, waiting for more feedback.

As the conversation continued, stories of change slowly emerged, such as the more direct and revealing conversation between Ann and my father during their road trip from Oregon to California for this second family consultation and his subsequent observation that Ann seemed "more at home with herself." That one observation felt powerful to me, not only because it described what I think is core to this work, the "at-homeness" with oneself and one's family, but it reflected the sensitivity of my father to even notice and report this kind of observation. Simple alertness to emotional process and a willingness to speak about one's consciousness, as my father showed here, are fundamental signs of a family's hopeful evolution. I was also proud of my sister for having had the courage to speak honestly to my father. During the past year I had experienced that feeling of greater integrity and lightness in my relationship with him; perhaps Ann was on the same road.

Simple shifts were happening in our midst, in our very conversations together in the family meetings as we were more alive, authentic, and direct speaking and listening to those issues that mattered. We were being different with each other as a concern about "no difference" was uttered! Yet, we were reluctant to both see and celebrate the small shifts that, indeed, were being reported in our conversation. Why this refusal to confidently acknowledge movement ahead? Were we afraid of hope, lest we again become disappointed? Were we victims of our own pride, not wanting to attribute too much change to the therapeutic process, something "done" to us from outside consultants? Perhaps both our religious heritage and our family temperament put more emphasis on suffering instead of joy, leading us to understate any positivity while punctuating an almost joyless obligation to suffer and serve anyway. As the conversation unfolded, we snuck in small victories of change, camouflaged beneath the dominant picture of struggle.

These references to positive change were encouraging. Katie noted how we siblings had collaborated in celebrating my father's birthday. More significantly, she also noted how we had come together as a sibling coalition to advocate for more fair recognition of our father at the college where he had served for over 25 years, writing a letter to the president of the college expressing our specific concerns about a portrait dedicated to him at the college. Katie also talked about supporting Lynn in her job search, and the family's quick response to our daughter Stacy's acute illness. Katie punctuated these memories with a confident, "I think things really happened."

These recollections of positive change were intermingled with disclosures of ongoing struggles. The most perturbing struggle in this family, distributed among all of us but less expressed by my father, was this profound yearning for acknowledgment, appreciation, recognition. We all seemed to be working so hard while hungering to be seen, desired, and credited.

This longing was hidden beneath distracting issues like the squabbles between Katie and me, debates and disputes around irrelevant issues.

As we all were more expressive about our yearning, I began to feel more aware of my own isolation in life and the emotional cost. Historically, I had managed our family stress through my distancing, busyness, and the drive for accomplishment and recognition outside the family. To compensate for the uncertainty of relationships in my family, I drove myself to pile up numbers as a form of credit—grades, sports statistics, hours worked, clients seen, accumulated money. This crediting by numbers felt more certain than the hoped-for crediting and acknowledgment from my family. Not surprisingly, however, crediting by numbers, regardless of how big the numbers are, does not begin to address the yearnings of the emotional life and the desire to be seen and loved that only relationships, especially family relationships, can offer.

More and more I was becoming aware in these conversations of the emotional deficits we incurred as we lived in a professional household with "all eyes on us" because of my father's academic position. The explicit, but more frequently implicit, message was to excel and do well and, concurrently, hide "not well." Getting into trouble, underachieving, challenging norms all seemed to not serve the goal of "doing well."

My brother Thomas, with his mental handicap and his unpredictable, bizarre, and embarrassing behavior, inadvertly fulfilled the role of acting out the "dark side" for all of us. Nothing was left for us, and thus we were compelled to make up for his deficit by driving to be even more excellent. None of this was overtly mandated. There were no explicit and conscious directives from either my father or mother to make up for anything or to protect anyone. Nonetheless, the unspoken emotional field in the family was powerful in directing our passions and aversions as we grew older and long after we physically left the family.

We were caught within this emotional trap as we repeatedly voiced our fragilities and yearnings for more aliveness between us, something deeper, more connecting, more human, less manicured and polished. Themes during these conversations centered on becoming more whole, integrating those split off parts of our family legacy that we had sacrificed in service of excellence.

Jim and Felise helped illuminate and amplify these lost dimensions of family life necessary for well-being. We were a busy, working family; we had not integrated the peace of relaxation, of doing nothing. We were a giving family, more focused on giving to others outside the family as "missions" than to those within the family; we had not integrated the ability to receive well and to generously acknowledge the giver. We were a serious family, prone to argue, debate, and contend with each other; we had not integrated having fun and enjoying life and one another. We were an ambitious family, typically striving for more as if what we had was not good enough; we had not integrated the ability to celebrate what had been accomplished as sufficient. We were inclined toward intellectual arguments; we had not integrated our emotions well into our life together. We felt pressed to look good in service of doing well; we had not integrated our courage to disclose fragilities and struggles.

These themes especially permeated this second family consultation as we were challenged to become more whole and less divided, rewriting the family script to integrate these disowned aspects of healthy family life. These stories also had been developing long before our family of origin, rooted in the generations that had preceded us as my father had alluded to in his description of his own family life. I wondered how typical these struggles were in most families. And yet, while wondering how different or "strange" we might be, I was increasingly believing that our family was struggling with issues central to all family life. I was feeling more encouraged in the honesty of our humanity.

One way or another, a family will attempt to integrate lost parts, usually indirectly. Now I began to understand the possible "reason" behind the long list of somatic complaints in our family, including mine. Somatic complaints were "acceptable" complaints and failures, in contrast to behavioral, psychological, or relationship concerns, which seemed to be linked more to the self and one's character. My brother cornered the market on psychological acting out, with my mother a close second. Somatic complaints, on the other hand, were more tolerable "failings," less under our control and volition, especially in a culture that so systematically separates the link between mind and body, the self and the soma.

No wonder I complained of headaches, pseudo brain tumors, and the prospect of imminent death because of some disease process. Somehow my dark, ailing side had to come forth but in a way in which my personality still could look "excellent." As I reflected on myself, I wondered about other family members and the emotional forces behind physical complaints and diseases. These physical complaints and failings also could generate more empathic responses than any personality failing or vulnerability. How was I fatiguing my life through indirect expressions rather than through direct and authentic declarations? Was this the source of much fatigue and distress in life—indirect, counterfeit communication?

I thought of another example. Why was I so preoccupied with death? I think the premature death of my mother certainly punctuated my fear of early death and staying alert for warning symptoms. But there was more here. With the family's rigorous attention to "acceptability" and a history of being preoccupied with the functioning of my brother and mother and the marginalizing of the rest of us, an emotional "megaphone" seemed necessary to be heard. Something big needed to happen to redirect attention. Perhaps I had to focus on death for acknowledgment. Having suffered the loneliness that comes from "doing well," could I find affection and connection by ringing the bell of death? These preoccupations and expressions of my concerns certainly were not by conscious design.

I wanted to work toward being less indirect, not using my body to speak for me, especially in my search for affection and care. These family conversations were challenging me with the adventure of integration and authenticity sparked by more awareness of myself in relationship with others in the family. I believed that if I were moving more in this direction, I would not only help myself, but more directly through my actions invite other family members from a busy hardness into more soft tenderness and closeness.

We were shifting in these conversations between tenderness and hardness, fragility and arguments. We were conversing about closeness more than ever before, tilling new emotional soil for this consciousness and more possibility of behavioral changes. We were raising the bar on the conversation about our needs, sustaining the discomfort and perhaps cocreating more capacity in us for this kind of talk and feeling. Felise and Jim kept us from escaping. Perhaps one role of family consultants is to function like loving prison guards—prevent escape and shine the bright lights so that we all come out from our shadows to more of a live encounter. As tough as it was, a greater human give and take was emerging. As I described my experience of isolation, for example, Lynn remarked, "I think I'm hearing you for the first time . . . seeing you as a human being."

I felt more give and take with my sisters but, strangely, I also began to be aware of my loneliness as the one brother with three sisters and one handicapped brother. I had spoken more harshly in these meetings about my suspicion that my sisters were talking about me. I challenged them to be more direct with me, to gossip less. Behind this commanding challenge was a more fragile feeling of being alone as the brother with sisters; as close as I might try to be with them, I could never cross the gender barrier and, for that reason, I believed I would always feel "left out" to some extent. And I was aware of their understandable preference to talk with each other, especially Katie and Lynn.

I felt like an outsider, like an only child. My father was my father; increasing comfort and peerhood with him still bumped up against the generational barrier. My brother was unreachable as a peer. His status as a handicapped brother, although evoking compassion and care from all of us, created an unpenetrable sibling barrier. In so many ways, I have felt like an only child, determined around my self-sufficiency, feeling more isolated, uneasy in relating, and trying to connect with others in ways that don't often feel engaging to others. I also began to acknowledge that I have felt more comfortable around females than males, sometimes feeling like I was attempting to relate to other women as substitute sisters if I couldn't get closer to my real sisters. I had a sense that I was searching for my "substitute brother" with my two sons, real male companionship. Whatever the motivation, Annie did observe that I was actively involved in the lives of my sons with affection and interest. I also felt more intentional and committed to this work of being in the lives of my children after these family conversations about longing for relationships.

Nonetheless, I faced some primary challenges with my siblings. How could I continue to work on developing closer and more open relationships with my sisters, knowing, in the end, that I would be an alien male? How could I work on embracing my brother as a male sibling, finding new ways to also be more intimate with him while recognizing and accepting the inherent limitations between us? How could I deepen my intimacy with my father, accepting the generational barrier as a challenge to develop friendships with other males rather than retreating to further isolation? I had a beginning appreciation for the importance of sibling relationships as sustaining across the life span and the criticalness of including siblings in these family consultations so that the future can be more directly negotiated and sustained.

Our lives continued to evolve as the months passed after the second family consultation. We seemed to be enacting in small ways our commitments for more closeness and honesty. For example, Lynn did get married about two years after the family consultation. After the wedding celebration in Ohio, my father, Katie and her family, and I and my family, all crowded into two cars on a family tour through three states. We visited my father's boyhood home and neighborhood as he told stories about his early years, stopping by his family's church and school, which he attended and where his father had taught for over 50 years. Before leaving his hometown, we gathered around the graveside of both his parents. We then traveled to Indiana, to the hometown where Katie, Thomas, and I grew up, walking through our old home where we had lived in over 30 years previously and touring our old grade school, peppering our tour with anecdotes from our own recollection. Our children seemed to be more interested in the motel swimming pool—so much for these family stories that begin to fade as the generations pass.

There seemed to be more desires to visit each other. Phone calls increased slightly and were used as opportunities to inquire further about our personal lives instead of merely "doing business" with each other. Emotional versatility appeared to increase; we expressed worry, concern, irritation, struggles, pleasure, hope in more open ways with each other. I experienced this openness, for example, on a trip with my father. I had invited him to go with me to a professional conference, using the trip as an opportunity to talk about his history, my mother, and our relationship. I felt more free to invite him, not out of obligation, but out of care. He was more open with me, sharing more intimacies of his life with my mother, which helped me better appreciate her passion and joy for life.

A year after this trip, my father was in trouble one night during a business trip to California. From his hotel room, he called Linda complaining of a pain in his chest, attributing the pain to acidic discomfort after his dinner. Linda called Katie and me because she was worried; we all got on the phone and strongly pushed my father to go to the hospital, fearing that his pains signaled more ominous problems. I couldn't help recollecting the death of my mother. Sure enough, my father was in the process of suffering a heart attack. Linda, Katie, and I quickly changed our plans, boarded a plane the next morning, and were off to California, convening at the airport and speeding to a rural hospital in the heartland of California's agricultural belt.

Coming into this rural hospital, it didn't take long for us to find the cardiac care unit. We all walked gently into the room, talked to the nurse, and were directed to my father's bedside. As we approached him hooked up to wires, tubes, and the beeping monitors, our eyes met his. We bent down, softly embracing him in bed, quietly crying as we touched him. He could talk. He was stabilized. We found out his heart had suffered damage, but the damage had been contained. He was safe and the story of my mother's sudden death would not, at least for now, be repeated. We felt a care, a rush to respond without hesitation, an urgency to be with each other.

Families often respond in these ways, with or without family of origin consultations. But I thought there was a deeper texture to our coming together beyond the urgency of our physical presence. It felt like we all were being held by a greater emotional strength, a resiliency that was too deep for words. I even had the fantasy in that moment that my father's life had been saved, in part, because he was held by his confidence in the family's emotional presence with him, generated through the two family consultations and sustained by our continuing work over the years.

I and other family members have continued our lives, sometimes recollecting our family consultations, but more often simply living through the comings and goings of ordinary life. I believe these family meetings have given me and our family continuing opportunities to evolve in new and different ways.

We all have wondered from time to time whether these consultations did really make any difference, especially during those times when we all have succumbed to old behaviors as if we had not learned anything.

And yet, I feel a new resilience within myself and the family as we have faced interesting crises that appear in the lives of most families. It seems like we believe, more than before, that change is possible, not only in the future, but in the past. G. K. Chesterton once said that "history is the remembrance of our remembrances." We were remembering differently as these family conversations unfolded, shifting the way we thought we had been. And so our past was changing as our memory of the past was changing.

The past also seemed bigger and richer as we collectively amalgamated our recollections; there was more substance to our history than what existed on the thin scaffolding of our individual view. And that substance of our history felt less intimidating as the stories flagged as untouchable "minefields" in our collective unconscious were touched and unpacked. Locked up secrets suck a family's vitality.

Although we drift into our own private lives and are occupied by the urgencies of our own families, there does seem to be more intentionality of linking up with each other. Conversations can be more adventuresome and daring, diving with less hesitation toward authenticity regardless of the emotional tone from joy to irritation. It has felt like we have more confidence in our mutual ability to bounce back. There has been more inquiry and curiosity about our private lives, feeling not intrusive but supportive. Secrets and assumptions have been challenged and demythologized, opening a more human but risky adventure. We are more willing to tell the truth and hear the truth, the reciprocal obligations of authenticity. We're still having problems with joyfulness, although aging is helping loosen the tight ropes of having to appear competent and committed to suffering service. I certainly have had my share of the challenges in parenting and marriage. But I believe I have been a better father and more interested in evolving into a better father and husband as a result of this ongoing work with my family.

All this evolution comes mixed with the reality of disappointments, drifting into inattention, lapses of disinterest, some crises that are quite challenging and seem insurmountable, and complaints of unfairness and lack of support. But this is life with all its accompanying suffering. With less illusion, we have more courage to continue to evolve with hope and possibility. I have greater trust in myself, but more importantly, greater confidence in our collective life together. I believe we will help each other become better people. And I am more confident that we have the strength as a family to live our ordinary lives with imagination and hope.

PART IV

EPILOGUE

Chapter 13

AUTHORS' TRIALOGUE

JAMES L. FRAMO, PhD
TIMOTHY T. WEBER, PhD
FELISE B. LEVINE, PhD

In the latter stages of writing this book, the three authors of this book got together and tape recorded an unrehearsed discussion of the whole experience of the family-of-origin consultation with Tim's family. During the intervening years we had been doing the detail work of organizing the book as well as continuing our own clinical practices. The discussion was transcribed word for word and the informal nature of the conversation was retained.

In this trialogue we covered a wide range of topics: We compared our ideas about family-of-origin work; the place of family-of-origin consultations in the realm of treatment methods; the results of Felise's follow-up phone interviews with the members of Tim's family; the almost visceral resistance on the part of both clients and therapists to involve their families in treatment; the value of cotherapy; the timing, spacing, and length of sessions; why intergenerational therapy is not more widely used; and so on.

As a participant observer, Tim evaluated his personal experience of the process; his appraisal of how Jim and Felise conducted the sessions; changes that occurred as a result of the procedure; and his critique of how the method could be improved.

Excerpts from the transcript of the discussion follow:

LEVINE: Tim, what was it like for you as a member of a family undergoing the family-of-origin experience? It has been some years since our initial and follow-up consultations with your family, Tim. The passage of time gives us a unique opportunity to reflect upon the consultations themselves, and also to discuss the family-of-origin consultation as a treatment method.

FRAMO: I see two levels here, Tim. Actually, one is you as a member of the family, and you as a therapist, theoretician.

WEBER: Right. Yeah. So let me just comment as a member of the family, and then discuss how my personal experience informs my theoretical views.

FRAMO: I want to hear about your experience as a family member. When you originally contacted me about bringing your family in, you had an agenda of things you were concerned about that you wanted to deal with. Do you feel they were dealt with?

WEBER: Yes.

FRAMO: Was anything on your agenda that was important that you never got to?

WEBER: Yeah, there were some things like that. I've written some notes that helped me to think about the usefulness of this: How was this useful to me, how was this whole experience useful?

LEVINE: What came to mind when you were jotting down some thoughts?

WEBER: What came to mind was that this experience was useful because it cleaned up a lot of unfinished business.

LEVINE: Like with Mom?

WEBER: With Mom, with father, with siblings. We had never really had any extended conversation of substance about our history and our relationships. That never really happened.

FRAMO: You mean all together?

WEBER: Yeah.

FRAMO: Twosomes were doing it all the time.

WEBER: Well, twosomes were doing it on a hit-and-miss, sometimes in an ambush fashion, as I think happens in most families. But there had never been any sustained conversation of substance in the system about our life and history and our future and our relationships. And I found that I was stuck frozen. There had been issues such as Mom's death, my relationship with Dad, relationships with siblings, Thomas's retardation. I wanted to know how I was seen by other members of the family. I wanted feedback about myself . . .

FRAMO: You found that out, too.

WEBER: Yeah. I did.

LEVINE: You'd do it again, it sounds like.

WEBER: Oh, I would do it again, because it widened the lens and it deepened our relationship, you know. It was sort of like, just from a kinesthetic point of view, the lens widened and the relationships deepened.

LEVINE: Do you think other family members would agree with you about that? For example, if Dad were sitting here would he say that relationships have deepened? Because when I did the follow-up phone interviews everyone's consensus was that this family hadn't changed as much as you had changed. Your sisters reported that they were responding mostly to the changes in you, Tim; and that their main change was that they were less bothered by some of Dad's behavior, such as his distancing. They were more accepting of him, but they primarily saw you as the person who changed the most.

FRAMO: So they ended up with more acceptance of Dad as he is.

LEVINE: *We* would say that that's a huge change in the system, even though they didn't recognize it as one.

FRAMO: Yes, that *is* a change.

LEVINE: That's in many ways what we hope people would get from these sessions.

FRAMO: Well, when they said that Tim had changed did they say in what way?

LEVINE: They said that Tim was more accessible, that he's more in the family. They noted that they were getting to know Tim better, and felt closer to him. They were a little protective of Dad. They worried that his feelings were hurt.

FRAMO: I think they're leaving out what Tim's talking about, though. He feels that all relationships in the family have deepened. It's the first time that the family members got to know what's been going on inside each other family member, that they had never talked about before as a family together.

LEVINE: But that's something that *we*, as family therapists, value. Not all families value openly sharing feelings or discussing sensitive issues in front of one another. In fact, in some cultures family members experience openness as disrespectful, as a violation of privacy, and as a threat to family harmony. Family therapists assume that openness leads to deeper relationships. Maybe this isn't always true. That's why I asked you, Tim, about whether your father and sisters would agree with you that the family relationships have deepened.

WEBER: I think they're very global in terms of their cognitive awareness. I think, globally, they would say, "Well, perhaps we're a little bit more connected with one another." I think they would say that perhaps Tim's a little bit more open. I think those are the two things they would say, but I don't think they would go much beyond that. I think they would probably say it probably hurt my dad.

LEVINE: Which they did say. Each of your sisters was very concerned that they and you said things in the sessions that hurt your father's feelings. Yet, when I asked him about this he said no, that his feelings were not hurt.

WEBER: And I think they would probably say Dad hasn't changed much.

LEVINE: Right. That's exactly what they said in response to my phone questions.

WEBER: I think they would acknowledge little change, or little awareness about themselves and about the family. They might acknowledge that it was probably good to talk about Mom's life and death— we got that out. It was a much needed cathartic experience. But I don't think they would talk much about the spreading effects— that the sessions impacted other close relationships. I don't think they'd say they learned anything stunningly new.

FRAMO: A spreading effect was when you and your dad and Thomas, after the session, took a trip together to visit Mom's and Dad's families of origin. That's a spreading effect.

WEBER: Yeah. But I don't think they'd acknowledge that. See, I think there's been enormous spreading effects. And I think the family reports spreading effects, as they did in the follow-ups, at the same time saying nothing changed.

LEVINE: Like what?

WEBER: Well . . . Remember the follow-up session, when the question was asked, "Has anything changed?" The response was, "No." And then they'd tell about the changes. I think there's a disconnection between the incident, the family-of-origin consultation, and their observations. I don't think they would correlate these events.

FRAMO: But, you know, some parts of the first two hours were very painful for family members, particularly around Mom. And you don't want to say, "That was a good experience, and I got a lot from it." Mourning is very difficult. There was a lot of pain around Mom. Everybody was crying. I mean, that's not a pleasant experience.

WEBER: I think they think that that recollection probably hurt my dad.

FRAMO: The recollection about Mom?

WEBER: Yeah.

LEVINE: In the follow-up phone interview, when I asked Dad about that, he didn't report feeling hurt.

WEBER: Right. I don't think he's as hurt as my sisters thought.

FRAMO: Well, protectiveness of Dad was a family theme from the time you were a little boy.

LEVINE: But I think you are right. I suspect your dad isn't nearly as hurt as your sisters thought. Because when I interviewed him on the phone in the follow-up, he said quite directly that he was not hurt. But when you say that you've noticed certain changes. For example, if Katie is having a problem is she likely to call you up and talk about it with you? Or if something's on your mind and you want to run it by a family member, are you likely to call someone up?

WEBER: Right. Here's how I think this work has been useful for me and for the family. This is my own judgment, even if they don't acknowledge it. One is that it's cleaned up some unfinished business, so that things such as jealousy, envy, subsystems, alienation, secrets, feelings, and thoughts that are not shared were demystified. A lot of that's been cleaned up, so instead of there being a cloudy lens over the family it's a lot clearer. And there's not a lot of energy put into maintaining old secrets from unfinished business. More of the energy is freed up to be here-and-now in the future.

FRAMO: Well, I think that's good. Having gone over the transcripts, I'm more familiar with some of the actual words. So, for example, I thought in the session when Katie really opened up about what it was like for her to come and see this family, she said, "Am I thin, am I fat, nobody's interested in what I'm doing"; and said to you, Tim, "You don't even know me as a person." I thought, you know, it's the first time she really opened up like that to you. So you have some idea of what she's been struggling with. Then when you opened up, "This is what I struggle with: I have trouble relating," they got to know more about what was going on inside you. We got to know a hell of a lot more about what was going on inside Ann. Prior to the family meeting Ann was only talking to Lynn. Do you see what I'm getting at here?

WEBER: Yes, I do.

LEVINE: Tim, in your earlier statement you mentioned putting some closure or some ending on some of the old business. Then the energy in the present doesn't go back to maintaining the old patterns, the old resentments, the old feelings that "I have to protect myself." You can truly be present and enjoy each other in a new way. I think that's one of the really big benefits of this work. And part of what you're saying is that, even though they might not attribute it to the session, there's a positive change there.

WEBER: Right.

FRAMO: I think this is relevant to all psychotherapies. There are a lot of people, at the end of a psychotherapy experience, whose life has changed. They're organized a lot better, et cetera, but you ask, "How was that therapy for you?" and the reply is, "Oh, not much. I didn't get much out of it." I mean, this happens, I think, with a lot of patients at the end of their psychotherapy. I don't know how you account for it.

WEBER: I have a cognitive correlation.

FRAMO: What do you mean?

WEBER: They don't attribute the particular outcome to a particular stimulus. If you did outcome research based upon physiological and relationship changes you might see a difference in the client's attribution about what changed in psychotherapy.

FRAMO: I've also seen the opposite. People didn't get much out of the therapy at all, but they go around telling everybody what a wonderful therapy experience they had, and they're still engaged in the same old behavior. Have you seen that: praising the therapy without change?

WEBER: Yeah. I want to add some other ideas about changes that are correlated with family-of-origin consultations. I think relationships become clearer. There's more smoothness in relationships, in that I could go to anybody without regretting that I haven't talked about something. That the resources—the psychic, the relational resources—are used for present and future. And I'm not thinking that this is a pseudo mutual relationship . . .

LEVINE: So you're not pretending.

WEBER: No. There's not any barrier.

FRAMO: It's more real.

WEBER: Right. There's not an incongruency.

FRAMO: . . . fewer secrets.

WEBER: Yeah. Like, I can go to my dad . . . Everybody in the family could die right now, and I would not regret not having said something to them.

FRAMO: That's good.

Levine: I think that's a critical statement for you to make, Tim.

FRAMO: It is, it is.

LEVINE: If all relationships cease as of the next moment, you wouldn't regret how you've been able to be with them, and them with you.

WEBER: Yeah.

LEVINE: Jim, this is the essence of your work. If I were to say to someone what was Jim Framo's dream when he did this work, I would say that that's probably, in the simplest language, what your dream is.

FRAMO: Nothing important is left unsaid.

LEVINE: Yes. And there are no regrets. When death comes, when people lose a family member, they feel the relationship has come to a point where the important things have been said.[1] They've worked out the old stuff, so they can be free to love each other, or they could be free to let each other go if they need to.

WEBER: There's a real freedom. I mean, I think that's a critical point.

FRAMO: Let me ask a concrete question. As you notice, if you look through the transcript, I kept saying, "How much are you going to call each other in the future," and I even made a joke about whether you're going to make the telephone companies rich. I said I'll wager that in the future there's going to be a lot more contact. You know, because years went by with only minimal contact.

WEBER: Right. There's been more contact.

FRAMO: Do you call Ann, Katie, Lynn . . .

WEBER: Yeah. I'm the one. I would say that if you had my sisters here they would say, "He's the one who actually calls." There's glitches, but we . . .

FRAMO: Do they ever call you?

WEBER: One of my concerns is that, no, they don't call much. Dad calls. Thomas calls. Dad and Thomas call. They don't call unless there's a logistical issue that we have to work out. They don't call to just talk.

LEVINE: How come?

FRAMO: I was just talking to my sister a few minutes ago.

WEBER: I heard you.

---

1. Jim Framo died on August 22, 2001, as we were completing the editing of this book. Speaking as his wife, and on behalf of his daughters and his family of origin, we all agree that when he died the important things had been said. Jim lived his theories.

LEVINE: Jim calls his sisters and brother every week. Or they call him. I think the close ties in your Italian family have influenced your work, Jim.

FRAMO: Also, we're all getting old. We used to call each other every four or five months. And at the end of the conversation now we say, "I love you." We never used to say that.

WEBER: In our family, we know we can count on each other. We now have family reunions once a year, or maybe once every two years.

FRAMO: So if I said to you why don't you call each one of your sisters with no agenda, no appointment, just to say, "How are you?"

WEBER: I did that.

FRAMO: Oh, you do do that.

WEBER: I took Ann out for a lunch two weeks ago. We went to this nice restaurant in Seattle, we just sat down, we talked. We talked about matters of substance. Ann was ready, I was ready. We just made the date, and we said let's do this once every couple of months.

FRAMO: I think Katie saw some of your pain. All the sisters did. They saw you originally as way out there on this pedestal; Tim is this "accomplished person," they admired you. But you weren't real to them until you opened up about your pain.

WEBER: Well, I think everybody's role is demythologized in some way. That's another result of these meetings. There's more fluidity in role perception; there's less rigidity. There's a demythologizing of who people are—as the hero or the father. There's just much more, I think, fluidity in how people . . .

LEVINE: Tim, were there other changes resulting from the family-of-origin sessions?

WEBER: We're more of a resource for one another. There's more responsiveness, there's less resentment. There's a freedom in relating, and there's a sense of family as opposed to individuals. The "self" and the "we." There's more substance to who I am other than just myself. I'm part of a history of an evolving group. So, I think I've become a stronger self, but I'm also more conscious of my we-ness.

LEVINE: Whitaker talked about that in terms of family nationality, a sense of belonging to the nation of your family, with its history and identification with the unit, with the group. But it's without sacrificing the individual's autonomy, integrity.

WEBER: Yeah. The twin paradox is that the self, I think, becomes much more strong in those experiences. It's so much like when you climb a peak, you're sitting on the summit of the peak and you're looking out, and you can see for hundreds of miles. It's that kind of experience that I'm much smaller in a much larger universe. That's the spiritual piece.

FRAMO: There are those who try to apply family systems theory to other systems: work situations, businesses, et cetera. I make the point that nothing, no other system in this world, will ever even come close to the family. It's just utterly different from all other systems. So I'm endorsing what you're both saying, now, about a sense of family. I think it's extremely important. In my judgment, people who don't have a family or don't even have a sense that they belong to one are much worse off than people who do.

WEBER: A sense of belonging.

FRAMO: That's right.

WEBER: You know, more and more these other systems seem so tenuous . . .

FRAMO: Your work situation is never going to become like a family, although stuff from the family can be acted out at work. But you can always leave your job. Try to leave your family.

WEBER: Right. Where I work is not a place where if I come to the door they have to take me in. I think these consultations are like catalytic experiences, also. I think they release potentiality for the future. I don't think that all the changes are quite addressed or opened up in the moment, or even in the ensuing moments.

LEVINE: Oh, I agree with you. I think, Jim, you routinely say at the end of your sessions, "We've just begun a process here."

FRAMO: Yeah, I just get the ball rolling.

LEVINE: We're very enthusiastic about this method, but it's important to let other people know that this process is not magical; not all the changes happen in the session.

FRAMO: Certainly not right away afterward, either.

LEVINE: Right. It's like hiking Mount Everest, and you reach the first base camp; that becomes the new launching pad for climbing to the next base camp. I think family-of-origin sessions create a new launching pad for the family over the years to address their relationships. And that also may be why people don't attribute so many of the changes directly to the family-of-origin session: because the change is in creating a new launching pad, which generates subtle changes over time.

FRAMO: And they don't make the connection between the family-of-origin sessions and the subtle shifts that take place in the family system over time.

LEVINE: Right. And also, I think, the family member who initiates the sessions probably does a lot of work to sustain the changes, which I suspect the other family members don't do as much. I also think the organizer of the session is also the family member most likely to continue launching from that new pad.

FRAMO: Tim, in your family, Lynn was sort of a second family healer. I thought she would continue the work and push for more changes.

LEVINE: It was very interesting, because in the phone follow-up interview two years after the California meeting, she was the least enthusiastic about the outcome of it, which absolutely surprised me because in the session . . .

FRAMO: She was the most open in the session.

LEVINE: But she felt guilty because she was young and impetuous and in hindsight feels she spoke too harshly about things, especially about Dad.

FRAMO: There was one point where she confronted her father and said, "I hate it when you talk in those abstract ways. Be real with me!"

LEVINE: I know. But I think that over the years it hasn't sat well with her. She feels that she hurt her father. Your dad hasn't said that he was particularly devastated. This is an example of how perceptions of family members can change following family-of-origin sessions. Jim and I did a family-of-origin session with one of my clients and she was extremely negative about the experience afterward. She just said it didn't help, it was a waste of time. But the spreading effect, in terms of her relationships with her daughters, was where the payoff occurred. A year later she felt very positive about her family-of-origin session. If hopes are raised or promises made, clients feel disappointed when the glow of the session wears off. If they don't continue to work on these disappointments and come to terms with the limitations in the family they are likely to feel the sessions are a waste of time.

WEBER: And in our family, when there was an absence of glow during the sessions and afterward, still positive changes were reported, although not necessarily attributed to the family-of-origin sessions.

FRAMO: It reminds me of major surgery. If you ask someone immediately after their surgery they feel crummy. But if you ask them later they view it differently.

LEVINE: Were there areas that you felt, Tim, could've been covered more?

WEBER: There's a limitation of time, and there's always a prioritizing, but here's some areas. The mental retardation of Thomas was touched upon, but I think the family sort of steered away and moved away from that. And I'm wondering if that area should have been opened up more.

FRAMO: I kept bringing him into the conversation.

LEVINE: But you mean a discussion . . .

WEBER: A discussion of his mental retardation.

FRAMO: They didn't want to talk about it. We gave them plenty of opportunity. You're the only one who did. Perhaps their hesitation was a response to being interviewed in front of a live audience.

LEVINE: I think that was part of it. One of Tim's sisters told me she was quite aware and inhibited by the audience presence.

WEBER: Yeah. Okay. So now the question would be, and this has something to do with process, too: at that point would it have been useful to have a discussion about the decision not to talk about the mental retardation, and what that's like in the family?

LEVINE: I think at any one moment in time the therapist can go down a lot of different roads. I think, Jim, your focus was on going back to the relationship issue about Mom, and their grief, and that didn't feel finished. And then there was the theme about Dad being saintly compared to Mom, who was seen as out of control and dangerous. I think it's useful to use cotherapists in family-of-origin consultations, because they see different things. For example, I might have said, "You know, earlier, Tim, you mentioned how hard it was for the family to talk about Thomas, his retardation. Is that something the family feels uncomfortable talking about?" It would then be up to you to ask your family why not. Because we don't, as family-of-origin consultants, have an agenda for the family.

FRAMO: I think they were trying to protect Thomas.

LEVINE: Oh, absolutely.

FRAMO: I think they were quite aware of how out of control Thomas could get, with psychoticlike behavior. And they must have witnessed some of these outbursts, so they figured it would make Thomas feel terrible if it were discussed.

LEVINE: I think it could have been useful to say, "It seems like such a difficult thing for this family to talk about. Can we understand that?"

WEBER: A meta conversation about the content.

LEVINE: Absolutely.

FRAMO: How do you think Thomas would've reacted had they reminded him of some of his more bizarre behavior?

WEBER: If we had had a sustained conversation about it, he would've become a little bit more, I would imagine, agitated. I don't think he would've been upset, actually. I think he would've been—in some of my fantasies—he might have been relieved, actually.

LEVINE: You'd have to ask him, though. You need to ask the person if it is okay to discuss him.

WEBER: Depends on his mood.

LEVINE: This raises another issue. Should every issue in a family be talked about?

FRAMO: No. I have, in many of these family-of-origin sessions, made a deliberate choice not to deal with certain things. We've both done that.

LEVINE: Now I would agree with you, but I think we're probably in the camp that says people have a right to their fantasies, to their private thoughts, to their private feelings . . .

WEBER: Well, in the paper you and I, Felise, have written, we make the point that people have a right to a private existence (Weber & Levine, 1996).

LEVINE: Absolutely. That's why I wanted to put that in the paper. I don't think that families have to, or should, talk about everything that goes on. For example, if Thomas does not have the capacity to truly make a choice about participating in a discussion about him he may not understand the implications of the choice. Is it fair to him for the family to talk about his retardation with him when he has a limited capacity to talk about himself? This is a legitimate ethical question. We don't want to give the family the impression that this topic is too powerful to talk about. Yet we need to be fair to all family members.

WEBER: Let me also just quickly mention some other content areas I wished we had discussed. One was Dad's death, not just Mom's death. Maybe a little bit more on the future and when Dad dies.

LEVINE: You mean, does everybody worry about Dad?

WEBER: Yeah, and his aging. You know, we've lost one parent, what about him? More on the emphasis of the potential loss of him. I'm curious about what would happen with that. The stepfamily issues . . .

FRAMO: Remember in the prep interview, you said, "Somebody's going to die"? And the theme of killing was mentioned a number of times. It was even mentioned in the second two hours. When everybody was criticizing Dad, you said, "I'm afraid we're going to kill him."

WEBER: Uh huh. I was protective of him.

FRAMO: But it's interesting that you didn't think we were going to hurt Dad's feelings. You jumped to the extreme: killing. That's an old theme: that you thought Mom's behavior was going to kill him.

WEBER: Yeah. [laughing]

LEVINE: I think that's Tim's style. When Tim decides he wants to deal with something he will use language almost to the absurd to shock the system.

FRAMO: I think this killing thing . . . There's a lot of it in the preparation interview. This is more than Tim's style. I think it's an unconscious preoccupation.

WEBER: There's a piece of Whitaker in me that helps me. I do amplify certain metaphors to get to a particular point. I also think that we had sort of a pseudo-mutual family in many ways, for a long period of time. I think that's less so now. But I think that part of my concern was that in the midst of pseudo-mutuality, there was rage, there was anger, there were suicidal and homicidal tendencies. So I think part of it was tapping into that . . .

LEVINE: Yeah. I think part of what you were picking up is, you know, you wonder, really, how emotionally present your father was with your mother. You wonder whether or not he hated her at times, as all husbands hate their wives and wives hate their husbands sometimes. I think you were using the language of love and hate when we were talking about murder. That's how I understand it.

FRAMO: And Ann felt she had killed her mother.

LEVINE: Yes. There are a lot of unspoken fantasies about death, murder, suicide. So you would have wanted us, Tim, to talk more about the fantasies around Dad's death, losing Dad. I think the stepfamily issue, we probably would not have gotten as much into.

FRAMO: We didn't get into it. You mean Dad's second marriage? We didn't deal with that.

LEVINE: No. But Tim is wondering why not talk about the stepfamily issues.

FRAMO: Did we in the follow-up consult?

WEBER: A little bit.

FRAMO: Oh, we did. Something having to do with money or something?

LEVINE: I think that we would, with stepfamily issues, have probably put some limits on the discussion around your father's second wife, Linda, and just have the family deal with your dad about what there was about his blended family that was specifically upsetting them. Because it's real easy to talk about the member who's not there, and put the blame on that member. I think we did, in the second consultation, get to some of the concern that there was a double standard around money, and that your siblings and you felt that your father had made a contract that was not fair to him.

WEBER: Uh huh.

LEVINE: Maybe, perhaps that's changed. I don't know. But you had hoped to have gotten into that in more depth in the first consultation?

WEBER: No, probably not in the first. And I have more mixed feelings about that, because of that very reason: These are people who aren't there, and it starts to widen the lens much farther. But I do think, at the same time, that there were issues between my dad and all of us regarding how Dad was handling certain things in the stepfamily. For example, he would come to—especially my sisters, less so me—and talk about feelings of unfairness. He would just throw out specific information that would create an alliance immediately between him and one of my sisters against Linda.

LEVINE: One of the things that I think we would and have done is that when we've seen things like that happen, we'll make a referral for the parents—the father and the stepmother—to go into couple's counseling, which is what they did. So your father must have gotten something out of the session and the discussions that followed the session that maybe made him more aware that he had some work to do in the new family that he'd created.

WEBER: Reluctantly, he went into counseling with Linda, but I think this experience freed him up to do it even though he didn't take the initiative, I don't think. It freed him up to be more responsive later on.

LEVINE: Well, there's a discussion in the session about Ann's request to go to family therapy, and your father's regret about not responding then, and perhaps not responding to your mother when she had obviously been struggling emotionally. I think you're right. I think the session probably did free him up to say he's not going to let this chance go by again and not be a participant. And maybe also the family-of-origin consultation gave him some familiarity with this kind of experience so he had more mastery under his belt.

WEBER: Uh huh. Just enough to . . .

LEVINE: Just enough to say, "Okay. I know what this is about. I can do this."

WEBER: I think it really did open him to be more receptive to interpersonal conversations later on in couples counseling. I think it did have that sense of mastery like, "This isn't so alien to me to be in these kinds of conversations. I can do them; I can get through 'em."

FRAMO: Are there other things you want to cover now, Tim? Because I have a list of things, too.

WEBER: Well, yeah. There's the questions about your own style, and I have some thoughts about how I think your style is useful.

FRAMO: How would you characterize the style?

WEBER: Your style, how it was useful, areas where I would have done something different, now, reflecting on things.

FRAMO: Overall, what I did in those sessions, how would you characterize that style?

WEBER: Okay. In one sentence? How's ten?

FRAMO: Go ahead.

WEBER: Well, I've come to believe certain things about you from this experience, and from reflecting on this experience and getting to know you more. I don't know whether I believed all this at the time. This is sort of an accumulated image of you. I think that one of the major things I think you do is that you create a more naturalistic context for a conversation between human beings, as opposed to a psychiatric context. Your person, your self-disclosure, your humor, your personhood creates a naturalistic context for the experience to be much more human.

FRAMO: So I don't make it seem like psychotherapy.

WEBER: No. It's more naturalistic as opposed to a psychiatric context. So I think you create that space in which the humanity of the participants is more free to emerge—because of how you bring your own presence into that.

FRAMO: Also my use of everyday language? Down-to-earth language?

WEBER: Yes.

LEVINE: Also your ability, I think sometimes, to divert into more chitchat or just some social discourse. Then you'll sometimes reveal some things about your background . . .

FRAMO: In the service of the therapy, I hope.

LEVINE: In a way, you level the field, Jim, saying, "I'm a man; I'm a real person; I've lived life; I'm not just this famous family therapist with all these diplomas on my wall." I see that routinely in sessions. I see how easily parents relax in your presence, Jim. And I agree with Tim, your openness, humor, and down-to-earth language are very helpful. I also think you are not afraid to hone in on deep feelings and you know when to back off. You track affect better than any therapist I know.

FRAMO: Sometimes doing this I get blunt; I can be blunt in sessions.

WEBER: Well, I think so. I think that within that context then other things happen. I think you . . .

FRAMO: What'd you call it, the way I treated your family?

WEBER: Respectful irreverence.

FRAMO: Respectful irreverence. I like that.

WEBER: Because I think you do create, really have, a respect for the people there. You have this multidirectional partiality that Ivan Nagy talks about. You have this humanity. You're respectful of each person's experience. But there's a certain irreverence; like you don't take it too seriously, pomp and circumstance are not all that moving and intimidating to you. You move right through in a respectful way.

FRAMO: The irreverence example came up with your dad, when I would kid him.

WEBER: Right, about his . . .

LEVINE: The saintliness.

WEBER: Yeah, the pecadillos and . . .

FRAMO: When I said, "Well, there are no saints, except for Dad, of course."

WEBER: And this thing about unconditional positive regard with my sister. Now, you regret your part in how you responded in that moment, but . . .

FRAMO: Which sister?

WEBER: Katie. When you told her not to expect unconditional love as an adult.

FRAMO: Oh yeah. That was a mistake.

WEBER: But at the same time it was close to illustrating the same point. There was some respect there, so you don't take these sort of conventional terms and then get organized by them. I mean, I think you're willing to humanize even those idealistic concepts.

LEVINE: Absolutely. Jim told the truth. Even babies don't get unconditional love, although the longing for it seems life long. This is fantasy, and Jim, you will challenge illusions and inappropriate expectations.

FRAMO: I also do a lot of breaking of family rules. All the way through I tried to challenge the family belief that you only exist to serve the world. And when I said charity begins at home . . .

LEVINE: You know, Jim does not treat his clients like patients. He doesn't tiptoe around them, and he just says what he thinks, but in a very caring but direct way. He has been called the "velvet hammer."

FRAMO: But some people are bothered that I'm not treating them like patients.

LEVINE: This is true. I think that certain individuals who are much more easily hurt and are highly sensitive would have a little more trouble with Jim's style. I tend to be a little softer, or a little more indirect with my feedback. I'll work with some of the narcissistic wounds in a different way than Jim will.

FRAMO: Yeah, you're more indirect. What you do is you make the unpalatable palatable.

LEVINE: Or I'll sort of set up something. I'll say, "I want to give you some difficult feedback, are you up for it?" So I'll try to prepare someone to be less defensive.

WEBER: Right; some novocaine on the swab.

LEVINE: Yeah. A little bit. Whereas Jim will just say what occurs to him. And I think some of that is just Jim. Jim is like that with everybody, whether you're a client or not. He just sort of blurts things out. It's not always politically correct and supersensitive, but he's just being himself. Jim, you are one of the most consistent people I know. You are you, no matter who's there. There's no pretense.

FRAMO: Well, I say what I think. My mother used to say, "My mouth is where my heart is." [laughter]

LEVINE: A lot of families, particularly parents who have not had much therapy experience, they come in and expect to be blasted. Jim's availability, his personal way of doing the session, and respectfulness helps parents relax and be open. I think he did incredible work with your dad.

WEBER: He did. One of the things that I noted was his being able to link with the sponsor of the family. I think it was critical there.

FRAMO: I don't think you heard this, Felise, because I told Tim, but look at the transcript of the last two hours, then look at the father's speech in the beginning of it. Notice how his speech gets more concrete and real as the session progresses. He left the stratosphere. He stopped quoting Bacon and all the philosophers and started getting more real. His language changed.

WEBER: Well, I would think that, above all that you do—the self-disclosing, the humor, respectful irreverence—you value connectedness. I think the mission I perceive you having—my inference is that the mission you have—is to bring family members together.

FRAMO: Well, what could I have done differently that might have made it more productive?

WEBER: Well, I just want to note some of the contributions first, before some of the differences.

FRAMO: You're about to say, "I have something difficult to tell you." [laughter]

WEBER: You unpack the secrets. You lead with the father sponsor. I think you're very contextually oriented, in the sense of Nagy's work, give and take, fairness and justice. I think connectedness, fairness, and openness would probably be the three things that I would attribute to you, in terms of your values. Demythologizing, secret unpacking, establishing connections between family members, and the give and take are the three sort of tripod values I perceive you holding. And they're very powerful, Jim.

LEVINE: What do you think your father would say was most helpful about Jim's presence in the session?

WEBER: That he was a real authentic human being. He was a mensch, you know, as he . . .

LEVINE: My favorite Yiddish word!

WEBER: You were not a psychologist; you were not shrinking heads. You were a real human being. And he can have a conversation with you.

FRAMO: Even though I challenge family myths; no, not myths, beliefs.

WEBER: Yeah. But you do that within a context of trust. I think you create an enormous context of trust.

FRAMO: Except Dad believed all his life that you're here on this earth to serve others. And I was challenging that. You know, you're here on this earth to serve others—servanthood he called it. And I challenged that; don't you think that would make him uncomfortable?

LEVINE: It did. He quipped that you and he could engage in quoting scriptures in the Bible.

FRAMO: I'm saying to your dad, "Your kids are here, they want you; forget about the world."

LEVINE: Well, you weren't saying forget about the world. You were saying refocus your attention. There are some things right in front of you that need some attention.

FRAMO: Yeah, make it secondary or even make it balanced, more integrated. By the way, when I read the transcript I noticed something. This whole idea of circular questioning has been brought
up as a great new discovery, and I found that I often use it. I
never labeled it circular questioning, you know, "Ann, what do
you think Katie thought when she . . . ?" I did quite a bit of that,
but I never knew it was circular questioning.

LEVINE: Well, that's one aspect of circular questioning. The other aspect
is heightening differences.

WEBER: Right, ranking before and after questions . . .

FRAMO: Well, I noticed sometimes if you ask a direct question and they
don't answer you can ask somebody else to give their answer.

LEVINE: Well, that's a piece of circular questioning.

WEBER: Well, I think what you also do is, a frequent line that you have is,
"Katie, did you know this about Tim?" You ask people if they
know "this," so I think you open up multiple realities.

FRAMO: I want them to take in what somebody is saying; for instance, I
want Katie to hear you.

WEBER: Yeah.

LEVINE: I would say that it is a question I often hear you ask in family-of-
origin sessions, or even couples therapy, to the listener: "Did you
know that?" I'm not sure, Tim, when you ask that question, what
do you mean? Because you may be imbuing more or something
different than Jim would.

WEBER: I have my own story around it.

FRAMO: I can tell you what I mean by it. Tim will say, "You all think I'm
this perfect person and I'm happy, and I've got my life in order.
Well, I've got a lot of problems." And I ask Katie, "Katie, did you
know that? What Tim is struggling with? Are you aware of this, or
can this change your perception of him?" That's what I mean.

WEBER: Here's why I think that's useful: I think you build up a connectedness in that question. Connectedness is one of those tripod
values for me. And I think that by asking the question you create
a relational experience out of the report. You know, a person can
report an internal something, but now it becomes a relational
experience: "Did you know?" "Are you part of it?" "I didn't know
all of it." And now it becomes a dialogical experience as opposed
to an individual experience.

FRAMO: Well, I wanted the family members to get to know each other.

LEVINE: That's the focus on relationships. I think Tim is right. You build
connectedness through your questioning. I think you also en-

courage curiosity when you ask, "Did you know so-and-so felt that way?" That's a steppingstone to building empathy.

WEBER: Yeah. I think that's what it does. Because now people have a phenomenon that becomes a relational phenomenon, as opposed to somebody just describing their own emotional experience. So it builds up this sort of web of the connecting of multiple realities.

FRAMO: People in family sessions often ascribe traits or characteristics to the other person that that person rejects. And they'll respond, "You don't know me at all. I'm not these things that you say I am." So I say, "Let's work on getting to know each other." Because people are always ascribing things to one another in families. [turning to Levine] Remember those three men we saw recently in a family-of-origin session? Three brothers?

LEVINE: Yes.

FRAMO: Look at all that stuff they threw at that one brother. He was the black sheep of the family, he was a crook, and this and that and the other. He said, "You don't know me at all." So I said, "Let them get to know who you are." I thought that was a very successful family-of-origin session. Tim, do you have some other points for us to cover?

WEBER: Yes. Here's where group process work would come into play. I think that there are times where maybe more attention to the actual interaction in the room, apart from the content, would be more interesting. For example, there were a number of sequences where I really was protecting my father in different ways. What I might have done, from a group process point of view, is focused on not only the content of what we were talking about, or even the history of it, but what was actually going on in the room in the moment. So, as a therapist, I might have said, "Tim, I've noticed that in the last few moments, when I asked your dad a question, you came in and answered for him. My belief about that is that you were concerned about your dad's vulnerability in that moment. What was that like for you and . . . "

LEVINE: I'm more likely to intervene in that way. In our cotherapy, Jim will be much more focused on exploring the content and getting to the in-depth issues, and I might stop that every once in a while and move to process.

FRAMO: Although in my commentary I talk repeatedly about your protecting your dad.

WEBER: You do. Well, let me amplify that one example, because I'd go even further than that. In fact, this may be a fifteen-minute conversation in the session where I might say, "Tim, I was curious about what was going on for you," so I could get to Tim's internal experience. Then I'd turn to the dad and ask, "What was it like for you when he interrupted? Do you depend upon him to do that?" Then I'd turn to other family members and ask, "What was your observation of what happened to . . . ?" So the conversation now continues, and it might go off in an entirely different direction.

LEVINE: I agree. I think there's use to a way of close process monitoring. I tend to go more to the immediate process as it's unfolding. I will attend to transference issues, or countertransference issues, or transference between family members.

WEBER: In the moment.

LEVINE: Yeah. We diverge there in our directions. But I think there's a great use to each direction. What other things do you think you would have done differently, Tim?

WEBER: Let me mention three more points. And as I say all these things I'm thinking, gee, Jim, I'm giving *you* feedback. I'm just consciously aware of the here-and-now moment. [chuckling]

LEVINE: The de-idolization of the moment. [laughing] Is it okay, Jim?

FRAMO: What?

LEVINE: That he de-idolizes you.

FRAMO: Oh yeah, I eat it up.

LEVINE: No, DE-idolizes you.

FRAMO: Oh! [lots of laughter] There goes my narcissism.

WEBER: Three other things. One is that sometimes I think there can be more of an emphasis on a dyadic or triadic subsystem of families, so that if something's going on between two people the tendency toward triangulation and actually spreading the conversation might actually dilute the work that two people could do.

FRAMO: I handle that, Tim, by offering subsystem sessions after the family-of-origin sessions: a mother and son, a father and daughter, mother and father . . .

WEBER: But I think, in the moment, one thing we frequently do in group process would be to actually take the two people in the family and bring them into the middle, into a fishbowl. I'd say, "Bring your chairs into the middle," so it now becomes a structural intervention, and, "I want you to talk to each other about how you believe you've been acknowledged or not acknowledged in this family. Katie and Tim, I just want you to have this conversation."

So everybody in the family is on the outside, these two members now are in the middle—or they may turn their chairs—and now I become the minimal facilitator of that conversation. It becomes a dyad that gets worked and deepened. And then that conversation may go on for five minutes, I may stop it and make an observation, then invite participants on the outside of the fishbowl to comment on their experience of the dyadic conversation. There are times where, I think, that could have actually intensified . . . Another example of turning up the heat; that's a variation on that previous thing of turning up the heat.

LEVINE: I like your suggestion: that group process fish-bowl technique. I think that would be real useful. That's where your group therapy training and group process training help. Also, you have a structural therapy background that adds much to your work.

FRAMO: I like your ideas. It sounds like an interesting technique also.

LEVINE: For me, the subsystem work generally is in the follow-up in family-of-origin work. I would say that, in Jim's method, the emphasis on dyads would come in later sessions, if the family chooses to have follow-up or an additional session.

FRAMO: The hardest thing for people to do is talk directly face to face to the person, the family member, and say what's in their heart. What else is on your list of things you would do different?

WEBER: Most of my ideas have to do with the management of the session. Such as the use of kinesthetic circular questioning. I'll give you an example of the kinesthetic circular questioning. The method is primarily a verbal-audio method. The hardest thing is for two family members to sit face-to-face with one another and say what's in their heart.

FRAMO: That's right. Say what's in your heart, Tim. [still laughing]

WEBER: The method really relies on a conversation. What I was wondering is: Are there times when it might be useful to break up the conversation and actually have some kind of movement interaction? I'm thinking of two examples; one is of Peggy Papp's work with sculpting.

FRAMO: Or Minuchin—moving the chairs?

WEBER: Well, a little more imaginative than just the structural moving of the chairs. I think that would be an example, but I mean a Satir or Peggy Papp sort of format. As in Satir's four styles of communication that there are different ways that families position themselves to illustrate a metaphor. Here's a variation of kinesthetic circular questioning that we do in group process. We might ask all the family members to "stand up, and line up in the order of those of you who've been most affected by Mom's death. I want you to stand in the order of here's the most affected to here's the least affected, and I want you to rank yourself." So five family members line themselves up, then I'd ask, "Dad, would you change this order around?" "Katie, would you change this order?" "Tim, would you?" And on down the group; so it takes a few minutes. And then people sit down and comment on the rank order. I think, sometimes, it might be useful to break up the conversation, do something that's more kinesthetic or structural.

FRAMO: That's quite outside the range of what I'd do. I can see, for example, I can admire Virginia's and Peggy's work, and other people who have a different style, but it just doesn't fit for me. I can see its value.

WEBER: In my family-of-origin session, if we had done something like that for five minutes and sat down, it might have had this emotional impact that words can't convey. We're a verbal family, and sometimes I think by doing something nonverbal, especially for a verbal family, we get outside of our preferred mode of behaving and it starts to impact in different ways.

FRAMO: I understand what you're saying.

WEBER: Just a few more things quickly; one is the time. I think that two-hour meetings are too short. I've come to believe that over time. Had there been a little more time, like had there been three two-hour meetings, or six to eight hours, it might have been a little bit more time to unpack some of the baggage. I'll share a couple other things. I would use genograms with the family to gather data. It's data-gathering time, but it also is an intervention in terms of people sharing different family stories, beliefs, mythologies. It's a very useful way to get on board with the family, to sort of unearth the family stories and themes, to set an agenda for the ensuing consultation. And it's not just a conversation; it's a visualization of the genogram, and then the themes of the family are noted on another piece of newsprint that's also put up.

FRAMO: There again, I think there's value in genograms. Again, it's not my thing. Felise does it.

LEVINE: When we do the prep interview, I take notes and highlight themes and construct the genogram. But it's not on large newsprint paper for the family to see.

FRAMO: Tim, you're adding another dimension to this work. It's also a good way to start with a couple—collect the genogram information in front of each other.

LEVINE: Right. And I think when we work together, we tend not to use those techniques because, Jim, you're a conversationalist. You're less into the nonverbal techniques.

FRAMO: That's true.

WEBER: Another method I have used to help family members prepare for family-of-origin consultations is to send a preparation letter to each family member a couple of months before the consultation. This letter describes the values and purpose that undergird the consultation, the consultation process and how family members can best prepare, and concludes with a set of fifteen questions I want family members to reflect upon to help enhance the learning and growth of the consultation conversation. I and my colleague, Cheryl Cebula, have been working on refining this methodology over the last several years. We then have a thirty-minute telephone interview with each family member after they have received the letter. This phone interview helps us develop a more collaborative frame for the consultation and gives us an opportunity to punctuate certain themes and gently coach individuals on how to maximize the benefits of the upcoming conversation.

FRAMO: You certainly put a lot more effort into preparing people than I do. You know, we've had some people call us and say, "Is there anything I can do to prepare for the sessions?"

LEVINE: Well, it's a very interesting difference. You take a little bit more responsibility for the session than Jim or I do, Tim. We leave it up to the client to prepare the family.

FRAMO: If I'm working with an ongoing client I have that person take responsibility for the agenda for the sessions. I coach the client to prepare the family. This helps the client to find better ways of dealing with their family and prepare the family for dealing with the hard issues.

LEVINE: Jim will give the client his 1976 family-of-origin article, for the family to read, and then his book is a reference if someone wants to read his book (Framo, 1976, 1992). But it's all focused on the organizing client; we do not have direct contact with the family members beforehand unless they call.

WEBER: They don't call up?

FRAMO: Sometimes we've had people call.

LEVINE: And ask questions. We leave that open. We say it's fine if your family has questions, they're free to call. Or the client may say, "Is it okay if my brother or sister calls and asks you . . . " You have a very nice preparation letter, Tim. Jim, you do some of that in your informed consent in the beginning of the session. You'll state that the purpose of the meeting is for them to clarify misunderstandings and get to know each other as real people. You normalize the process letting them know that all families have struggles, and that this is an opportunity for them to say what's on their mind. You prepare them to expect that they might feel angry or upset, and that these feelings are stages in working out more fulfilling relationships.

FRAMO: Why has there been such resistance to bringing families of origin in?

LEVINE: Resistance comes from two directions: clients and therapists. Therapists overidentify with the anxiety of the patient about bringing in the family. I think even most family therapists, although we would hope they would be different, have not worked out issues directly with their own families of origin. I think that most family therapists have talked about it, but most have not experienced it themselves. Maybe they've done couples therapy, but how many of them bring in their clients' families of origin? And I don't think you can do this work unless you've done extensive work on your own family-of-origin relationships.

FRAMO: You think one needs the experience.

LEVINE: I think so.

FRAMO: So, theoretically, it doesn't appeal to people.

LEVINE: I think, personally, it doesn't appeal to a lot of therapists. They figure, "Well, I've moved away from my family of origin. I only have to deal with them twice a year. Why bring this up. My parents are getting older." It's the same resistance as the clients.

FRAMO: But I remember a therapist once saying to me, "You mean you actually bring in parents and brothers and sisters?" I said yeah. He says, "Boy, I'd never do that with my family!" So that's a piece of it. There's also an inherent kind of thing about the family being sacrosanct—you can touch me as an individual patient, but don't you dare touch them. I'll bring in my spouse or my kids, but my parents—that's *personal*! And there's this enormous protectiveness of the sanctity of the family. I think that runs through our entire culture; and it varies from culture to culture. It's stronger in some cultures than others.

LEVINE: I think you're hitting on something important: Many therapists, as well as patients, feel the family-of-origin method is somehow dangerous to the sanctity of the family.

FRAMO: I think that's true.

LEVINE: Also, there are many therapists who would say history doesn't matter so much. Let's just do some brief problem solving, positive solutions, reframing, externalize the symptoms, all this other work that could be helpful.

WEBER: Most therapists, I think, are reluctant to bring *any* other member in, let alone family of origin. Because I think a cozy therapeutic relationship creates a pseudo-mutual conversation about somebody else who's not in the room; I think that's how a lot of therapists prefer to work. And then to bring somebody else in—a child, a spouse—I think, creates more of a challenge in embracing multiple realities. Then to bring in the family . . .

FRAMO: Some clients have said to me, "When I was in individual therapy my mother was in town, and my therapist recommended that I have a session with my mother." That's as far as the individual therapist would go: Bring in one member, usually it's the mother, not a sibling. From my point of view, in terms of object relations theory, I think the internal objects undergo some kind of transformation; and that the inner objects, which have gotten projected onto the other, affect the relationships. The family members perceive each other differently.

LEVINE: One of the things that you say, Jim: That there is a re-projection process where adults have transference to their parents. They still perceive the parent in adulthood as the parent of childhood. And one of the things that happens is that when the parent becomes more real, and there's a leveling or rebalancing of hierarchy, they begin to know each other as adults. They also can relinquish the introjected parent-of-childhood.

FRAMO: There's also the recounting of events from the past that in the light of more information gets reinterpreted. The best example I can remember is a woman who asked her mother during a session, "When I was a teenager, you sent me to the hospital, and I was convinced you were trying to get rid of me, didn't know how to take care of me." And then the mother told this elaborate story about how ill she [the mother] was, and she was forced to send her, and so forth. With that new information, the client said, "Thank God. All my life I've been carrying around that misunderstanding." So that can cause change.

LEVINE: Right. What you're also talking about is how the child interprets events from the child's own cognitive and emotional limitations; and that thinking influenced by the childhood superego colors how the child interprets events. So the parents may be experienced as much more harsh than they really were. Now, sometimes parents are, in fact, as punitive as the adult remembers them to be. But a lot of times that's not the case. In family-of-origin sessions, when the parents reveal more of themselves the adult son or daughter has to reconcile the affectively held parent of childhood with the real, more human parent of adulthood. There is an internal psychological shift.

FRAMO: I think that the very fact that the parent comes to the session at all indicates their openness to change.

LEVINE: The parent showing up, you're saying, is a statement that also provokes change. It is a statement of change, but also provokes change.

FRAMO: Right. Also, we've met some parents that were just as impossible at the end of sessions as they were in the beginning. I mean, they were really mean people. We couldn't stand them. They were not amenable to change at all, or any intervention.

LEVINE: When parents are troubled, the adult children may have to do the work of being the forgiving parent for the parents, as Donald Williamson talks about in his book *The Intimacy Paradox* (1991).

FRAMO: Regardless of how awful and cruel and rejecting the parents are, the grown children often keep seeking love from them.

LEVINE: One problem in the family of origin is that sometimes the adult son or daughter continues to try to get from the parent, but the parent is bankrupt. I know you have said in sessions, Jim, "Your mom or dad cannot give you what you need; can you let go of that?"

FRAMO: Some people can't. I might say, "You're never going to get what you want from your mother."

LEVINE: Right. But our hope would be: Can you live with that? I mean, *that* sometimes is the outcome of the family-of-origin sessions.

FRAMO: I try to aim in the direction of getting needs filled elsewhere: spouses, friends, work, et cetera.

LEVINE: Jim, I think this is very important. Sometimes people think the family-of-origin session is going to get them what they fantasize about an idyllic relationship with the parent.

FRAMO: I discuss this in my book. Sometimes people have to give up the dream. Another question I'd like to ask Tim: When should these sessions be held in ongoing treatment? At what point? Early on? What has to happen in ongoing therapy for you to bring it up?

WEBER: When I am working with an individual, and after we have been working for three to six months, we decide to widen the lens. Widening the lens may involve some subsystem work first, and then eventually the whole family.

FRAMO: You would start with subsystem? I want to start with the whole family, then go to subsystem.

WEBER: Well, in the ideal world I'd probably do it that way. But in the way it often shows up with people, and as issues emerge, sometimes there's subsystem work and then the lens widens and other people are included in.

LEVINE: Jim, you've changed over the years that I've known you. You will wait, now, until later in the therapy to bring it up. You've talked about this at conferences. You used to bring it up in the first or second session.

FRAMO: I used to bring up the idea early on of doing it sometime in the future. I was losing too many clients. Now I wait until I have an established relationship.

LEVINE: And I think that's probably true for me as well. I wait a little bit, until I know the client a little better, until they're more comfortable.

FRAMO: Now here's a question: Under what circumstances do these sessions improve the marriage of a couple you're treating, or even adversely affect the marriage?

LEVINE: I don't think we can understand that. I don't know that I could even answer that.

FRAMO: We've all had the experience of people saying, "My marriage didn't improve, but I have a better relationship with my father."

LEVINE: Yeah, but I don't know how the theory could explain that.

FRAMO: The follow-up study that Fran Baker did on my work found the same thing: A number of people said the relationships of the family of origin improved a great deal but that the sessions with the family did not have that much effect on their marriage (Baker, 1982).

LEVINE: I think a lot has to do with how the follow-up is done, and how the client is helped to rework and reexamine the process.

WEBER: I think the most effective family-of-origin work I'm doing is based on this premise about follow-up work. It's this family where we have the three two-hour meetings in February. Once every three or four weeks we get together for two hours with the same group, and we continue the follow-up work; and there is subsystem work that's even adjuncted to that.

FRAMO: Here's my next question: length of sessions and spacing?

LEVINE: Intensive marathon weekends get the ball rolling. That's not where the working through happens. That just becomes the template, or the reference point. I think things happen over time, there's a continual revisiting and reworking, kind of like a spiraling coil. If you follow the line of the coil it eventually gets to the other end. But if you just look at a small segment of the coil it looks like it moves forward a while, then moves backward a while, slowly progressing forward with a constant forward–backward modulation that happens over time progressing.

WEBER: So an intensive piece does not address that question of integration and pacing . . .

LEVINE: No, I don't think so. I think it's cathartic; I think it reshifts some realities. But I think it's important that people reflect. They can't reflect in ten seconds, you know. You need time to digest a good meal.

WEBER: In the organizational development [OD] field, there are two different ways to intervene with organizations and companies. There may be a controversy around the utility of these different ways of intervening. One is called training; the other is called consultation. Training is where you go in for an intensive week or two, you contract for a training experience with an intact work team. You present something, there's an intensive emotional experience, people's awareness gets heightened, they make agreements and promises, and then they're gone and that's it. You train them around some skills, and then hope that they utilize them fully. Consultation, which may include training, is where you do that, but then there's a follow-up consultation with subsystems. It may be the whole system, it may be subsystems, but it's an ongoing contract with an organization. And a lot of the OD people say that training really doesn't produce change. They say it's a heightened emotional experience where people maybe feel good or have some kind of refurbished vision of where they're headed. But it's the consultation piece, sort of being in the trenches in an ongoing way, over time, that really begins to shift the culture.

LEVINE: I agree, Tim. I like the consultation model. To me, it's like making the first cut in surgery. The intensive weekend is like splitting open the chest, then you've got the heart there. Once you're in you've got to do the work, and you don't do that work in ten minutes. It takes many hours over time. And then there's the recovery and integration of the experience. I like the idea of training plus consultation. I think there's usefulness to go in, radically, open the system, and then allow for the follow-up.

FRAMO: Okay. Can I get to the next question? Cutoffs are usually repaired in these sessions. Do they ever get worse? Do they ever get more wide, do you think? Like a brother and sister not talking to each other for many years, then we have the session and they say at the end, "I want nothing to do with you." In other words, under what circumstances can the family-of-origin session make things worse?

WEBER: I had a session, a subsystem meeting, between a woman and her father. We had four hours. So this wasn't the entire family. Her basic message to her father was that she really . . . She didn't attack him, but she said she really wanted to let him know that she really hadn't appreciated their relationship, and didn't know if she wanted to have anything to do with him.

FRAMO: Was that following a family-of-origin session?

WEBER: No. That was in the subsystem meeting between daughter and father. She said the only reason she would want to have her father in her life was for her son, because she believes he has a right to have a relationship with his grandfather.

FRAMO: Was that an incest case?

WEBER: No. But there were incidents in the family history where she had felt very betrayed by him. There was a court situation where the parents divorced and she testified on behalf of the mother. The father, in response to that, took away her college fund or something. What was interesting about that was, by acknowledging her pain and anger, in the ensuing months, she felt more freed up and she began to feel less reactive to interactions with her father.

LEVINE: So she could be in a relationship with him?

WEBER: Yeah. It was limited, and pretty circumscribed. But the question I had, at that point, was that the risk was that the father would hear that and say, "If that's the way it is, then I don't want to have anything to do with you either." But with support and encouragement and coaching, he was able to stay in the conversation and work it through.

LEVINE: You know what? I think it's an interesting thing, what you're saying, Tim. I think the father knew he was going to hear that. I think that parents, when they agree to come in, are already prepared to hear how their children feel. If they've had too many of their own personal problems, they may not know, they might truly be surprised. But I think most parents intuitively know what several of the issues are that their kids are going to bring up. I think they expect to be blasted, and so the very act of coming in is a statement of their willingness to hear some of that stuff.

FRAMO: It's a statement of love.

LEVINE: Because the father or mother who would fall apart in the face of criticism is really not likely to show up. I think they'd select themselves out. It's our hope that family-of-origin consultations don't make things worse. Although sometimes, you know, a can of beans can be opened, especially in families where there's a lot of mythology and illusion about how perfect things were. I'm sure the family will have to grieve the loss of what they thought, what they pretended was happening. But, on the other hand, I think we have to trust that on some level they unconsciously knew that this was not authentic.

FRAMO: I think this is my last question, it's about family-of-origin sessions affecting symptoms. The clearest example I can remember is a father calling me up several months afterward and saying this is the first time in twenty years his wife hadn't had an asthma attack—since that session. I had gotten other reports about symptoms being removed following the family-of-origin sessions.

LEVINE: Many years ago, you did a demonstration session where the father was an alcoholic, and after the family-of-origin session you got feedback that he had stopped drinking.

FRAMO: Yeah. But I have no real data on symptom removal. I've never studied it on a systematic basis. It's impressionistic.

LEVINE: If the assumption is that it's a result of psychological or relational conflict, and that conflict gets resolved in the family-of-origin session or follow-up, that could explain symptom relief. What about you, Tim? You have the opportunity to follow up on your cases more than we do.

FRAMO: Have you seen symptoms get relieved?

WEBER: I was just thinking of a client. I don't think he would report that his marriage has terrifically improved. I don't think he would report that.

FRAMO: No, I'm actually thinking about clinical symptoms like depression or anxiety states.

WEBER: He says everybody in the family comments positively about that experience. They say it was useful, and they're continuing to work on things. He's noticing changes in terms of relationships and more openness. I asked if he could summarize in one sentence what really was the major benefit of those meetings. He said something like, "We can tell the truth."

FRAMO: That's a meaningful statement.

WEBER: He reports that in work systems, and in marriage that he doesn't withdraw sexually. He finds more courage to really stay present, to stay as connected as he can, and to work through something without a dreaded fear and anxiety. So that would be an example of a symptom change.

LEVINE: You know, it's also an example not just of a symptom change, but of a structural change in his internal world. His psychic structure, his capacity to tolerate anxiety, has increased. Whatever the underlying fantasies were of what it would mean to say the truth, they were demythologized. The catastrophe didn't happen in the family-of-origin session; he was able to tell the truth, there was no retaliation, he didn't feel guilty. In other words, although we don't know what the fantasized loss was, he feels less conflicted and less anxious. Just before we wrap up, there is a subject I want to talk about, and that is cotherapy. Tim, you mentioned that you often do family-of-origin with a female cotherapist. Jim and I work as a cotherapy team, so when we try to teach this method generally we encourage therapists to do this work as a cotherapy team. There are certain things that are very important if we want to model for people how to do cotherapy. There are certain sensitivities like gender issues. I think we need to be clear, as a male-female team, no matter how egalitarian we may be together, that families may not always treat us as equal cotherapists. It is important how we model a non-gender-organized way of collaboration. I will refer back to Jim and credit him in sessions, he will credit me and refer back to me in sessions, regardless of whether the family treats one of us as more senior to the other.

FRAMO: You know, one technique we've developed that's very effective is to stop the session; in essence, we turn to each other and discuss the case.

WEBER: In front of them?

FRAMO: In front of them. We give our different views of what's going on with them.

LEVINE: There are many different styles of cotherapy. I would say Jim and I tend to work on parallel tracks. We sometimes go in different directions. We're collaborative, but we are in there as two separate therapists, not as echoes of each other. Tim, what are your thoughts about cotherapy?

WEBER: I have worked with a female cotherapist, Cheryl Cebula, for several years now in these family-of-origin consultations. I have found that our gender diversity, different styles of engagement and conversation, and differences in what we punctuate will deeply enrich our work with families. We broaden the range of what we see and who we connect with in our partnership. I think we bring more balance to the work and have sort of built some self-corrective mechanisms so that we don't become too excessive in one direction. It also helps to share the load when the depth and intensity is fatiguing. I think we recapitulate the parent system in our duo and evoke more emotional and provocative material. And frankly, I just want to have a partner to share the passion and joy of this work. Throughout the three days we are with each family, so many times beyond using each other as consultants, we are deeply moved by this work and the richness of relationships unfolding in the room. It would be hard to feel this alone.

FRAMO: Well, I can say that I much prefer doing family-of-origin sessions with a cotherapist than doing them alone.

LEVINE: Why is that?

FRAMO: Because I think it's a different kind of therapy than other kinds of therapies; because the feelings can get much more intense. I share with every other therapist the apprehension about opening up the insides of a family, and I like the idea of a surgeon standing next to me. As you know, things can get pretty hot and heavy, and these adult children can sometimes confront the parents in a brutal fashion. Sometimes people need to be protected, rescued, calmed down.

WEBER: A difficult job on the part of the therapist.

FRAMO: Yeah, and I want my flank protected so that if I make an intervention that offends people my cotherapist can jump in to sort of smooth things over. Now, I've done family-of-origin sessions with male cotherapists, but I prefer the male–female thing because I really do think men and women think differently and notice different things. I think it takes a woman to really understand a woman, a man to really understand a man. And vice versa, there are some things that only a man can understand about a woman and that a woman can understand about a man.

LEVINE: In a way, Jim, when you're saying you want your flank protected, you're saying you want someone to turn to and lean on and not feel like you have to do it all, because there's so much happening.

FRAMO: Now, I don't feel that when I do individual therapy. I don't feel that when I'm working with a couple—that I need backup. But I do feel it in family-of-origin sessions. Do you share that, Tim?

WEBER: Uh huh.

FRAMO: They're different, aren't they? Family-of-origin sessions are different from other kinds of work we do. It might have something to do with the therapists' associations to their own families.

WEBER: Well, they're more extensive, they're more epic interviews as op-
           posed to problem-oriented interviews. And it makes a difference
           for me to have a woman by my side.

LEVINE: In what way for you?

WEBER: I believe that I can link with the family better, in terms of the
           family's own experience. I'm more of a team. I believe I'm per-
           ceived as more engaged, with more fluidity and flexibility on the
           part of the members of the family. That would be one piece. But
           from my perspective, I believe I'm more alert with a female. I
           think we see more, we experience more, there's more of a whole-
           ism.

FRAMO: You can sit back and take a rest while your cotherapist takes over.

LEVINE: It's true that four hours of intensive work, sometimes six if the
           sessions are extended, is a lot of intensity to handle as a single
           therapist.

WEBER: Right. Somebody to spell me.

LEVINE: There are times that I can tell Jim's getting a little tired and I
           move forward, or he may sense that I'm losing a bit of a focus or
           losing the big picture, then he moves forward.

FRAMO: There have been times when we've each covered up for the other:
           if one of us makes a dumb remark. And there have been times
           when we've rescued each other. One person can get lost, and the
           other's still more objective.

LEVINE: Uh huh. Also, the potential for countertransference reenactments
           is really high in these sessions, because we all can identify with
           any of the issues the family is bringing up. I think the other thera-
           pist is there to pull you out if you get triangled in.

FRAMO: In contrast to regular family therapy, I think that family-of-ori-
           gin sessions are more likely to touch upon your own family stuff.

LEVINE: Absolutely; I think that's true. I feel that.

FRAMO: Somebody might be like your father or your brother. They may
           be dealing with some issue that you had to deal with. The par-
           ents' marital relationship may be similar to your own parents'
           marriage.

LEVINE: And in ongoing family therapy, when that happens you have the
           time between sessions to process it. I'll think about what I did
           last session, recognizing that I got caught, then I'd have a week to
           talk, think, consult with colleagues to work it through. But in the
           family-of-origin session there isn't that time to reflect, because
           you're always "on" and focusing on what's happening in the
           moment. Having a cotherapist there just spells you for a few min-

utes so you can step back and ask yourself, "Okay, what just happened here?"

WEBER: It keeps me psychologically in the foster parent role, and not the adoptive parent role.

LEVINE: Right, à la Carl Whitaker.

WEBER: Right. That power in the family system, the emotional field of having parents and siblings there who have all that history in the room is so enormous, so seductive, that I need somebody that's anchoring me on the other side of the line.

FRAMO: I think there is another reason for cotherapy. With these family-of-origin sessions, there's always the danger of opening up a can of worms. I mean, a big family secret, such as incest, the father molested a child, or somebody spent time in prison, or there's a lot of drug dealing going on. Family-of-origin sessions, I think, present a greater threat for something unexpected like that to come up, and that's another source of anxiety and a reason to have a cotherapist if anything is revealed. Somebody else is there to help you deal with it.

LEVINE: Sometimes in the preparation session we'll try to ask if there are any loaded topics. Are there things the client wants to be sure are dealt with? Are there secrets they have a hunch about and want to explore? We'll try to clarify with the client exactly what we'll be working with, so we can be prepared as well.

FRAMO: Although we've had clients say, "There is this thing that happened in my family, and I absolutely refuse to bring it up; I will not talk about it." Have you had that, Tim? Usually it's something like incest.

WEBER: I really have not had that happen, in part because a lot of my work is an extension of ongoing therapy. So I have a different kind of context. I'm thinking of the various avenues for doing intergenerational work. One would be just simply cognitive awareness, making synaptic connections between then-and-there and here-and-now.

LEVINE: You mean talking about your family of origin in individual therapy?

WEBER: Right; and then making connections. That would be one way. A second way would be the conversation and enactments of family scripts within a group setting, sometimes using group members as surrogate family members.

LEVINE: Like Satir.

WEBER: Right. That would be a second way. Another method is a coaching—using a Bowenian format.

LEVINE: Where you coach the family member to go back to their family of origin and work things out.

WEBER: Right.

FRAMO: Not only working things out, but changing by increasing their own level of differentiation within their family.

WEBER: Assignments are given, and the therapist now is a coach. Another avenue would be a more highly structured, strategic approach such as Donald Williamson uses with a selected system focusing on the primary triangle between adult sons and daughters and their parents (Williamson, 1991).

LEVINE: He has people prepare in his group therapy, get the emotions out in the group therapy, and then more or less report to the parents.

WEBER: Right. Siblings are not included. So it's a highly orchestrated, strategic approach.

LEVINE: Shifting the topic, I think Tim's family was enormously courageous for doing this. But isn't that a strange word to use about seeking therapy: courage? I mean, for something that is so beneficial. We don't normally say to someone when they go to the doctor to get treated for a problem, "It took courage for you to go." "It took courage for you to go to surgery." It's not the language we use, but we'll say very easily, "It took great courage to bring in your family," and then we're buying into the fears. We'll even say to a family, "It took great courage for you to come in." I've said that. But why are we using this language? It's a language of fear and anxiety.

WEBER: Maybe it's a realistic assessment of what in fact is there.

LEVINE: I do think it is courageous, because it is a big thing to do.

WEBER: Are you saying it shouldn't be that big?

LEVINE: I don't know; I'm wondering.

WEBER: I think it's sort of like death: If you're on the other side you realize it wasn't such a big deal as before. [laughter]

LEVINE: [laughing] That's an interesting analogy—death and family-of-origin therapy.

FRAMO: But I honestly do believe that family of origin work can bring about more deep change than any other therapeutic intervention. I really believe that.

LEVINE: But I think that, you know, when Tim, in his prep interview, used the language, the drama of murder and suicide . . .

WEBER: You're saying I amplified things.

LEVINE: You amplified things. But are we also saying that there is a shared unconscious fantasy in families and even among family therapists that these are the risks of bringing family in.

FRAMO: I think what people are most afraid of is that the family will be torn asunder, and they'll lose their family. What could be worse than losing your family?

WEBER: My bimodal fear was either this would be the most boring experience ever, that nothing would happen and everyone would be disappointed and then angry for having wasted their time, or somebody would die. But I think that the fear of boredom was an antidote to the homicidal fear. So I think that's probably where that came from. It was a complementary fear.

FRAMO: Okay folks, it's time to bring an end to this trialogue. As we close down I would like to provide closure to this discussion by doing a version of what we do at the end of family-of-origin sessions— namely, expressing our appreciation to each other. Since we don't have time for all of us to do this, I'll just speak for myself. I have enjoyed our discussion immensely. I prize the collaboration on our book, but more, I appreciate both of you for the excitement of the sharing of ideas. I have been stretched by the experience of jousting with two fine minds.

REFERENCES

Aponte, H. (1992). Training the person of the therapist in structural family therapy. *Journal of Marital and Family Therapy, 18,* 269–281.

Baker, F. (1982). *Framo's method of integration of family-of-origin with couples therapy: A follow-up study of an intergenerational approach.* Doctoral dissertation. Counseling Psychology Department, Temple University, Philadelphia, PA.

Bank, S. P., & Kahn, M. D. (1982). *The sibling bond.* New York: Basic Books.

Bank, S. P., & Lewis, K. Z. (1988). *Siblings in therapy.* New York: Norton.

Boszormenyi-Nagy, I., & Krasner, B. R. (1986). *Between give and take: A clinical guide to contextual therapy.* New York: Brunner/Mazel.

Bowen, M. (1978). *Family therapy in clinical practice.* New York: Aronson.

Chasin, R., Grunebaum, H., & Herzog, M. (Eds.) (1990). *One couple, four realities.* New York: Guilford.

Fairbairn, W. R. D. (1954). *An object-relations theory of the personality.* New York: Basic Books.

Ferber, A., Mendelsohn, M., & Napier, A. (Eds.) (1973). *The book of family therapy.* New York: Science House.

Forward, S. (1989). *Toxic parents.* New York: Bantam Books.

Framo, J. L. (1968). My families, my family. *Voices: Art and Science of Psychotherapy, 4,* 18–27.

Framo, J. L. (1970). Symptoms from a family transactional viewpoint. In N. W. Ackerman, J. Lieb, & J. K. Pearce (Eds.), *Family therapy in transition* (pp. 125–171). Boston: Little, Brown. Also reprinted in Kaplan, H. S. & Sager, C. J. (1972). *Progress in group and family therapy* (pp. 271–308). New York: Brunner/Mazel.

Framo, J. L. (1976). Family of origin as a therapeutic resource for adults in marital and family therapy: You can and should go home again. *Family Process, 15,* 193–210.

Framo, J. L. (1982). *Explorations in marital and family therapy: Selected papers of James L. Framo.* New York: Springer.

Framo, J. L. (1992). *Family-of-origin therapy: An intergenerational approach.* New York: Brunner/Mazel.

Freeman, D. S. (1992). *Multigenerational family therapy.* New York: Haworth.

Greenson, R. R. (1954). The struggle against identification. *Journal of the American Psychoanalytic Association, 2,* 200–217.

Hargrave, T. D. (1997). *Families and forgiveness: Healing wounds in the intergenerational family.* New York: Brunner/Mazel.

Headley, L. (1997). *Adults and their parents in family therapy.* New York: Plenum Press.

Hovestadt, A. J., & Fine, M. (Eds.) (1987). *Family-of-origin therapy.* Rockville, MD: Aspen.

Keeney, B., & Silverstein, O. (1986). *The therapeutic voice of Olga Silverstein.* New York: Guilford.

Kerr, M. E., & Bowen, M. (1988). *Family evaluation.* New York: Norton.

Levine, F. (1997). The girl who went on strike: A case of childhood diabetes. In S. McDaniel, J. Hepworth, & W. Doherty (Eds.), *The shared experience of illness: Stories of patients, families, and their therapists* (pp. 58–72). New York: Basic Books.

Lewis, J. M., Beavers, W. R., Gossett, J. T., & Phillips, V. A. (1976). *No single thread: Psychological health in family systems.* New York: Brunner/Mazel.

Napier, A. Y., & Whitaker, C. A. (1978). *The family crucible.* New York: Harper & Row.

O'Neill, E. (1955). *Long day's journey into night.* New Yaven, CT: Yale University Press.

Paul, N. (1967). The use of empathy in the resolution of grief. *Perspectives in Biology and Medicine, 11,* 153-169.

Paul, N. L., & Paul, B. B. (1975). *A marital puzzle.* New York: Norton.

Roberto, L. G. (1992). *Transgenerational family therapies.* New York: Guilford.

Satir, V., & Baldwin, M. (1983). *Satir step by step: A guide to creating change in families.* Palo Alto, CA: Science and Behavior Books.

Searight, H. R. (1997). *Family-of-origin therapy and diversity.* New York: Brunner/ Routledge.

Strobe, M., Greene, M. M., Gergen, K. J., & Stroebe, W. (1992). Broken hearts or broken bonds: Love and death in historical perspective. *American Psychologist, 47,* 1205-1212.

Walsh, F. (Ed.) (1993). *Normal family processes,* 2nd ed. New York: Guilford.

Weber, T. T., & Levine, F. B. (1995). Engaging the family: An integrating approach. In R. Mikesell, D. Lusterman, & S. McDaniel (Eds.), *Integrating family therapy* (pp. 45–71). Washington, DC: American Pschological Association.

Weber, T. T., McKeever, J. E., & McDaniel, S. H. (1985). A beginner's guide to the problem-oriented first interview. *Family Process, 24,* 357-364.

Whitaker, C. A. (1989). *Midnight musings of a family therapist.* New York: Norton.

Whitaker, C. A., & Bumberry, W. M. (1988). *Dancing with the family: A symbolic-experiential approach.* New York: Villard Books, division of Random House.

Williamson, D. (1997). On not taking illness too seriously: Aging with diabetes. In S. McDaniel, J. Hepworth, & W. Doherty. (Eds.), *The shared experience of illness: Stories of patients, families, and their therapists* (pp. 242–250). New York: Basic Books.

Williamson, D. S. (1991). *The intimacy paradox.* New York: Guilford.

Wolin, J., & Wolin, S. (1993). *The resilient self: How survivors of troubled families rise above adversity.* New York: Villard Books.

Wynne, L. C., McDaniel, S. H., & Weber, T. T. (1986). *Systems consultation: A new perspective for family therapy.* New York: Guilford.